3   The Expanding World of Man

1215   **1240**   **1275**

Newsweek New York N.Y.

Editor Neville Williams

1320

1348

1381

The Expanding World of Man

3

1431

1453

1492

Library of Congress Catalog Card No. 72–103156

Printed and bound in Italy

EFFIGIES DOCTORIS MARTINI LVTHERI
AVGVSTINIANI WITTENBERGESIS
1520

1512   **1521**   **1533**   **1543**

1571   1573   1588

Contents

Introduction

Sixteen milestones of history—all of which occurred between the early thirteenth and the late sixteenth centuries—are authoritatively discussed in this volume. Together, they provide a comprehensive picture of nearly four hundred years of world history. Any increase in the number of contributions would diminish the significance of each chosen event; while any reduction in the number of selections, by focusing on a few "epoch-making" battles, would eliminate the spiritual, artistic and scientific achievements of the era.

Although European events dominate the first half of Volume III, the theme of the whole—as the title makes plain—is *The Expanding World of Man.* Accordingly, milestones in the history of Russia, China, the Americas and India have been included. And despite Sir Edward Creasy's assertion—in his 1852 study entitled *Fifteen Decisive Battles of the World* —that all milestones of history are necessarily military or naval actions, no more than seven of the sixteen essays in this book are primarily concerned with warfare.

The Peasants' Revolt in England is considered a milestone in history despite the fact that it failed—for the English rising led to similar rebellions in France and Flanders and, collectively, those outbreaks altered the social structure of feudal Europe. In much the same way, it was subsequent interpretations of Magna Carta, coupled with the constitutional and historical significance ultimately attached to the document, that elevated the signing of the Great Charter to an event of singular importance. Some of the milestones included in this volume have more than a single claim to attention. In the field of cultural history, for instance, Dante's *Divine Comedy* stands as one of the half-dozen finest works of poetry in all of Western civilization—yet we learn more about the Christian spirit of the Middle Ages from Dante's masterpiece than we do from any other single source.

The Expanding World of Man is concerned with more than simply the discovery of new continents and the interaction of civilizations. From the mid-thirteenth century, man's intellectual horizons were also expanding. The philosophical treatises of Roger Bacon and the subsequent development of humanism —which affected art, letters and every aspect of human life—paved the way for the Renaissance. The rediscovery of Greece added a new dimension to classical scholarship, which had hitherto been limited to the civilization of Rome. The humanist outlook, which embraced a fearless search for truth and beauty, questioned the fundamental purpose of man. That search led, inescapably, to dispute with authority, especially the authority of the Church. The new theology of Luther, Zwingli and Calvin was as much an "expansion" of man's world as Columbus' voyage or Copernicus' theory of the universe were— and the renewed theology of Catholicism, born at the sixteenth-century Council of Trent, was itself an expansion of the medieval system perfected by St. Thomas Aquinas. Erasmus' detachment from theological controversy and Montaigne's quizzical open-mindedness in matters of faith both exemplify a broadening of outlook that would have been considered heretical in the age of Innocent III (1198–1216).

With the beginning of the Age of Discovery, Europe ceased to be a Mediterranean continent. There was a shift of emphasis to northwestern Europe and to the development of Antwerp—not merely as the commercial capital of the world but as the center of banking and finance as well. The new capitalism of the Antwerp Exchange and of such great European banking houses as the Fuggers of Augsburg is certainly an expansion of the system of

Introduction

medieval credit built up by Jewish money lenders and the banks of Florence. Never before had society been so fluid: careers in the service of monarchs like Louis XI of France or Henry VIII of England were open to talented members of all classes.

The sixteen essays in this volume are not presented in isolation; the unique events with which they deal are placed in historical context by means of narrative passages that link each essay to its successor. These linking passages make no effort to cover world history with textbook comprehensiveness. Instead, their function is to provide this volume with a greater cohesion than would otherwise be the case, and to offer a general survey of *The Expanding World of Man* in these four remarkable centuries.

Each linking passage deals with the events, the people and the achievements that set the stage for the "milestone" that follows. There was more to the High Renaissance than the Sistine Chapel, and more to the Continental Reformation than Luther's Bible—and the essays that describe those events are amplified by the narrative links that precede and follow them. These linking passages describe the characteristics of the epoch (such as chivalry or anti-clericalism), the tendencies and movements that underlay it (the rise of the universities and vernacular literature, humanism and the demand for Church reform), the economic changes that gave it shape (decline of feudalism, apogee of Venetian trade with the Levant), and the developments in art and architecture that gave the era its unique style.

In general, the links discuss events that were of great moment in the history of a particular country but are of insufficient importance to rank as "milestones" in world history. For example, the execution of the accused heretic John Huss at the Council of Constance (1415) was a seminal date in the rise of Bohemian nationalism, but Huss' martyrdom had little long-term effect on the development of Europe. Other seemingly significant lives and events have been rejected as "milestones" and relegated to the linking passages for similar reasons: the legacy of the remarkable Holy Roman Emperor Frederick II, whose contemporaries dubbed him the "Wonder of the World," was purely negative; the life's work of Pope Boniface VIII proved basically unconstructive; and even Henry Tudor's victory at Bosworth Field was no more than a domestic event ensuring a change of dynasty on the English throne.

In their own fields, Tycho Brahe's charts of the heavens and Vesalius' anatomical studies of the human body were tremendously important, yet none can be described as epoch-making in broad historical terms. Such achievements are accordingly described in the linking passages.

With the closing of the Middle Ages the pace of change quickened. The globe was shrinking as rapidly as man's knowledge of the universe was expanding. In the maelstrom of the Reformation both art and science strove to escape from the straitjacket of clerical control—and Christendom came under attack from within as well as from without. National states hardened under the rule of strong kings, and Europe was plunged into a series of dynastic wars that lasted until 1763.

As a result of those developments, the history of the sixteenth century is richer and more varied than that of the previous era. Consequently, three essays each have been assigned to the thirteenth, fourteenth and fifteenth centuries, while the sixteenth century—with full justification—has been treated in seven separate essays. This imbalance creates an unevenness in the time span covered in each of the linking passages: there is half a century between Marco Polo's arrival at Peking and Dante's writing of the *Divine Comedy*, and half a century between the Peasants' Revolt and

Joan of Arc's death—but only ten years separate the Copernican theory from Luther's Bible, and the Battle of Lepanto and Akbar's entry to Gujarat occur within two years of one another. Nonetheless, it is fair to say that no individual of importance or event of significance has been omitted.

In the ensuing pages the reader can trace the changing facets of Christian experience from St. Francis of Assisi and St. Louis through Wycliffe, Thomas à Kempis, Savonarola and the Protestant reformers to St. Francis Xavier and St. Ignatius Loyola; he can observe the evolution of the papacy from the time of Innocent III through the pontificate of Sixtus V; and he can survey the politics of the West from the accession of Henry III of England through the assassination of Henry IV of France. As the essays progress, the reader moves gradually from a world of monastic chronicles, written in Gothic script and beautifully illuminated, to an age in which printed books with elaborate woodcuts are a commonplace. Warfare persists: crusades against the Turk, the Hundred Years' War between England and France, the wars of religion and frequent civil wars—all fought during this period—suggest that sophisticated Europe was basically no more politically advanced than India or Persia, China or Japan. Those conflicts are fought against a background of changing tactics on land and sea, and with increasingly efficient weapons.

Dynasties fall, boundaries change, enterprise supplants the chivalric ideal, and written languages take shape in this era. There is a new urgency about man's quest for fulfillment as he attempts to explore the unknown, exploit his environment, understand the purpose of life and come to terms with reality—and in so doing, "expand" the world of man.

NEVILLE WILLIAMS

Agreement at Runnymede 1215

In the summer of 1215 King John of England affixed his seal to Magna Carta, a crude bill of rights drawn up by his rebellious barons, and thus unwittingly hastened the decline of omnipotent, "divine-right" monarchs not only in England but in Europe as well. The "firm peace" that was reached at Runnymede proved to be an enduring one : the Great Charter survived subsequent civil wars, numerous rewritings and even annulment by the Pope.
In ensuing generations, Magna Carta was reinterpreted and expanded to the point where it became the "irrepealable fundamental statute" of English law. And five and a half centuries later the personal liberties guaranteed by the Charter served as the basis for the Bill of Rights of the United States Constitution.

On June 15, 1215, a remarkable confrontation took place at Runnymede, a meadow located a mile or so to the west of the Thames-side town of Staines and twenty miles southwest of London. This unusual assembly, a formal meeting between King John of England and a party of his subjects who had been in rebellion since the beginning of May, had been called to settle the dispute concerning the King's rule and the general conduct of the government. As such, the gathering at Runnymede was unprecedented in English history.

When the antagonists met on June 15, the broad terms of agreement had already been settled through official envoys. The confrontation at Runnymede was the final stage of a long and complex series of negotiations begun by representatives of the beleagured King and his rebellious barons on May 25, 1215. On June 19, a final settlement, described in the records of the meeting as a "firm peace," was finally reached.

Nonetheless, King John and his opponents continued to meet at Runnymede through June 23, for the King was compelled to fulfill immediately some of the concessions he had promised. From June 15 to 23, therefore, John and the rebel lords rode out to Runnymede daily; the King and his supporters from his castle at Windsor, the rebel party from the town of Staines.

The rebel party, made up of a group of barons and their supporters, was dominated by England's most powerful landowners, who held title to their estates in return for military and other forms of feudal service to the King. The final settlement therefore assumed feudal characteristics that now seem antiquated and inadequate: the rebels renewed their homage and fealty to the King; the King and his leading supporters swore a solemn oath to observe the terms of the settlement; and the execution of the agreement was secured by a treaty that placed the barons in charge of London, the capital of the realm. The terms of the settlement were written in a charter, one that came to be known, because of its large size,

as Magna Carta, or the Great Charter.

At the time, the charter form seemed the most suitable vehicle for the terms of peace. Charters were frequently used in the early 1200s to record grants of land, rights or privileges; they were the most solemn and formal documents available for such transactions. In 1215 England had no statute laws and but a rudimentary concept of legislation. Hence this part of the settlement took the form of a solemn concession, an apparently voluntary act of self-restraint, whereby John promised to right the wrongs alleged against him and to limit both his own and his successors' actions in the future. Magna Carta was traditional and familiar in form, a fact that seemed to give it strength and permanence.

King John did not actually affix his signature to the Charter; instead it was sealed with the impression of the Great Seal and witnessed by the Archbishop of Canterbury and other great men. The document, written in Latin and which later came to be divided into some sixty numbered chapters, originally was written without such aids to reference and ranged haphazardly over most aspects of government.

First, Magna Carta sought to regulate the feudal relationships between the Crown and its immediate tenants by laying down rules about payments due on the succession to estates, about the custody of wards and their lands, and about the marriage of heiresses. Second, it provided for regular justice in central and local courts and sought to ensure that the King would only act against his subjects by recognized legal procedure. The most famous and most significant chapter of Magna Carta, Number 39, states :

> No free man shall be taken or imprisoned or deprived or outlawed or exiled or in any way ruined . . . except by the lawful judgment of his peers or by the law of the land.

Third, the Charter attempted to regulate the King's financial power, seeking to control his right to tax and the manner in which his officers collected debts or sought to increase royal revenues. Fourth, it demanded that the King restore rights and property

Pope Innocent III, at first John's enemy, but later his ally against the barons.

Opposite King John, from his tomb at Worcester Cathedral.

An attack on tyranny

King John; Magna Carta attacked his power.

Chateau Gaillard, a great English stronghold in France, which John lost to Philip Augustus of France.

that he had seized or acquired by unjust agreements. Fifth, it arranged for the election in every county of juries of knights who were to inquire into the activities of the sheriffs and other local agents of the Crown. Finally, the Great Charter established a body of twenty-five barons—originally twenty-four of the rebel leaders and the Mayor of London—who were to hear and adjudicate complaints and claims against the King under the terms of the Charter.

In all, Magna Carta was a radical, indeed a revolutionary document. "Why," King John is purported to have asked, "do they not demand my kingdom?" The Charter had been inspired by deep and bitterly felt grievances, focused for the most part on King John himself. Unlike his brother and predecessor, Richard I, who spent most of his brief reign (1189–99) fighting abroad, John (1199–1216) was largely resident in England, and was personally responsible for his government. John was an active and inventive monarch, but he was faced with several major problems. The Continental empire accumulated by his father, Henry II (1151–89), was breaking up; Normandy, England's remaining Continental holding, had fallen to the French in 1204.

John responded to his problems with energetic defiance, mustering all the resources of his realm for military and diplomatic victory on the Continent; war plans and war finance dominated his policies. He achieved a settlement with the Pope in 1213, but failed in a great counterattack against King Philip of France in 1214. This defeat led immediately to the outbreak of a rebellion which had been developing in England for some time. The opposition exploited the King's failures abroad—soon after the loss of Normandy he was nicknamed John Softsword—but it fed on the resentment produced by his policies at home. This welling discontent was caused by the King's financial demands, by his exploitation of feudal relationships for his own political and financial interests, and by his increasing readiness to inject political and personal considerations into his exercise of justice. John's subjects were further outraged

by his use of patronage, which sharply distinguished those in from those out of favor, and by his reliance on a number of skilled foreign advisers who came to England from the lost lands on the Continent and enjoyed increasing influence and reward as sheriffs, custodians of castles and husbands of native heiresses.

Magna Carta dealt with all these injustices and inequities, but it was not concerned with them alone. King John's transgressions were not novel, and many of the grievances that the Charter dealt with considerably antedated John's reign. Richard I, the King's brother, and Henry II, their father, had also found the task of defending England's Continental possessions to be demanding and expensive; they too had been forced to muster armies and levy heavy taxes. Nor were John's policies really new. He and many of his most important officials had been brought up in the administrative traditions of Henry II's court, and for the most part they simply adhered to those traditions.

The political theories and assumptions that the Charter embodied were likewise issues of long standing. In the course of the twelfth century men had become increasingly familiar with two notions, both of which they owed in large measure to the increasing law and order provided by the Crown. One assumption derived from a growing readiness to accept and expect regular justice according to routine procedures in a court of law; from that notion emerged the idea of an established custom of the realm. The other concept derived from the fact that kings sold, and subjects bought, rights and privileges. Local communities—first towns and then counties—had rapidly acquired privileges in this way, possessing and defending them in common, and chartered liberties held by individuals or groups had become common features of English feudal society. Magna Carta, which sought to equate the custom of the realm with the rights of all free men, summarized both these trends. English law and political thought were profoundly affected by the Charter, which

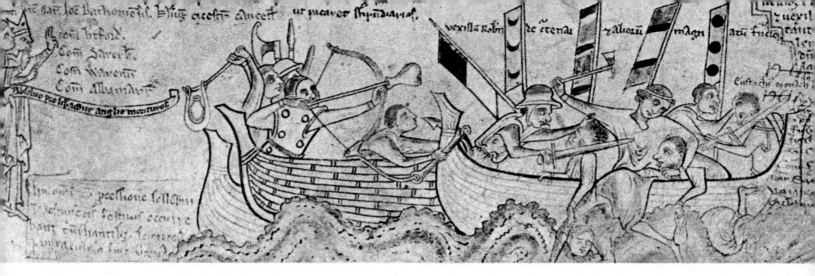

equated law with liberties and ultimately law with liberty.

The rebellion of 1215 marked a new departure. It was not simply another example of feudal anarchy, but rather a political and legal program, a statement of general rather than individual aims. As the crisis deepened in the early months of 1215, the argument turned increasingly on defining the customs of the realm, and upon erecting a largely fictitious "ancient custom" to challenge the innovations of Henry II and his sons. Out of these arguments grew a list of preliminary demands, which the rebellious nobles submitted to their king in April. John failed to meet the baronial demands, and in May of 1215, the barons went to war. On May 17, the rebels seized London, and the King was forced to open negotiations at Runnymede.

However, the June settlement was only a temporary one. On the one hand, it was a compromise that failed to satisfy the most intransigent of the King's opponents; on the other, it was equally unacceptable to the King himself. In time, inquiries into local government provoked outbreaks of lawlessness. The restoration of lands and privileges to individuals revealed a number of irreconcilable cases soluble only by force of arms. By September the country was drifting into a new civil war. The Charter itself provided the King with a rationale for attack, for although its text asserted that the Charter had been freely granted, the supporters of the document knew that their demands had been exacted by force. On these grounds, Pope Innocent III, to whom both parties had appealed for arbitration, annulled Magna Carta on August 24, 1215. The civil war that ensued was a bitter affair that continued for a year after John's death in October, 1216. Although the war ultimately involved the French, Magna Carta remained the central issue. Peace was secured only by reissuing the Charter in November, 1216, and November, 1217. These versions owed a great deal to the approval of the Pope and his agents in England. They omitted many of the purely temporary sections of the Charter of 1215 and abandoned the court of twenty-five barons and many of the provisions concerned with financial administration. With John dead and the new king, Henry III—a boy of nine at his accession—less of a threat to the barons' power, these chapters were no longer as essential. It was the 1217 version, slightly amended in 1225, that was incorporated into the law of the land. The 1217 and 1225 versions of the Great Charter were accompanied by a Charter of the Forest specifically concerned with the administration of the royal forests. In subsequent confirmation the two were usually associated.

The Charter's transformation was both curious and unique. Originally, Magna Carta was simply part of a settlement to end a civil war; it was in force only during the summer months of 1215, until its annulment by Pope Innocent. Yet it became, in the works of the great legal historian, F.W. Maitland, "the nearest approach to an irrepealable fundamental statute that England has ever had"; nine of its chapters still stand on the statute book. This transition from peace treaty to "fundamental statute" makes Magna Carta significant.

England was not alone in having such a charter of liberties; they were common features of European politics in the thirteenth and fourteenth centuries. Hungary had the Golden Bull (1222); Germany had both the Confederation with the Ecclesiastical Princes (1220) and the Statute in Favor of the Princes (1232); Aragon, the General Privilege (1283) and the Privilege of the Union (1287); and France, the charters of privileges of Normandy, Burgundy, and other provinces (1315). All these concessions sprang from situations analogous to that of England in 1215: war, financial pressure, harsh administration and discontent. No contemporary would have selected the English Magna Carta as the one most likely to survive, and yet it did while the other charters were soon defunct.

Magna Carta survived and flourished because it became inextricably linked with the processes of English government and political life. As early as 1215, careful measures were taken to ensure its full publication—a copy was sent to each shire, and the

A battle at sea between the English and the French.

Philip Augustus unhorsed at the Battle of Bouvines (1214) —one of the series of battles in the endemic war between France and England.

"The Charter walks abroad"

The sufferings of prisoners arrested without trial. This was banned by Magna Carta.

Magna Carta; an attempt by the barons to increase their power at the expense of the King became in time the foundation stone of constitutional liberty.

sheriff was ordered to read it out in the county court. This procedure was repeated in 1216, 1217, 1225 and again in 1253. As time passed, even greater emphasis was given to publication: a twice yearly reading in the county courts became law in 1265, a twice yearly reading in the cathedrals followed in 1297, and a reading four times a year in the county courts was decreed in 1300. On this last occasion, English was specified as the appropriate language, apparently for the first time. As a result, the Charter was well known, and copies proliferated in monastic or cathedral archives, in legal text books, and even

in the hands of the knights who did much of the work of the county courts.

However, the story of the Charter did not end with the feudal politics and law of the thirteenth century. Its longer survival depended on two features of the original document that were preserved in all subsequent reissues: first, the Charter was a grant in perpetuity intended to last for all time; and second, it stated broad general procedures and principles rather than detailed and transitory points of law. Thus each generation could reinterpret the Charter to fit new circumstances. Between 1331 and 1363 Parliament passed six statutory interpretations of the famous Chapter 39, which developed it in directions unimagined in 1215. These interpretations equated the "lawful judgment of peers" with trial by jury, a process that scarcely existed in thirteenth-century England; they identified the "law of the land" with "due process of law," a phrase that would have been all but incomprehensible in 1215; and they replaced the words "no free man" of the 1215 version with "no man whatsoever estate or condition he may be," a change that extended Magna Carta's protection to the villeins, or the majority of the population, who were thus brought within the scope of a provision from which they had been hitherto excluded.

Such reinterpretation became common and was extended to other chapters, particularly in the seventeenth century. Even in contemporary times,

lawyers have appealed to the chapter of Magna Carta that states that widows are to have their dower and marriage portion without delay in order to secure the prompt payment of a widow's pension, and to the chapter that permits free entry and exit from the realm in order to challenge the requirement of a passport for foreign travel.

Lawyers have been encouraged in this practice by the peculiar prominence that Magna Carta has acquired in English common law. The Charter was always given pride of place as the first item in the printed collection of statues published in the sixteenth century, and by the late thirteenth century—at a time when men were first becoming acquainted with the notion of statute law—Magna Carta already figured prominently in the manuscript collections of statutes that lawyers were then beginning to compile as books of reference. In a sense, Magna Carta became the origin of statute law. In 1215 this was unintended, at least by the rebel barons; their legal theory did not carry them beyond the idea of chartered privileges. Nevertheless, the 1215 charter contains a number of provisions concerned with the detailed administration of the law that do not seem to have been part of the rebels' demands, and which were probably inserted by the lawyers of the Crown simply in order to reform existing laws. The reissues of 1216 and 1217—particularly the latter—contain additional and more important material of the same kind, concerned with the conveying of land and the sessions of local courts. Much of the Charter of the Forest is made up of similar detailed regulations. Each of these successive documents show progressively better drafting, and all are marked improvements as legal drafts on the 1215 petition, known as the Articles of the Barons, in which the King's opponents first stated their demands.

These revisions of the original Charter were the work of men experienced in the administration of the courts, who used the Charter as a means of legal reform. Hence, Magna Carta was both a program of rebellion and a statement of law. The former characteristic was the more prominent in 1215, the latter in the revisions of 1217 and 1225. The former characteristic led to the demand for its confirmation in later crises; the latter made it a starting point for a growing body of legislation in the thirteenth century. The Provisions of Merton of 1236, the Statute of Marlborough of 1267, and the Statutes of Westminster of 1275 and 1285 were all in part concerned with points of law first formulated in Magna Carta, and as a result the Charter has become embedded in English history as a fundamental law. In the constitutional conflicts of the seventeenth century, Magna Carta was the obvious weapon to use in defending Parliament and the common law courts against the prerogative of the Stuart kings. "I shall be very glad to see," Sir Benjamin Rudyard declaimed in a Commons debate on the Petition of Right in 1628, "that old, decrepit Law Magna Carta which hath been kept so long, and lien bed-rid, as it were, I shall be glad to see it walk abroad again with new vigour and lustre . . ."

In the hands of Sir Edward Coke, first the Chief Justice and then the bitter constitutional opponent of the Stuarts, the Great Charter was used to attack royal monopolies, prerogative taxation and the prerogative court of the Star Chamber. All these Coke denounced as injurious to the freedom of the individual or to established judicial process. Others used the Charter to justify the principle of habeas corpus and the claim, advanced in the Petition of Right, that there should be "no arrest without cause shown." Coke was the first to equate the "liberties" of the Charter with the liberty of the individual, and it was the legal writings of Coke that carried the Charter to North America and planted the principles that he had found in Chapter 39 in the constitutions of the early colonies and ultimately of the United States. By this time, the Charter was considerably altered; the feudal liberties of the thirteenth century had given way to liberty as conceived by Coke and the American Founding Fathers, but some of the characteristics of the original charter still remained. Coke and his fellows regarded Magna Carta as a statement of fundamental, incontravertible law which itself went back beyond 1215 to the days before the Norman conquest of England. The men of 1215 had made no claim as bold and precise as that, although they had maintained, somewhat falsely, that their program was but a statement of ancient custom. Indeed, it was their myth that provided the foundation for Coke's modern legal structure—which continues to influence much of British, and American, legal thought today.   J. C. HOLT

Parliament in the reign of Edward I; the growth of parliamentary liberties sprang from Magna Carta.

Henry III and later successors of John reissued Magna Carta.

3/17

St. Francis and St. Dominic found their

Five months after King John was forced to grant the Magna Carta at Runnymede, Pope Innocent III—who was then at the height of his power—opened the Fourth Lateran Council in Rome. As a young man, Innocent had mastered Scholastic philosophy at Paris and canon and civil law at Bologna, but his pontificate (1198–1216) revealed him to be a man of action as well. In 1215, the fifty-four-year-old Pope seemed likely to dominate Europe for years to come. "The Lord left to St. Peter the governance not of the Church alone, but of the whole world," Innocent proclaimed—and he appeared bent on putting this claim into effect. "Princes have power in earth, priests over the soul, and as much as the soul is worthier than the body, so much worthier is the priesthood than the monarchy," he preached.

The unity of Christendom was Innocent's cherished ideal. To this end he inspired the Fourth Crusade, demanded rigorous treatment of the Albigensian heretics, and summoned 1,500 archbishops and other dignitaries to Rome to hear his plans for Church reform. The decrees that Innocent required the Lateran Council to endorse—almost without discussion—emphasized the universality of the Church and the significance of its sacraments, redefined dogma, and laid down detailed rules for episcopal elections, monastic life, the qualifications of the clergy and theological instruction. The Pope expected that those decrees would pitch spiritual life in a higher key, leaving no man in doubt of what the Church required of him. The Council, which ended in 1216 with the summoning of another crusade, capped the career of the greatest of the medieval popes—for Innocent died shortly after the Council dispersed.

Francis of Assisi

Through his patronage of both the Franciscans and Dominicans, Innocent associated the papacy with the new spiritual movements. The wisdom of Innocent's alliance with those new orders cannot be underestimated, for through the genius of Francis of Assisi (1182–1226) the religious life of the West was to be completely transformed. St. Francis, born Giovanni Bernardone, was the son of a wealthy Tuscan merchant. His childhood companions nicknamed him Francis ("the Frenchman") because of his penchant for French romances and troubadours' songs.

While in his twenties, Francis experienced a sudden conversion and told his friends that he intended to marry "a fairer bride than ever you saw, who surpasses all others in beauty and excels them in virtue" —the Lady Poverty. He renounced his possessions to lead a life of prayer and poverty in the hills—and soon attracted a substantial band of followers. In ragged habit and bare feet, he tended lepers, collected alms for the poor, preached the brotherhood of man and animals, and put the message of the Gospels in the language of the troubadours. Holy poverty seemed to bring a gaiety of spirit to the Franciscans, earning the Tuscan mendicants the nickname "God's jesters."

Detail of a reliquary of St. Francis.

Pope Innocent gave his cautious approval to the Order of Minorites (or Gray Friars) and Francis returned to Assisi to organize additional groups of friars in the area. Such religious groups were soon established throughout the West. Francis traveled widely—even arguing his case before the Sultan of Egypt—before relinquishing the rule of his Order to Brother Elias of Cortona in 1220 in order to devote himself to simpler tasks.

One of Francis' final tasks was to draw up a Rule for his friend St. Clare and her "Minoresses." These female counterparts of the Gray Friars, known as the "Poor Clares," were similarly dependent on alms, but like all other orders for women— and unlike the Franciscans—they were strictly enclosed. Two years after his death, St. Francis was canonized and his followers began to formulate plans for a great church at Assisi. Ironically, it was to be richly endowed and superbly decorated by the greatest artists in Italy—which was supposed to honor the apostle of poverty.

The Dominicans

In these same years the Order of the Dominicans, or Friars Preachers, was founded by the Spaniard Dominic de Guzman (1170–1221), who had been sent to Provence to help convert the Albigensian schismatics. If heresy was to be combated, he argued, there was an imperative need for an educated, preaching ministry in the towns; therefore, study was to be an integral part of the Dominican's vow. While St. Francis spurned possessing so much as a crucifix of his own, St. Dominic insisted on books for all his brothers.

Albigensian Heretics

The Albigensian heretics of Provence—who took their name from the town of Albi on the Tarn River —professed a total disregard of all authority, spiritual and secular. They classified believers into two groups: "the perfect," who renounced property, marriage and the world at large and on death passed directly to a state of glory; and "other believers," who could live as they chose, provided they received before death the sacrament of the *Consolamentum*, an act of absolution which could be performed only once in a lifetime, however, and those who recovered from their death beds were expected to commit suicide. The sect quickly took root in Provence.

The Albigensians did not attract much attention until Count Raymond VI of Toulouse joined the movement. Zealous priests were sent to wean the Albigensians from their errors, but their descriptions of the Christian life smacked too much of asceticism for those nurtured on Provençal vernacular literature. When his priests' arguments failed, Innocent III obliged Philip II of France to proclaim a crusade against the Albigensians, whom he called "heretics worse than the Saracens." Raymond soon submitted and restored Provençal churches to orthodox use, but many of his subjects held out.

The young Henry III

Henry III was only nine at the time of his accession to the English

An elephant that was presented to Henry III, from Matthew Paris' *Chronicles*.

throne and control of the government was placed in the hands of William, Earl of Pembroke.

Upon Pembroke's death, the papal legate Pandulph was appointed regent. Archbishop Langton soon persuaded the Pope to recall Pandulph, however, and power passed to Hubert de Burgh, England's chief justice, who was anxious to restore strong government and free England from interference by foreigners. After coming of age, Henry III dismissed Hubert and attempted to rule England alone. He foolishly appointed the Frenchman Peter des Roches as chief justice, and Roches promptly appointed his kinsfolk to high office. His actions provoked the English barons to renounce their fealty to Henry and threatened his position. Following in the steps of Stephen Langton, the saintly Archbishop Edmund Rich warned the king that his attempt to rule the realm without the cooperation of his barons would end in disaster. Henry wisely expelled the French officials.

Henry found fulfillment for his religious ideals and cultured tastes in his buildings at Westminster. The reconstructed Abbey, which housed the relics of Henry's mentor, Edward the Confessor, was the first building in England with double

The head of Henry III.

tiers of flying-buttresses and bar-traceried windows. "As the rose is to other flowers," ran an inscription on a tile in the Chapter House, "so is this house to other buildings." The nearby Palace of Westminster was no less splendid. Its *tour de force* was the Painted Chamber, an enormous, richly decorated room that the king ordered his clerk of the works to have finished by a certain date, "even though you have to hire 1,000 workmen a day."

Curiously, in the business of

The seal of Philip Augustus.

government proper, Henry showed no such drive. His rival, Philip II of France, on the other hand, was an energetic and forceful king. During his long reign (1180–1223) the kingdom of France tripled in size (largely as a result of Philip's conquest of Normandy and Poitou from John of England). Philip thoroughly reformed the financial and judicial administration of his realm by employing a corps of professional officials. By playing off one great feudal landowner against another, he likewise reduced the powers of the barons. In consequence, French feudalism became firmly established, and military obligations to the Crown were reaffirmed. Philip walled and paved Paris, built the original Louvre (as a fortified palace) and endowed the Cathedral of Notre-Dame. Indeed, the layout of the capital remained much as he left it until the age of Napoleon III.

This was also the age of French romances, of courtly love and chivalry. It was the age of the fables of Chretian de Troyes of Champange, of the *Chanson de Roland* and of troubadours improvising their songs as interludes between recited passages of prose (the lay, vernacular counterpart to the monks' Latin plainsong, which was sung between the spoken prayers of divine offices). The schools of Paris, now in their prime, produced drinking songs as well as disputations on Scholasticism. And contemporary crusades—

even in the Age of Faith—were as much adventures on the frontiers of Europe as campaigns against the dreaded Infidel.

Frederick II and the Holy Roman Empire

The sudden death of Emperor Henry VI in 1197 plunged Germany into fourteen years of civil war. The struggle for the throne was resolved in 1211, when the German princes deposed the already excommunicated Guelf emperor Otto IV, and invited the eighteen-year-old Frederick, a Hohenstaufen, to be their king. Frederick, the son of Henry VI and Constance of Sicily, had been under the guardianship of Pope Innocent III since his mother's death.

Despite his early pledges that he would not attempt to unite the Empire with his inherited kingdoms of Sicily and Naples, Frederick did precisely that—and the resulting confederation hemmed in the Papal States. Moreover, Frederick refused to confirm the enormous privileges over the German Church that Otto had granted to Rome—and he created additional friction by his crusading. At his coronation in Rome in 1220, Frederick renewed his pledge to deliver Jerusalem from the Infidel, but he found political conditions in Naples and Sicily such that he was forced to restore order there before launching his first crusade. In 1227 he set sail for the Holy Land but was obliged to return to port a few days later when he became quite sick. Alleging that Frederick's illness was feigned, Pope Gregory IX excommunicated him.

Frederick II's successful operations in the Holy Land and his command of the Arabic language enabled him to extract a ten-year truce from Malik-al-Kamil, the Sultan of Egypt, a truce that granted him control of Jerusalem, Bethlehem and Nazareth. On Gregory's orders, the Patriarch of Jerusalem refused to celebrate religious services in Frederick's presence. In defiance, the Emperor, who had married the daughter of the late king of Jerusalem four years earlier, crowned himself king in the Church of the Holy Sepulcher.

Frederick's feud with the papacy became even more bitter when Innocent IV replaced the aged Gregory IX in 1243. Fearful of his life, Innocent fled to Lyons where, in 1245, he gathered a synod, demanded Frederick's removal and

put forward his own candidates for Emperor. Despite the Emperor's offers of reconciliation, the Pope would not retract his demands and even went so far as to preach a crusade against him.

Known as *Stupor mundi*, the wonder of the world, Frederick II amazed his contemporaries and leaves posterity puzzled. Some have called him "the first modern man to occupy a throne," and certainly his remodeling of his Italian kingdom, with its remarkable code of laws, and his passion for science foreshadow the autocratic princes of the Renaissance. Yet Frederick left Germany much as he found it: a conglomeration of feudal principalities utterly divided on the nature of the Empire and the person of the Emperor.

A brilliant linguist with a real passion for scholarship and the arts, Frederick was as much at home with the philosophy of Aristotle as with the study of natural science. He wrote a remarkable book on hawking, translated Arabic works and found a niche for the Provençal poets expelled during the Albigensian crusade. After his own crusade, he installed Saracen garrisons in Italy and his court was exposed to the esthetic influences of Moslem civilization; the courtyards of his palace were decorated with fountains, the rooms were luxurious with cushions and colorful silk hangings, perfume and exotic fruits. He turned his court into a university, noting that "science must go hand in hand with government, legislation and the pursuit of war." He founded the University of Naples, the first university to owe its origin to royal initiative, and endowed a medical

Frederick II with a hawk.

Marienburg, headquarters of the Teutonic knights.

school at Salerno, which admitted women as well as men.

The Emperor's patronage of the Teutonic Knights, whom he reorganized as a crusading, military order in 1226 to combat the Mongol invasions, led to German colonization beyond the eastern frontiers of the Empire, notably in Prussia. The flag followed the Cross and resulted in a considerable German migration towards the northeast.

Mongol incursions

From the steppes of Central Asia in the eleventh century came the Mongol Tartars, who were to dominate Russia for 250 years. After a prolonged struggle for supremacy, the chieftain Temusin was acknowledged Genghis Khan, or "Very Mighty King," by an assembly of the leaders of Mongol tribes at Karakorum in 1206. Genghis Khan led his nomadic followers into northern China and northern Persia, and even penetrated as far west as Bokhara in southwestern Russia. Led by Subotai, the Great Khan's chief of staff, the Mongols swept on across the Caucasus and onto the steppes of Polovtsk. The prince of Kiev and the rulers of southern Russia hastened to the aid of the Polovtsi, but were defeated at the battle of the Kalku River in 1223. By the time of his death in 1227, Genghis Khan had consolidated his empire in North China, and ten years later Genghis' grandnephew Batu began a systematic conquest of southern and central Russia. He took Kiev in 1240, and marched on Novgorod, a city then ruled by the Grand Duke Alexander Nevski.

The Russian Giant Stirs

The thaw of 1238 was a particularly heavy one in northeastern Russia and flood waters accompanying it forced the apparently invincible Mongol chieftain Batu to withdraw to the steppes of Central Asia. Batu's retreat saved the city of Novgorod from certain sack and spared its adolescent Grand Prince, Alexander. The significance of Novgorod's escape became apparent two years later when Russian troops led by the young Prince defeated the vast armies of King Erik of Sweden on the banks of the Neva River. In rapid succession, Alexander (who had added Nevski to his name to commemorate his initial victory) routed the Germanic Knights of the Teutonic Order and turned back a Lithuanian invasion. Having secured Russia's frontiers, Alexander devoted the rest of his life to interceding with the Tartars on behalf of his people. His selfless diplomacy led to Alexander's canonization in 1380.

The Archangel Michael; the Orthodox faith alone held Russia together in the thirteenth century, when it was attacked from all sides.

Opposite St. Boris and St. Gleb: these national saints appeared to Nevski's army in battle and scattered the enemy.

Russia began to emerge as a European power shortly after the middle of the ninth century A.D. The Grand Duchy of Kiev, cradle of the Russian empire, was founded during that century by Normans and Slavs—men of Indo-European rather than Asian origin—who built their city along the river route that leads from the Baltic to the Black Sea. Around Kiev arose a great cluster of principalities that were eventually united under the house of Rurik. This powerful dynasty of Scandinavian origin married its daughters to the kings of France, Hungary, and Norway, and to the Emperor of Germany, while contracting other family alliances with the Byzantine Emperor and the King of England. Converted under Vladimir the Saint, the Kievian state became a bulwark of Christendom against the nomads of the steppes. Linked with the great European commercial centers by her flourishing trade routes, "the Mother of Cities," as the Russians fondly called Kiev, rapidly became one of the most active and civilized metropolises on the Continent.

A Mongol invasion at the beginning of the thirteenth century put an end to Kiev's promising development, and for the next two hundred years the Russian nation was dominated by Asiatics. After the devastation of Kiev and the banks of the Dnieper by Mongol hordes, or armies, a large part of the population scattered to the north and east, where the virgin forest remained impenetrable to the enemy. The Grand Duke of Kiev, a descendant of Rurik's dynasty, transferred the center of government to the region of the Upper Volga and the Oka rivers, to the principalities of Rostov, Vladimir and Suzdal.

As a result, the whole aspect of national life was transformed. Intermarriage among the colonists and the indigenous Finnish tribes gradually produced a race of Great Russians—bearded, snub-nosed men of sober habits, the hard-working builders of the future empire. With the exception of Novgorod, a great commercial city in northwest Russia that was allied with the German Hanseatic League, the towns of the Suzdal, remote from the stream of commerce, preserved a clearly provincial character. The princes of the Suzdal appeared as nothing more than wealthy landowners, principally concerned with the administration of their large estates. Eschewing the incessant competition for the succession that preoccupied their relations and neighbors, the Suzdal princes transformed their own possessions into hereditary fiefs, a move that greatly strengthened their power.

Nonetheless, these princes were threatened from all sides by the gravest dangers. They had become vassals of the Mongols, and each of them was obliged to appear before the lieutenants of the Great Khan, who were established in the Lower Volga region, to make humble application for their investiture. In addition, the power of the Grand Duke was scarcely recognized over the immense territory—extending from the Gulf of Finland to the approaches to the White Sea—which belonged to the free city of Novgorod. Rich merchants, the real rulers of this patrician republic, chose and dismissed their local princes as they saw fit, with the sole purpose of ensuring the defense of their frontiers—although they generally gave preference to the increasingly powerless descendants of the Grand Duke of Kiev. Only a definite threat from without caused the merchants to request the aid of the younger sons of the house of Suzdal. To all this was added the increasingly strong pressure exerted on Russia by her western neighbors, the Swedes and the Teutonic Knights, who were representatives of more developed civilizations, which were capable of wiping out the last traces of the Russian national idea.

Alexander Nevski stands out in great clarity against the somber background of this tragic period of Russian history. In his spiritual and physical beauty, the clearness of his gaze and the purity of his soul, he represented the archetype of the princely saint as envisioned by Russians in the Middle Ages. In him the themes of patriotism and Christianity

Victory at the Neva

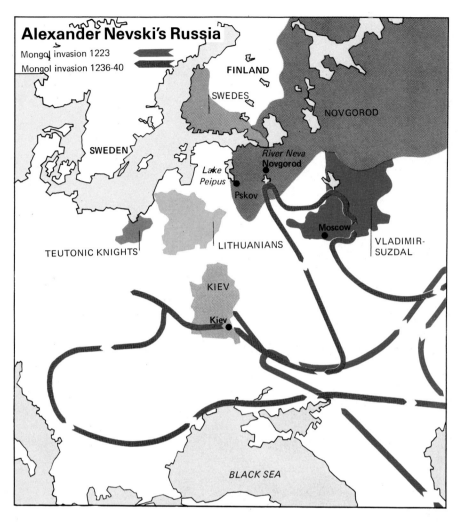

Alexander Nevski's Russia

Mongol invasion 1223
Mongol invasion 1236-40

FINLAND
SWEDES
NOVGOROD
SWEDEN
River Neva
Novgorod
Lake Peipus
Pskov
Moscow
TEUTONIC KNIGHTS
LITHUANIANS
VLADIMIR-SUZDAL
KIEV
Kiev
BLACK SEA

A copper cross of thirteenth-century Russian origin.

became interwoven and eventually merged into one another.

Alexander was born in May, 1219, at Pereyaslavl, a fief that was owned by his father, who was of the house of the Grand Prince of the Suzdal region. He spent the first years of his life in this small city, which stood on the shores of a lake among trees and meadows and was defended by a simple wooden palisade. He was scarcely three years old when his father was elected Prince of Novgorod and resettled some six miles away from that ever-unruly city in order to preside over its fortunes.

At the age of nine Alexander and his elder brother Theodore were left alone at Novgorod under the guardianship of certain nobles. Their father, who had grown disgusted with his office, rarely returned to Novgorod after 1228, and during a subsequent civil crisis, the children were obliged to flee the city under the leadership of a tutor. Theodore died prematurely some years later, and when his father, in 1236, became Grand Prince of Kiev—that is, the ruler of all Russia—Alexander fell heir to the fief of Novgorod.

The adolescent found himself faced with terrible responsibilities. A great Mongol invasion of the north of Russia occurred the following year. Led by Batu, grandson of Genghis, the invaders swiftly de-

feated the Volga Bulgars and swept into north-eastern Russia. By March of 1238, the barbarians had advanced to within sixty miles of Novgorod. Alexander's fief appeared doomed when Batu, fearing that imminent spring thaws would trap his forces in the heavy forests around Novgorod, suddenly withdrew to the steppes.

Alexander's memorable reign at Novgorod lasted for sixteen years. Alexander made it his business to combat the separatist tendencies of the city, to strengthen its links with the central power, and to weaken the economic and political power of the *boyars*, or local grandees. In 1239 he married the daughter of the Prince of Polotsk, a feudal neighbor. During the next few years Alexander frequently enjoyed the pleasures of the chase, and hunted bear armed only with a sling—but such diversions never swayed him from his administrative duties.

Alexander's first military victory, won in 1240 on the banks of the Neva, had world-wide repercussions and earned him the name of Nevski. In an attempt to conquer those parts of Russia that had not fallen under the dominion of the Tartars—and to cut off Novgorod's sole outlet to the Baltic Sea—King Erik of Sweden gathered together a great army and placed it under the command of his son-in-law Birger. The Swedish sovereign derived some encouragement in this undertaking from a bull issued by Pope Gregory IX in 1237, and addressed to the Bishop of Uppsala. That edict summoned the Swedes to a crusade against the Finns, who had abandoned their Catholic faith under the influence of their neighbors the Russians. King Erik's interpretation of this papal message was clearly somewhat forced, but it appeared to furnish him with some justification for his aggression against Russia.

Alexander had foreseen the danger, and in 1239 he had organized the defense of the routes from Novgorod to the sea, and had placed sentries on both sides of the Gulf of Finland. Pelguse, the chieftain of the local tribe and a convert to Christianity, warned Alexander that a Swedish army was disembarking on the banks of the Neva, and the Prince hastened to meet the enemy. Reviewing his troops before their departure, Alexander uttered the phrase—an allusion to the Psalms—that has remained his most famous: "God is not on the side of force but of the just cause, the *Pravda*." The word *pravda*, employed in modern times as the title of the most important Soviet newspaper, is not easy to translate; it means at the same time "truth," "justice," "social equity," and "just cause"—and embodies, even today, the deepest aspiration of the Russian people.

In order to engage the enemy, Alexander's troops were forced to march over marshy land, a region around modern Leningrad that still presents a rather gloomy appearance. Pressing on swiftly, Alexander's army arrived at the mist-shrouded banks of the Neva several hours after dawn. There, according to Russian legend, the local chieftain Pelguse had witnessed a curious vision as the sun rose. He saw a boat bearing several mysterious ghosts coming slowly down the river. As the vessel drew near, the shades

were revealed to be two holy princes, Boris and Gleb, and their heavenly oarsmen, who were coming to the aid of their "brother Alexander."

The battle, which began a short time later, caught the Swedes unawares; they were convinced that the Novgorod forces, deprived of the assistance of a Suzdal army recently destroyed by the Mongols, would be in no position to offer them resistance. Birger, the King's son-in-law, and many of his knights were installed in a gold embroidered tent, but the main body of the Swedish army had not yet disembarked. The Russians carried out their attacks with lightning-like rapidity; while Alexander himself wounded Birger with a blow from a spear, his men-at-arms cut the bridges joining the boats to the river bank. Panic seized the Swedes, who fled in utter disorder. According to legend, archangels swept down from Heaven and wiped out the Swedish knights on the opposite shore of the Neva.

Similar scenes occurred in the following year, when Alexander inflicted total defeat on the Knights of the Teutonic Order, a German crusading force that had acted in concert with the Swedes. The Knights had seized Izborsk, and broken the Truce of Pskov by burning the outskirts of that city before the boyars could open the gates to them. Having crushed the Swedish offensive, Alexander made ready to go to the aid of Pskov. Prevented by the boyars from carrying out this plan, Alexander withdrew to his father's estate at Pereyaslavl. It was not long before he was recalled by his subjects, who had at last realized the true extent of their danger. Alexander returned with regiments raised in the territory of Suzdal, and set off for the western frontier at the head of the combined Russian forces.

Sergei Eisenstein's film classic *Alexander Nevski* has made the public in the West familiar with this battle, in which the steel-clad Teutons initially drove a wedge through the Russian lines, forcing them to retreat out onto the ice of Lake Peipus. There the Russians regrouped, attacked the enemy on two flanks and brought down or put to flight hundreds of German knights. Alexander's victory was complete, and the German advance was arrested for centuries. The battle, which salvaged the very existence of the Russian nation, was supposedly joined by heavenly armies, similar to those that had brought aid to Prince Alexander at the Neva.

Alexander's father, the Grand Prince Yaroslav, died on his way back from the Mongol camp at Karakorum, where he had been summoned by the Great Khan. Russian chroniclers, whose assertions agree with the testimony of Plano Carpini, the famous Italian traveler, suggest that Alexander's

Genghis Khan, the Mongol chief whose death in 1227 saved Russia from annihilation.

Above left Alexander Nevski leads the Russians into battle.

The city of Novgorod in the thirteenth century.

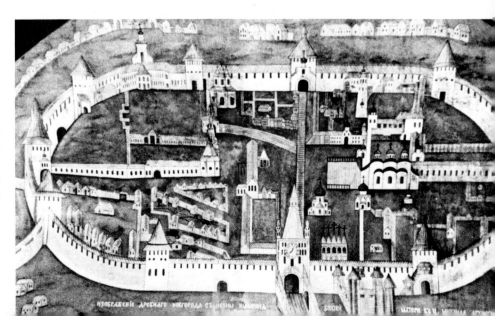

Medieval cathedral of Peroslave with the nineteenth-century statue of St. Alexander Nevski.

Bear hunting : a favored occupation in thirteenth-century Russia.

father was poisoned. The matter of the succession could not be settled without further intervention of the Tartar leaders. For reasons that remain unknown, it was not the deceased prince's eldest son, Yuri, but Alexander who was summoned, together with his brother Andrew, to appear before the Asiatic overlords.

Alexander was now faced with a tragic dilemma. Was the hero of the Neva and Lake Peipus to adopt the attitude of a humble vassal and recognize openly the loss of Russian independence—thus insulting the death-under-torture already suffered by some of Alexander's near relations? A Western knight might not have submitted to such a sacrifice of his honor, but Alexander was a Russian knight—an Orthodox prince—and, thinking solely of the good of his people, he preferred to submit to the Divine Will, and took counsel of the higher clergy. The metropolitan Cyril—head of the Russian Orthodox Church—gave his approval to Alexander's decision to leave for the Mongol camp on the condition that he worship no idols and not deny his faith in Christ.

Collaboration with the Tartars was, at that moment, a historical necessity. The term "collaborator" has been somewhat discredited in recent times, and has become synonymous with treachery. We consider it a patriot's duty to continue the struggle, as long as the slightest chance of success remains— but there was no chance for Russia in 1246. The nation could count on no help from outside, for the attitude of neighboring countries was entirely hostile.

The Prince becomes a monk

Moreover, Russia's armies, which had been sufficient to confront enemies as courageous as the Swedes or the Teutons in equal numbers, could offer no defense against the nomad hordes, who carried all before them as they advanced by tens, or even hundreds of thousands.

Subsequently, the Russians have recognized the great service that Alexander rendered them by sacrificing his pride for the sake of the Fatherland. The Mongols themselves were profoundly impressed by the conduct of this man, whose reputation had reached them some time beforehand; they granted him the honors due to his rank and spared him both the ordeal by fire and worship of the idols. Nevertheless, they did oblige Alexander to undertake the interminable journey through the deserts of Asia to Karakorum, and only allowed him to return to his native land after three years' absence. In the years that followed, Alexander returned to his masters' camp, situated north of the Azov Sea, on three occasions, to arrange current affairs and to implore the Mongols' mercy for his people.

Alexander's eldest brother was dead, and his second brother, Andrew, had taken to flight after an attempted rising, which ended—as could be foreseen—in terrible reprisals. Alexander thereby became the Grand Prince of Russia. It was his concern now to prevent further invasions, to inspire the Great Khan with confidence, to serve as intermediary between him and the Russian people, and to prevent rash insurrections even at the price of painful concession.

This superhuman task was made no easier by fresh attacks from Sweden, against which, in 1258, Alexander was obliged to conduct a new and similarly victorious campaign. Incessant unrest in Novgorod assumed an especially serious character when, in 1259, the Tartars exacted a tribute from the population of the land.

In 1262, when the exactions of the Tartars provoked another popular uprising, Alexander undertook his fifth journey to the Tartar headquarters, in an effort to ward off a punitive expedition. For a whole year he struggled to pacify the Great Khan and his henchmen, and eventually succeeded in dissuading the Tartars from their plan of raising Russian regiments for a war against Persia. But Alexander had come to the end of his strength. On the return journey, over roads made difficult by the autumn rains, he fell ill, and was taken to a monastery, where he died in November, 1263. Before drawing his last breath, Alexander gave up his princely rank and put on the habit of a monk.

In subsequent years, numerous miracles occurred at Alexander's tomb, which led to his being canonized locally in 1380, and by the whole Russian Church at the Council of 1547. Five centuries after Alexander's death—after the victorious outcome of his successor's war against Sweden—Peter the Great caused the relics of St. Alexander Nevski to be transferred to the new capital of St. Petersburg (Leningrad), where they lie today at the monastery that bears his name.   CONSTANTINE DE GRUNWALD

The dormition of the Virgin Mary: an icon of the Novgorod School.

St. George and the Dragon, representing the triumph of good over evil.

St. Thomas Aquinas finds faith to be

St. Louis of France.

Frenchmen look back upon the reign of Louis IX (1226–70) as one of the golden ages of the French monarchy. Few kings of France were as dearly loved by their subjects or achieved as high a reputation among contemporary monarchs as Saint Louis. His austere upbringing by Blanche of Castille (who was queen-regent of France during her son's minority) and his natural piety led Louis to model his life on the ideal of Christian knighthood— and consequently his reign was dominated by crusading ventures against the Infidel. His strategic ability did not match his enthusiasm, however, and his campaigns proved disastrous.

The Seventh Crusade

In preparation for his first campaign, the Seventh Crusade (1248–54), Louis IX laid out the port and town of Aigues-Mortes on an estuary of the Rhone in Languedoc. The French army, which sailed from Louis' new port, easily took the Egyptian city of Damietta, but when Louis advanced on Cairo he was captured and his army was massacred. The French king paid the Sultan of Egypt an enormous sum to ransom himself and many other Christian captives. Upon his release, Louis made a prolonged pilgrimage to Jerusalem, postponing his return to France for four years. The objectives of Louis' second crusade—officially, the Eighth Crusade, made in conjunction with Edward I of England in 1270—were changed at the last moment, probably at the insistence of Louis' brother Charles of Anjou, and the French monarch found

himself leading his followers across the sands of Tunis. The Anglo-French force was struck by dysentery and Louis died, still convinced that he could convert the Emir. Almost at once reports began to circulate of miracles being wrought by the agency of the King's relics, and before long he was canonized.

As Christendom's holy knight, Louis had been the chief promoter of peace in Europe. He had, for example, yielded the districts of Limousin and Perigord to Henry III of England on the condition that Henry become his vassal for the attenuated duchies of Aquitaine and Gascony and renounce all English claims to Normandy, Maine, Anjou and Poîtou. Unhappily, the Treaty of Paris (1259), which confirmed this arrangement, contained the seeds of the Hundred Years' War.

Men and nations turned to Louis as the natural arbitrator in their disputes. He advised on the succession to the throne of Flanders and in 1264, by the *Mise of Amiens*, adjudicated in favor of Henry III against the English barons. Royal power and administration increased in France during his reign, but the country was pushed to the verge of bankruptcy. Louis, who brought tremendous prestige to the French monarchy, was able to follow the Cross only because his grandfather Philip II had established a strong royal administration.

English Gothic

While Henry III was lavishing more money than he could readily afford on a shrine for St. Edward the Confessor at Westminster, bishops and priors throughout the country were collecting benefactions from the rich and humbler offerings from pilgrims in order to transform the country's Norman cathedrals and churches into truly English edifices. In time, masons and glaziers altered the pointed arches and vaulted roofs of those cathedrals

beyond recognition. The west fronts of Peterborough and Wells cathedrals, the transepts of Durham and York, and the chapter houses at Lichfield and Lincoln were erected in this period—demonstrating both the range of craftsmanship and the wealth that could be tapped to finance operations on such a grandiose scale. Salisbury Cathedral, perhaps the finest example of English Gothic architecture, was completely rebuilt in the comparatively short period between 1220 and 1258. In this formative age of religious festivals and mystery plays, pilgrimages—to Becket's shrine at Canterbury, to St. Hugh's tomb at Lincoln, to St. Alban's, Bury and Winchester—were commonplace.

Universities come of age

The thirteenth century saw the consolidation of the universities, which had grown from uncertain origins to become key institutions of the medieval state. The Paris schools had outshone all others in the days of Peter Abelard (*d.* 1142), but it was not until 1200 that the University of Paris received a royal charter, incorporating its guild of masters. (By contrast, Bologna, already the fountainhead of legal studies, was organized as a guild of students.) Paris was soon recognized as the home of theological study and there, in 1257, Robert de Sorbon, Louis' confessor, founded the Sorbonne, a college where both professors and students pursued courses in Scholastic theology. Young men from all over Europe flocked to the Sorbonne to sit at the feet of such renowned lecturers as Guillaume de St. Amour and Pierre d'Ailly.

Oxford had already become a *Studium Generale*—a home of doctors, faculties and students from all quarters—by the time that Henry II's dispute with Becket closed the Paris schools to Englishmen. A scholarly quarrel at Oxford in 1209 led to the establishment of a second

university community at Cambridge. There, as at Oxford, the Franciscan friars played a leading role. The first rector of the Oxford Franciscans was Robert Grosseteste—chancellor and later Bishop of Lincoln, the diocese in which Oxford lay—who became a staunch defender of the university's liberties against the king, barons and townsfolk.

After a seven-year apprenticeship, a student at either English university attained the rank of master. As public proof of his ability he gave a specimen lesson—and was then licensed to teach anywhere. In this era before collegiate foundations, there was a notable freemasonry among Europe's wandering scholars' life, for political events occasionally forced an entire teaching faculty to migrate to another center of learning for a season. When Walter de Merton founded his college at Oxford in 1266, he took the precaution of acquiring property at Cambridge also, for use in the event of just such a migration.

In the middle years of the thirteenth century the first collegiate foundations—William of Durham's

The library at Merton College, Oxford's oldest college.

Great University Hall (later University College), Balliol and Merton at Oxford, and, in 1284, Peterhouse at Cambridge—were established. They proved to be of great benefit to scholars, Church and King.

St. Thomas Aquinas

The Italian St. Thomas Aquinas (1224–74), the most respected of medieval philosophers, entered the Dominican Order to study at Paris under Albert of Cologna. Aquinas, who spent most of his life teaching at Paris, and at Rome and other Italian cities, dominated Scholastic philosophy with his encyclopedic

The west front of Salisbury Cathedral : perhaps the finest example of English Gothic.

knowledge and incisive mind. His principal work was to build an elaborate structure reconciling pure philosophy with Church dogma and substituting Aristotelianism for Platonism as the most specifically Christian philosophy. Although he eliminated from the Latin version of Aristotle's texts the errors perpetrated by commentators through the centuries, his acceptance of Aristotle was uncritical.

The core of Thomism was that philosophy and theology were independent disciplines within their own bounds: the task of philosophy was to examine the natural order in the light of reason, while that of theology was to investigate the supernatural order as revealed in God's world. For Aquinas, faith and reason were separate phenomena that the orthodox thinker must satisfactorily reconcile—he was personally convinced that faith was rational; and reason, divine.

In his *Summa Theologica (Sum of All Theology)*, he attempted to create a perfect, all-embracing system, unfolding all that was known of the relationship between God and man. Aquinas' literary method was that of dialectical disputation, the familiar form of argumentation at the universities. He began by asking such questions as whether God existed, whether He was perfect, whether He was eternal. He painstakingly resolved all objections to each answer before passing from one point to the next.

The *Summa*, a monumental work that was impressive for its scholarliness and force of argument, irrevocably united philosophy with the medieval Church. As a result Aquinas came to be regarded as the most representative and the most balanced of the "Schoolmen."

Roger Bacon and medieval science

A systematic thinker of a very different kind was the English Franciscan friar Roger Bacon (1214–92). "Suspected novelties" in his lectures at Paris and Oxford led to his being disciplined by his Order. Indeed, the significance of Bacon's work lay in the very modernity for which he was disciplined. He gave up teaching the philosophy of Aristotle in order, as he said, "to acquire knowledge of all the sciences and their use in the field of theology," and for twenty years he labored in pursuit of that great design. During that time Bacon spent nearly five thousand dollars

on "secret books, different kinds of instruments, tables and other things." For him mathematics was "the alphabet of philosophy," and experiment, not speculation, was the keystone of science. Although Bacon did not actually invent eyeglasses, he did experiment with the use of convex lenses for correcting defects of vision, and although he is no longer honored as "the inventor of gunpowder," his contributions to scientific thought, as embodied in his great encyclopedic treatises, make him unique among medieval writers.

While Bacon's contemporaries were engaged in metaphysical disputations, he was describing and defining what he called "experimental science." "Experimental science alone," he wrote, "can ascertain to perfection what can be effected by Nature, what by art, what by fraud. It alone teaches how to judge all the follies of the magicians, just as logic tests argument." Bacon paid a high price for his role in the transmission of Greek and Arabic knowledge into Western scholarship: for many years he was obliged to work in strict secrecy; his superiors accused him of practicing "the black arts"; he was barred from England and he lost his family's financial support. Pope Clement IV ultimately recognized the friar's genius, however, and he was allowed to return home.

Germany after Frederick II

Meanwhile in Germany, Frederick II had died, leaving the Empire to his son Conrad IV, and Sicily to his illegitimate son Manfred. Both Germany and the Italian kingdom were soon plunged into war. Manfred later succeeded in regaining southern Italy and Sicily but in 1266 Charles of Anjou, brother of Louis IX, eagerly accepted a papal offer of the Sicilian crown.

Even more disastrous was the "great interregnum" in Germany (1254–73), for it spelled the doom of the Empire as an effective political organization. The bizarre "double imperial election" of 1257 —which resulted in the rival candidates, Richard, Earl of Cornwall (Henry III's brother) and Alfonso X of Castile, each claiming a majority of the seven electoral votes—discredited all concerned. Alfonso never set foot in Germany, while Richard, glorying in his title "King of the Romans," failed to establish his authority even where support

Rudolf I : the first Hapsburg Emperor.

was strongest. The 1257 election did fix the number of electors at the arbitrary number of seven, however, and in 1273 those electors united in choosing Rudolf I of Hapsburg, a weakling prince who was no threat to them. For the next two hundred years the Emperor was a meaningless figurehead, while the German potentates, lay and spiritual, ruled their districts as they chose.

Simon de Montfort and the first parliaments

During his struggle with the Hohenstaufen, Pope Alexander IV had offered the Kingdom of Sicily to Henry III for his second son, Edmund "Crouchback," in return for a considerable sum. The "Sicilian business" proved a fiasco, but the Pope insisted on payment. Before he was permitted to raise taxes to pay the Pope, Henry had to agree to his barons' demands to be brought into partnership with him in the government of the realm. Their plan of reform was embodied in the Provisions of Oxford (1258) with "parliaments" meeting three times a year to discuss affairs and redress grievances. However, implementation of the barons' plan proved impossible while personal animosities remained. Louis IX's

arbitration in favor of Henry was rejected by the city of London, and civil war broke out. The leader of the baronial opposition, Simon de Montfort, defeated his royal brother-in-law at the battle of Lewes in 1264, and for fifteen months was virtual ruler of England. In 1265 he called a parliament composed of two knights from each shire and—in a revolutionary step—added two burgesses from each previously unrepresented borough. Lord Edward, Henry's elder son, led the conservative barons against de Montfort at Evesham later the same year, and Henry III was returned to the throne. The events that occurred after the Provisions of Oxford were signed permanently affected the development of English government, however. And when Edward I succeeded Henry, one of his first acts as king was to summon a parliament similar to the one called by his uncle, de Montfort.

The seal of Simon de Montfort, virtual ruler of England for a year.

Fighting in the East

In the middle of the thirteenth century there were also decisive battles in the Near and Far East. The Mongol chieftain Hulagu, grandson of Genghis Khan, captured Baghdad in 1258, executed the Caliph and established the rule of the Il-Khans in Persia. Hulagu next took Aleppo, and seemed likely to overrun Syria until his advance was checked by the Mameluke of Egypt at Ain Jalut in 1260 and the Moslem state was saved. The Mameluke's warriors took Jaffa and Antioch in 1268, and there held the forces of the Eighth Crusade at bay. News of his accession reached Edward I at the Crusader's camp before Acre, "the sink of Christendom," in 1272. A year earlier, a caravan of Venetian merchants had passed through Acre on its way to the Orient.

When East Met West

Thirteenth-century Europe was only vaguely aware that its imported silks originated in a land to the east called Cathay. China, for its part, knew about the West but was not especially interested in it. Then, in the summer of 1275, three travelers from Venice reached the court of Kublai Khan, China's Great Lord of Lords. The brothers Niccolò and Maffeo Polo and Niccolò's son Marco lingered in the Far East for twenty years, and when Marco returned to Italy he set down his impressions of those years in a book entitled, somewhat grandiosely, Description of the World. *Marco Polo's travel narrative fascinated generations of readers; two centuries later it stirred the ambitions of another seeker of Cathay, Christopher Columbus.*

Every year at the beginning of June, Kublai Khan, Great Lord of Lords, "the mightiest man that ever was in the world since Adam our first parent," was accustomed to leave his winter palace in Peking for a three-month-long vacation at his summer palace in Shangtu ("Xanadu"). This princely pile of "marble and other ornamental stones, marvelously embellished and richly adorned, with gilded halls and chambers" stood at the entrance to a spacious game-park which provided food for the imperial falcons. In a pleasant grove, in the midst of the park, stood another large palace—a portable structure of split bamboo poles, held in place by more than two hundred silken cords. This palace was "reared on gilt and lacquered pillars, on each of which stood a dragon entwining the pillar with his tail and supporting the roof on his outstretched limbs."

Here it was that Kublai was visited, one summer day in the year 1275, by three travelers from far to the west—the brothers Niccolò and Maffeo Polo, merchants of Venice, and Niccolò's son Marco. The elder Polos were no strangers to the Khan. Some ten years earlier they had journeyed to his court in the train of an envoy sent by Kublai's brother Hulagu, Il-Khan of Persia. The Polo brothers had been assured that Kublai had never seen a "Latin" and was very anxious to meet one. They had been royally received and plied with questions "about the emperors, the government of their dominions and the maintenance of justice; then about kings, princes and nobles; next about the Lord Pope and all the practices of the Roman Church and the customs of the Latins." Then, because the Great Khan's curiosity was still unsatisfied, the elder Polos had been sent back to Europe on a special mission to the Pope, with a request that "he should send up to a hundred men, well versed in the seven arts and skilled to demonstrate to idolaters and others by clear reasoning that the Christian religion is better than theirs."

Support for a missionary enterprise on such a grandiose scale was scarcely to be expected from any Pope. However, after some delay—caused by the two-year electoral deadlock that followed the death of Clement IV in 1269—his successor Gregory X gave the project his blessing and ordered two learned Dominican friars to undertake the task of converting the Mongols. Unfortunately, the friars' resolve failed soon after the expedition set out, and the Polos went on alone. If no attempt was to be made to convert the Great Khan to the Christian faith, at least he would not lack for instructors in the benefits of East-West trade—and if Kublai was disappointed at this imperfect response to his appeal, he was too polite to show it. We are told that, after the ceremonial preliminaries in 1275, Niccolò presented Marco, then a lad of twenty-one, with the words: "Sire, this is my son and your liege man." To which the Khan replied: "He is heartily welcome."

This episode, like all else that we know of the Polos' travels in the East, is described in Marco Polo's ambitiously conceived narrative, *Description of the World.* Marco dictated his account to Rustichello of Pisa, a professional writer of romances, while both men were being held as war prisoners in Genoa in 1298. It is disconcerting but not surprising to discover that the court scene described above reproduces, almost verbatim, an earlier account that Rustichello had written on the presentation of Tristan to King Arthur at Camelot. There are other passages in the book that can be ascribed with some probability to the romance-writer rather than to the traveler, but the work as a whole carries conviction, not only by its wealth of detail, much of it fully supported by contemporary Chinese evidence, but by its sheer matter-of-factness. Much of Polo's narrative is little more than a catalogue—but a catalogue whose items include a dazzling profusion of gold and rubies, silks and sables, perfumes and spices, exotic customs and mysterious arts. Written in French, the traditional language of romance, and extensively copied and translated, *Description of the World* implanted an enticing and indelible image of "the gorgeous East" in the mind of Europe.

By the thirteenth century, Europeans had been vaguely aware for some time that the silks that they

Kublai Khan, Emperor of China and grandson of Genghis Khan; Marco Polo spent twenty years at his court.

Opposite The Venice from which Marco Polo set out on his journey.

"A ruler surpassing the Caesars"

Niccoló and Matteo Polo receive missionary instructions from Pope Gregory X.
Missionary enterprise went hand in hand with commercial effort and exploration.

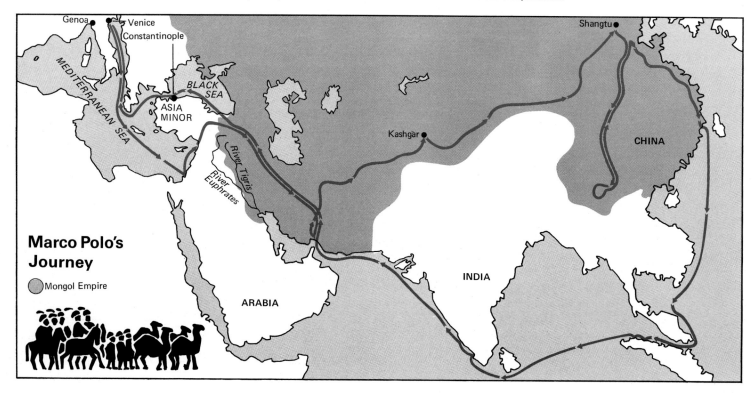

Marco Polo's Journey

Mongol Empire

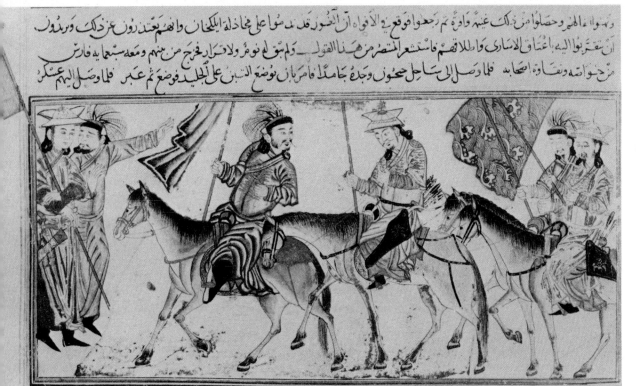

imported from the East originated in the land of the *Seres*. Since 1127, when northern China came under the rule of a nomad people, the *Kitai*, Europeans had taken to calling the lands to the east by the name *Cathay*. But neither of these names conveyed an image of the country or its inhabitants. The Chinese, probably thanks to Arab traders, were better informed about the West, particularly the Byzantine Empire, but they were not especially interested in it. Such trade as did trickle between the two regions passed through the Islamic states of the Middle East and Central Asia, and those nations deliberately interposed a barrier to direct commercial intercourse. The people most interested in penetrating the barrier were the merchant adventurers who formed the ruling class in the republic of Venice. Since the capture of Constantinople in the Fourth Crusade (1204), the Venetians had dominated the trade of the Black Sea and established a factory at Sudak in the Crimea. Their opportunity for further eastward expansion came with the meteoric rise of the Mongols.

Before 1206, the Mongols were inconspicuous among the numerous turbulent nomadic tribes of the Asiatic steppes whose periodic eruptions had vexed their settled neighbors since the days of Attila (A.D. 406?–453) and before. In that year, at a time when a social and economic upheaval had disrupted ancient tribal loyalties, the Mongols produced a leader with the genius to weld a miscellaneous band of hard-riding, sharp-shooting bowmen into an invincible army, whose numbers swelled with every victory. Assuming the title of Chinghiz (or Genghis) Khan, this Mongol leader conquered northern China ("Cathay") and then set out, in the words of Marco's *Description*, "to conquer the whole world."

By 1259, when the title of Great Khan devolved upon Genghis Khan's fourth successor, Kublai, the Mongol dominions extended from the Pacific on the east to the Mediterranean and the Black Sea on the west. The western territories were ruled by three subordinate khans—headquartered in Russia, in Persia, and at Bukhara in the heart of Asia—who soon became virtually independent. The European nations found themselves for the first time in direct and alarming proximity to an empire based in the Far East.

Marco describes Kublai as "the wisest man and the ablest in all respects, the best ruler of subjects and of empire and the man of the highest character of all that have ever been in the whole history of the Tartars." (Tartar was the current European name for the Mongols.) A Persian historian, Wassaf, declares that Kublai's reputation as a ruler "surpasses all that history tells of the Caesars of Rome." Even the Chinese annals, naturally prejudiced

Above A Mongol archer.

Above left Defeated Mongol troops retreat from Persia; from a Persian manuscript.

Elephants as well as infantry and cavalry were used by Mongol warriors.

Twenty years in China

against a foreign conqueror, praise him as a wise judge of men, a patron of letters, and one who truly loved his subjects. Under Kublai's protection the Polos were free to travel at large through China, all of which came under Mongol rule in 1279. Marco and the two elder Polos were able to observe at close hand a civilization far older and technically far more advanced than that of Europe—although as members of an alien ruling class, they never entered fully into the cultural life of the Chinese people.

What the Polos actually did during their twenty years' sojourn in the Far East is hard to say. No authentic references to them have been found in Chinese sources, and the few personal details given in the *Description* include some claims (perhaps added by Rustichello rather than Marco) that cannot be accepted as literally true. But Kublai, who could not afford to be wholly dependent on the loyalty of his Chinese subjects, employed many foreigners in positions of trust and authority, and there is no reason to doubt that Marco's extensive travels within the Great Khan's dominions, and beyond as far as India and Ceylon, were undertaken in an official capacity, even if we suspect an element of exaggeration in the language of the *Description*:

He had seen and heard more than once, when emissaries whom the Khan had dispatched to various parts of the world returned to him and rendered an account of the mission on which they had been sent but could give no other report of the countries they had visited, how their master would call them dolts and dunces, and declare that he would rather hear reports of these strange countries, and

of their customs and usages, than the business on which he had sent them . . . So Marco paid close attention to all the novelties and curiosities that came his way, that he might retail them to the Great Khan . . . Accordingly the Khan used to entrust him with all the most interesting and distant missions . . . and was so well satisfied with his conduct of affairs . . . and showed him such favor and kept him so near his person that the other lords were moved to envy.

Already we find a Venetian developing those special talents that were, at a later date, to make the reports of Venetian ambassadors one of the historian's most reliable and interesting sources.

Presumably the Polos did not forget that they were merchants, or that their mission had been intended to serve a religious purpose; and there are faint indications that they may have met with some success in both areas. Friar Odoric of Pordenone, who visited China soon after 1320, asserted that he knew of many people in Venice who had actually seen *Kinsai* (i.e. Hangchow, the former capital of Southern China). And the *Merchant's Handbook* of Francesco Pegolotti (1349) makes the startling claim that the overland route to Cathay was then "perfectly safe, whether by day or by night." Marco's interest in Chinese Christianity is shown by his numerous references to Nestorian churches and his lively account of a supposedly Christian sect investigated by him and his uncle Maffeo in Foochow. This interest must have helped to encourage the beginnings of Western missionary enterprise, leading up to the appointment in 1307 of Giovanni di Monte

Marco Polo's journey, from a Catalan Map.

Corvino as the first Catholic archbishop of Peking.

China under Kublai was open to foreign influence as it never had been before and would not be again for centuries. The enlightened Mongol ruler, who employed specialists from Egypt to teach the people of Fukien a better method of refining sugar, would have been willing enough to adopt any practical ideas the Polos could have taught him. But the only hint of such a lesson in the *Description* is a graphically told story of new-fangled siege-engines, constructed by craftsmen accompanying the Polos, that played a decisive part in the siege of Siangyang. Chinese sources confirm that foreign engineers were employed in this siege, but if we accept the statement in Marco's prologue that the journey to Peking took three and a half years, the Polos can hardly have reached Siangyang in time for a siege that took place in 1273.

There is an even greater likelihood that the Polos, after their return home, could have taught their fellow Europeans a thing or two; this may even have been a reason for Kublai's reluctance to let them go. But when the adventurers did return to Venice in 1295—after escorting a bride for the Il-Khan of Persia by way of Ceylon—the objects that they are reported to have brought home with them were more curious than enlightening: samples of sago—a food starch made from the pith of palm trees—and yak's hair, the dried head of a musk-deer, some brazil-wood seeds that failed to germinate, and earth from the shrine of St. Thomas, near Madras. Moreover, Marco's accounts of the manufacture of asbestos, porcelain, and palm wine—albeit fascinating—were non-technical, and could hardly have been put to practical use. Some Chinese inventions, including gunpowder and clocks, traveled to the West about this time, but they almost certainly arrived ahead of the Polos. If Marco had appreciated the importance of the Chinese art of printing, he might have anticipated Gutenberg by over a century—but the *Description* never even mentions printing.

Any immediate fruits that might have sprung from this first confrontation of East and West were nipped in the bud by the collapse of Mongol power in the years following the death of Kublai in 1294. In the west the Mongols were absorbed into a resurgent Islamic nation, which had become more militantly anti-Christian than ever. In the east the Mongols were supplanted in China in 1368 by the nationalistic and exclusive Ming Dynasty.

A Tuscan manuscript of the *Description*, written soon after 1300, appends an epilogue in which it is argued that the hand of God guided the travelers back to Venice, "so that men might know the things that are in the world." And there were restless and inquiring minds in the West on whom the knowledge contained in Polo's account was not wasted. It remained a potent element in the urge for expansion that led, two centuries later, to a second and far more momentous journey. A well-thumbed and heavily annotated copy of Marco's *Description* found a place among the prized possessions of Christopher Columbus.   RONALD LATHAM

Kublai Khan rewards his officers who have defeated an attempted rebellion.

A feast at Kublai Khan's palace.

Below Fishing for pearls.

Venice and Genoa compete for trade and

The power of the papacy had already begun to wane by 1274 when Gregory X urged his program of reforms upon the Synod of Lyons. The popes had become deeply involved in Italian politics, and those who followed Gregory were either puppets of Charles of Anjou, King of Sicily and son of Louis VIII of France, or supporters of his rival, Peter of Aragon. The rivalry between the Colonna and Orsini families of Rome dominated papal elections in this period and for twenty-seven months after the death of Nicholas V the College of Cardinals squabbled over his successor. In July, 1294, the cardinals settled on a hermit from the Abruzzi region of central Italy who became Celestine V. The new Pope soon sided with Charles and appointed the King's son, a layman not yet twenty-one, Archbishop of Lyons. The ascetic Celestine proved incapable of independent leadership, and after five months he abdicated. This time a successor was found at once in Cardinal Caetani. His election as Pope Boniface VIII (1294-1303) was not unanimous, however, and he took the precaution of imprisoning his predecessor.

Boniface saw himself as the true successor of Innocent III, reasserting the dominion of the papacy over all the kingdoms of the world. "The temporal power ought to be subject to the spiritual power," he declared, "and whosoever resisteth this power, ordained by God,

The papal coronation of Boniface VIII in 1303.

resisteth the ordinance of God. . . . Therefore we declare that for every human creature to be subject to the Roman Pope [is] altogether necessary for salvation." Yet Boniface failed to appreciate that by his day, with the rise of national monarchies, conditions in the West were very different from what they had been in the age of Innocent III. Formerly,

both secular and spiritual power had been—at least in theory—international, but the theory no longer fitted the facts: kings were not prepared to pay more than lip service to the ideal of an international spiritual power. And when Boniface attempted to establish his claims as both Pope and Caesar, his political weakness—and the weakness of the papacy—became apparent.

The Pope's major disputes were with the kings of England and France, natural rivals whom a more skilled negotiator might have played off against one another. By his bull *Clericis Laicos*, issued in 1296, Boniface forbade the clergy to pay royal taxes without his consent. Philip IV replied to this attempt to force him to accept papal intervention in the affairs of government by prohibiting the export of bullion from France, while Edward I outlawed the English clergy. The Pope was forced to retreat—and even agreed to canonize Louis IX. In 1301, Boniface, who had been imprisoned in England at the time of de Montfort's rebellion, claimed Scotland as his own fief and forbade the projected English invasion. Edward therefore summoned a parliament which denied that he should answer to the Pope for any of his temporal rights.

The Great Jubilee of 1300, celebrated at Rome with unprecedented pageantry, filled the papal coffers. Boniface intended to use those funds to found estates for his relatives—a plan that agitated and alienated the great families of Rome. The Pope himself then drafted the text of the bull *Unam Sanctam*, which stated the papal prerogative in its most extreme form. Those claims were too much for Philip of France, and when his appeal for moderation was rejected, he sent his vice-chancellor Guillaume de Nogaret to seize Boniface and bring him to France for trial.

Nogaret stormed the papal palace at Anagni on September 7, 1303, just as Boniface was about to pronounce sentence of excommunication against Philip IV. The chancellor tried to force the Pope to abdicate—a move that led Dante, who had branded Boniface "the Prince of the new Pharisees," to lament that "Christ in His vicar was made a captive and mocked a second time" at Anagni. Fearing public reaction against him, Nogaret fled after three days and Boniface was escorted to Rome by

Edward I defies Boniface VIII : Boniface quarreled chronically with Europe's kings.

the people of Anagni. There the Orsini, sworn enemies of the Colonna, confined him to the Vatican. He died a month later—some say by French poison. His successor condemned those involved in the "terrible day at Anagni" but spent his brief pontificate in exile in Perugia, for Rome was in a state of complete anarchy.

Papacy exiled to Avignon

Clement V was elected on the grounds that as Archbishop of Bordeaux he was a subject of Edward I and would therefore oppose Philip IV. The French king won the new Pope over by bribery, however, and saw him consecrated at Lyons in 1305. Rome became more turbulent than ever, and Clement moved the entire papal court to Avignon in 1307. This period of self-imposed exile, known as the Babylonian Captivity of the papacy, was to last for seventy years.

The Provençal city of Avignon was not technically part of France, a situation which permitted Clement to maintain that he was independent of Philip IV. Yet in truth all the Avignon popes were pro-French, and this was to prove a special hardship for England in the coming Hundred Years' War. The fact that Rome, the "Eternal City" and traditional center of Christendom, was without a pope struck many contemporaries as a contradiction in terms, and they roundly denounced the Captivity.

In order to avoid the unseemliness of a posthumous inquiry into Boniface's alleged heresies—an

inquest that Philip IV was advocating—Clement agreed to the abolition of the Knights Templars in France. Their trial for heresy was a travesty of justice; torture was used to extract confessions and the Grand Master of the Order and sixty-nine other knights were burned at the stake in 1308.

The crown under Edward I

Under Edward I the power of the Crown was extended so that England became a centralized monarchy. This was achieved not by high-handedness but with full respect for law. "The English Justinian," as Edward was known, systematized the law and its administration and overhauled the machinery of government, both in the central departments of state and in shire and borough governments. This was the formative age of common law as well as statute law; it saw the foundation of the Inns of Court in London (which offered training in the legal profession) and the first reporting of legal cases in Year Books. Edward's experience in the Baron's War had taught him that government was a partnership between the king and his baron knights, and during his reign parliaments met regularly (although not nearly as frequently as the Provisions of Oxford had laid down). In 1297, when opposition to the King's financial demands arose, Parliament framed the novel doctrine that taxation could only be levied with its consent.

During the last ten years of Edward's reign, following the Confirmation of the Charters in 1297, there were ominous signs of a reaction against the increase of royal power and the accompanying bureaucracy. Under Edward's weak successor, that opposition developed into an attack upon the monarch himself.

Swiss Confederation

The first momentous steps toward Swiss Confederation were taken by the peasant communities of Uri, Schwyz and Unterwalden in the forest valleys around Lake Lucerne at the end of the thirteenth century. The Lake itself was a unifying factor, as was the fact that each community, though distinct in its historical development, shared a common language, German, and a zealous desire to escape from the oppressive tactics of their Hapsburg overlords. Emperor Rudolf I first recognized the privileges of the Uri, but it was from neighboring Schwyz that the future federation of cantons, "Switzerland," took its name. In 1291 the three communities formed a Perpetual League (perhaps as an extension of an earlier alliance) for self-defense against would-be aggressors.

The Schwyz took advantage of the disputed imperial election of 1314 (in which Lewis of Bavaria successfully challenged the Hapsburg candidate Frederick) to seize the great abbey of Einsiedeln. Frederick placed the rebels under the ban of the Empire, but Lewis

A mail shirt of about 1300, probably English.

removed the ban. In November, 1315, Frederick sent an army of 20,000 men, led by his brother Leopold, against the Swiss, but a confederate force of 2,000 routed the Emperor's picked troops at Morgarten. As a contemporary noted, their encounter was not so much a battle as a massacre—"like a herd driven to the shambles by these mountain people." In December the victors formed a new league: the confederates were to be "as one person, like man and wife"; they were to respect their overlords, but they were permitted to withhold their services if those lords acted unjustly. Members were made to swear that they would not make treaties with outside powers without consulting the Confederation at large. This new league was solemnly recognized by Lewis IV.

France loses Sicily

After the death of Manfred, King of Sicily, in 1266, his daughter Constance, whose husband was the heir to the throne of Aragon, assumed the title "Queen of Sicily." She was not, however, in any position to substantiate her claim. Hohenstaufen rule had ended with the execution of her cousin Conradin, but bloodshed continued as Charles of Anjou put to death many of Conradin's supporters. As the papal nominee, Charles could do no wrong in Italy, where—in addition to being Duke of Provence and Anjou and King of Sicily and Naples—he was "senator" of Rome, imperial vicar of Tuscany and lord of many Lombard cities. Charles consolidated his rule in these considerable territories by outright oppression—then turned his ambitious eyes eastward to Constantinople. He persuaded the Pope to proclaim a crusade against the Byzantine Emperor.

While Charles was assembling a great fleet in Messina harbor during the spring of 1282, Peter III of Aragon, who was in close touch with the Greek Emperor, was making preparations for an invasion of Sicily. Peter's plan appealed to the merchants of Barcelona, who were so eager to supplant the Genoese in Sicilian trade, that they gladly rented ships to him.

It now became evident that Charles had sown dragon's teeth in Sicily. He was detested by the Sicilians, and his French soldiers were hated for their insolence. On Easter Monday, 1282, a French sergeant accosted a young married woman outside the Church of the Holy Ghost in Palermo and was stabbed by her husband. The people of Palermo rose as a man, crying "Death to the French!" And while the church bells rang for Vespers, they massacred the garrison. News of the "Sicilian Vespers" spread to other towns and they too proclaimed communas. At the end of April Charles' fleet mutinied, but it was not until August that a deputation from Messina and Palermo was able to reach Peter III in Algiers to offer him the crown of the Two Sicilies.

Venice and Genoa: trading rivals

While the French and the Spanish fought for the Two Sicilies, Venice and Genoa continued their struggle for exclusive trading rights in the Levant and the Black Sea. Genoa's concordat with the Byzantine rulers (which granted their merchants freedom to trade throughout the Eastern Empire, as well as possession of Smyrna and special privileges in Constantinople) was balanced by Venice's favorable treaty with the Turks.

In 1294 the Genoese closed the Dardanelles, but the Venetians forced the passage and sacked Galata. After capturing the Aegean islands of Chios and Phocaea from the Venetians, Genoese adventurers attacked their rivals at Curzola in 1299. Marco Polo, home from the East, was captured during that engagement and spent his imprisonment writing the tale of his travels. A peace treaty arranged through the mediation of Milan put an end to military operations in the eastern Mediterranean but the commercial rivalry of the two Italian states persisted.

At the turn of the century, the Venetians began building great galleys, which they intended to use in trading with northwest Europe, and in 1317 this fleet made its first voyage to Flanders. To their surprise the Venetians found the Florentines already well established in the capitals of northern Europe. Florence, once torn between Guelf and Ghibelline factions, had developed into an oligarchy of bankers. The "florin," first coined in 1252, had become the standard currency of international finance and members of the great Florentine banking houses financed government debts in England, France and Germany.

Florence

Florence rapidly became the artistic and cultural capital of the West. It produced Giotto, who broke away from the Tuscan-Byzantine school of "flat" painting and made his figures real and three-dimensional, and Dante, the poetic genius of the Middle Ages. Both men had artistic forerunners in Florence. Giotto's teacher Cimabue painted frescoes in the churches of Assisi and wrought a splendid mosaic in the apse of Pisa Cathedral. Giotto himself achieved much greater dramatic power than his master, however, and he can fairly be termed "the founder of modern painting." His fresco cycle of the Legend of St. Francis at Assisi and his decorations of Florentine chapels—all commissioned by successful bankers as a peace offering to the Church for having charged usurious rates of interest—show both a novelty of composition and a remarkable technique. In a passage on the brevity of human glory, Dante observed that "Cimabue thought that he held the field in painting, but now Giotto is acclaimed and the former's fame obscured."

Giotto's *Flight into Egypt* from the Capella degli Scrovegni all'Arena.

The Divine Comedy

Banished from his native Florence during a period of civil turmoil, Dante Alighieri composed his renowned allegory, The Divine Comedy, *to express his resentment and frustration over the enforced exile. The stanzas of his Christian epic contain scornful references to contemporary political figures, well-known clerics and personal acquaintances—but Dante's masterpiece is more than a catalog of grievances. In eschewing classical Latin for colloquial Italian, Dante gave new dignity to the vernacular and made his epic accessible to a vast new audience. And in tracing the Poet's journey through Hell and Purgatory and into Paradise, the Florentine genius provided a synthesis of contemporary political and theological ideologies that is unparalleled in world literature.*

Dante's political enemy, Pope Boniface VIII, consigned to the eighth circle of Hell—although he did not die until 1305, three years after Dante completed the *Inferno*.

Opposite Dante and Virgil, his guide through Hell and Purgatory.

On Good Friday in the year 1300, Dante Alighieri, a citizen of the thriving Italian city-state of Florence, found himself lost in a dark wood. Fleeing from its terrors, he encountered the ghost of his favorite author, the Latin poet Virgil. The poet told Dante that he could escape from the forest only by taking a road that led down into Hell and through it to Purgatory and Paradise. With Virgil as his guide, Dante crossed the river Acheron and began the terrible descent. Hell was a huge, funnel-shaped pit with ledges circling its sides, on which the ghosts of the sinful suffered pains appropriate to their offenses.

As Dante climbed down those tiers, he recognized both unimportant Florentine contemporaries and figures of Christian and classical history, such as Caiaphas—the Jewish High Priest who presided over the council that condemned Jesus to death—and Ulysses, the wandering hero of Homer's epic. At each level of their downward journey, Dante and his ghostly guide encountered sinners of greater guilt. At the lip of the funnel they found those who were merely lustful, but as the two journeyed onward, they passed heretics, seducers, perjurers, and traitors—and finally came to Judas, the betrayer of Christ, and Brutus, the betrayer of Julius Caesar, both of whom were being tormented by Satan himself at the cold center of the earth. Virgil led Dante through a tunnel past this final horror, and they emerged at the other side of the world.

The two eventually came to the foot of the mountain of Purgatory, which was in form the exact opposite and complement of Hell: a peak rising up into the skies. Like Hell, the mountain was a series of circles inhabited by those who had succumbed to various classes of sin: those guilty of the more destructive sins, such as Pride, were found near the bottom, those guilty of the more trivial, such as Lust, were at the top. Unlike the lost souls in Hell, the inhabitants of Purgatory were all working, with certainty of ultimate success, for release from the effect of their sins. When Dante emerged at the summit, he could see, across the river Lethe, the Earthly Paradise that

man had enjoyed in his original innocence. The pagan Virgil could not pass into this region, and he was replaced as guide by the shade of Beatrice, a woman whom Dante had known and loved as an adolescent in Florence, and who had remained a symbol of perfection ever since. After rebuking him severely for his life of sin, Beatrice led Dante into Paradise.

Once in the celestial regions, Dante's progress became a weightless ascent through realms of air and light. With Beatrice at his side, he passed through the levels above the earth that contained the planets, the sun and the stars, meeting souls whose earthly lives had embodied a hierarchy of virtues. He was carried before the apostles Peter and John, who examined his understanding of the Christian virtues of Faith, Hope and Charity. Finally the Florentine was admitted to the Empyrean of God and the Saints, where he acquired a new guide, St. Bernard. He was then led before the Virgin Mary, by whose intercession Dante was permitted to look into the light of the Trinity.

Such, briefly, is the story told in Dante Alighieri's *Divine Comedy*. The work itself is one of the most important epic poems and one of the greatest Christian allegories in literary history. Its one hundred cantos are divided into three equal sections: the *Inferno*, which concerns Virgil and Dante's descent into Hell; the *Purgatorio*, which deals with the two poets' ascent of Mount Purgatory; and the *Paradiso*, which describes Dante's voyage through the heavens, culminating in his arrival at the Empyrean of God.

Despite its length and weighty philosophical content, the *Divine Comedy* was an enormously popular work. That success was due in part to the fact that Dante had composed his materpiece in the vernacular, Italian, rather than Latin—a choice that scandalized many of the poet's scholarly contemporaries, but made the epic accessible to a far larger audience. In addition, the *Divine Comedy* was studded with topical references—to members of the papal court, Florentine officials, friends, and

A pictorial version of Dante's Hell by Orcagna.

Dante's Hell

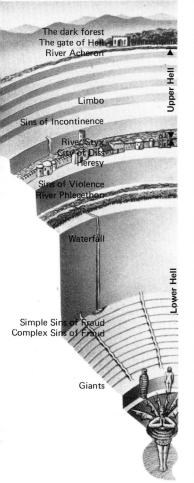

The dark forest
The gate of Hell
River Acheron

Upper Hell

Limbo

Sins of Incontinence

River Styx
City of Dis
Heresy

Sins of Violence
River Phlegethon

Lower Hell

Waterfall

Simple Sins of Fraud
Complex Sins of Fraud

Giants

local reprobates—which made the work lively reading. That liveliness was further enhanced by Dante's use of *terza rima* verse form, a rhyme scheme (aba, bcb, cdc, ded, . . . yzy, z) that linked each stanza to the one that followed and gave the *Divine Comedy's* narrative an easy flow.

Stylistic considerations aside, the *Divine Comedy* was, before everything else, the record of the author's own conversion, of his movement from Hell to Heaven. In the *Purgatorio*, Dante portrayed himself as a penitent, shedding the stains of his sins as he climbed through the levels of successful repentence. The Roman poet, Virgil, and Dante's contemporary, Beatrice, were the inspirations of his real life as well as the poetic symbols of Natural Reason and

Divine Grace. Thus Dante was, in one sense, compressing much of the anguish of his earthly career into the few days of his spiritual odyssey. We do not know much about the author's conversion, although, by comparison with his literary equals, Homer and Shakespeare, Dante's public life is rather well documented. The known facts give us some hints of the reasons why Dante fused the account of his own central religious experience with both an elaborate expression of a comprehensive religious and moral outlook and a commentary on the great men and events of his lifetime.

Dante was born into a middle-class Florentine family in 1265. He grew up—and no doubt expected to spend his entire life—in that great city, one of the

Art, politics and finance in Florence

most exciting, affluent, colorful, and turbulent metropolises of Europe. As a young man he became a good lyric poet, and composed a large number of love poems in the new style of Italian versifying that was becoming fashionable. He also fell in love with a girl named Beatrice, who married somebody else and died when Dante was twenty-five. About that time Dante began to lose interest in love poetry and became more interested in philosophy and theology.

Dante recognized and accepted the responsibilities of his class and, while in his thirties, took a reasonably prominent part in the politics of Florence, which was an independent republic run, for the most part, by its more well-to-do citizens. For anyone with principles, the political world was a dangerous one. Dante's period of political activity, which started in 1295 when he was thirty, was a period of bitter strife between the Black and White factions of the Guelphs, the dominant political power in Florence. It was also the period of the pontificate of Boniface VIII, one of the most aggressive of the medieval popes, who interfered in Florentine affairs on the side of the Blacks. In 1302, while Dante, who was a White, was absent on a peace mission to the Pope, the Blacks seized control of the city. Dante was one of those banished for life, and he spent the last twenty years of his life—years of increasing fame—condemned, as he said of himself, to "exile and poverty," "a ship without sails or rudder" wandering from one northern Italian patron or court to another.

Most of Dante's important writings were composed during his exile. It is not surprising, therefore, that the political circumstances of his age—circumstances of which Dante was so conspicuously a victim—should figure prominently in his great poem. Florence in his lifetime was at the summit of its material greatness. The thirteenth century had been a prolonged period of spectacular economic expansion all over Europe, and the great Italian commercial centers had played a role in this expansion not unlike the one that England would play in the nineteenth century. They had provided the western world with its textile industry, its great merchants and bankers, and—in 1252—with the florin, the first gold coin to be minted in Western Europe since the fall of the Roman Empire. Dante himself did not belong to a great mercantile clan. In fact, he looked back rather nostalgically to the days of his ancestor, Cacciaguida, who had lived in the simpler Florence of the twelfth century. Beatrice's husband, on the other hand, was one of the Bardi, famous merchants who trafficked with England and France.

The cloth industry and international trade had enabled Florence and several other larger Italian cities to become independent republics and to re-create the city-state spirit of ancient Greece and Rome. By the end of the thirteenth century, the traders, master-craftsmen and shopkeepers of Florence had largely established their freedom from the influence of the local noble families, who still retained a foothold in both the city and the country. This development was confirmed, about the time Dante entered politics, by the Ordinances of Justice (1293), a kind of constitution that based city government on the guilds, or trade associations of ordinary citizens.

Popular government inevitably involved faction. Throughout the thirteenth century, Florence had been torn by the strife between "Guelfs" and "Ghibellines"—broadly speaking, supporters of the Pope and the Emperor, respectively. This feud was traditionally traced back to 1215, when a member of one family mortally offended a member of the other by breaking his engagement to a girl of the latter's house. But for that, as Dante's forebear Cacciaguida

Dante and his poem by
Domenico de Michelino,
with Florence on the right.

said, "many would have been happy who are now sad." Rivalry between the Guelfs and the Ghibellines became an inseparable part of Florentine life. By the end of the century, the Ghibellines had ceased to be a serious threat to civil stability, but feuding between Black and White Guelf elements—which supplanted the original quarrel—led to the catastrophic turning point in Dante's career.

The Italy outside Florence, in which Dante spent his years of exile, was, in his eyes, a political "hostel of woe, a ship without a pilot in a great tempest . . . a brothel." Unlike other parts of Europe, which had been absorbed into such geographically large political units as the monarchies of England and France, northern Italy had no dominant power. The region was a mass of petty states, ruled either by republican cities like Florence or by lords like Can Grande de la Scala, the hospitable ruler of Verona to whom Dante dedicated the *Paradiso*. From our perspective, the political chaos of Italy seems one of the preconditions of the Renaissance, necessary to the

free and diverse development of life and thought; effective unification of fourteenth-century Italy would probably have been stultifying. But to Dante, who had suffered so much from the effects of that disunity, the vision of a stable order imposed from above was overwhelmingly attractive. There was no power in Italy with the resources or prestige to impose unity, and so Dante, like many of his contemporaries, turned hopefully to the German Emperors.

For several centuries the rulers of Germany, claiming to be the successors of the Roman emperors, had been trying intermittently to establish their authority in Italy. In former times several had been partially successful: Frederick Barbarossa, in the twelfth century, and Frederick II, in the thirteenth, had wielded a good deal of power in the peninsula. But the economic expansion of Italy made it increasingly unlikely that a backward German warlord would be anything but a tool of local politicians if he brought his retinue over the Alps. In this hope, as in other things, Dante was a romantic. While he was in exile

Italy: "a hostel of woe"

he wrote a book on monarchy, in which he argued, with references to philosophical and historical matter drawn from his classical reading, that men ought to accept the authority of a single ruler, the divinely ordained Roman Emperor.

The chief opponents of the German imperial claims in Italy were, of course, the popes, particularly Pope Boniface VIII (1295–1303), whose supporters in Florence were responsible for Dante's exile. In the *Divine Comedy*, which is set in 1300, Boniface is already expected in the eighth circle of Hell, three years before his death. This bit of literary revenge is part of the highly critical view of the papacy as an institution that permeates Dante's work. Earlier medieval popes, although greatly venerated as the successors of St. Peter, had not been very powerful, and the transition from claimed powers to exercised powers took place largely in the century before the *Divine Comedy*, when the fortunes of the papacy were roughly the reverse of those of the Empire.

At the beginning of the thirteenth century, the popes had become the effective rulers of a state in central Italy. More remarkable perhaps, they had acquired control over many aspects of the Christian Church beyond the Alps. The popes played an increasingly substantial part in appointing northern European bishops and rectors, whom they were then able to tax in order to subsidize their political ambitions at home. Boniface VIII was a particularly ambitious pope, who belonged to one of the great Roman families, Gaetani, and was an expert canon lawyer. He asserted the authority of the pope to correct all Christians, including kings, in a Bull published in 1302, which begins with the ringing words "*Unam Sanctam*—One holy, catholic, apostolic Church . . ." Boniface's whole career embodied the conception of the Church as a militant, temporally powerful institution—a conception that Dante denounced.

The papacy was not the only institution that was building up its power at the turn of the century. The most powerful man in Europe at that time was Philip

the Fair, King of France, and his ascendancy was indirectly to affect Dante's life.

One of the most significant movements of the poet's lifetime was the developing connection between the papacy and the French monarchy, a compound of attraction and rivalry between the two institutions with the largest claims to real influence over the Christian world. Pope Boniface invited Charles of Valois, brother of King Philip, to bring an army to Italy, and it was while the Pope's supporters in Florence were strengthened by the temporary

Pagan and Christian art contrasted: *Strength* (*left*) by Niccoló Pisano, and *Faith* by Giotto.

The Church Triumphant by Martini: Pope Benedict XI (1303–4) negotiates a peace treaty between Philip IV of France and Edward I of England, with Florence in the background.

The hierarchical universe of "The Divine Comedy"

presence of Charles' army that Dante was exiled. The poet therefore had every reason to hate the royal house of France—and he took the opportunity to denounce it when he met their remote ancestor, Hugh Capet, in the *Purgatorio*.

More spectacular events were to come. Boniface eventually was forced to devote much of his pontificate to a fierce struggle with Philip the Fair—a contest that became the central theme in the political history of Europe at this period. The Pope's claims to powers of taxation and jurisdiction in northern Europe brought him into conflict with the pretentious and ruthless French King. Boniface issued the famous papal Bull, *Unam Sanctam*—which was plainly directed against Philip. An exasperated Philip retaliated by sending a small expedition to Anagni, the Pope's birthplace and residence outside Rome. In 1303, the Pope was taken prisoner by the French king's troops—an atrocity that seemed, even to such an enemy of Boniface as Dante, to be the work of a new "Pilate," who was crucifying Christ's vicar.

Before Dante completed the *Divine Comedy*, the power of the French monarchy had led to the election of a French pope, Clement v, and the establishment of the papal court at Avignon, in southern France, where it was to remain until 1377. Whether this was an advantage or a disadvantage for the papacy is a question for debate, but there is no question that the "Babylonian Captivity" left Italy even more destitute of political leadership. The exiled Dante greeted with enthusiasm the election,

The ideal of *Good Government* in the city by Lorinzetti.

in 1308, of a German emperor, Henry VII, who was reputedly just and magnanimous, and ambitious to take control of the peninsula. Henry came to Italy in 1310 and remained for three years. His ambitions were ground down by the impossibility of overcoming opposition from various quarters—notably from Florence—and he died of a fever in 1313. It is ironic and rather disconcerting that Dante's political idealism, expressed in his book on monarchy and reaffirmed in the *Paradiso* (where Henry VII was promised a place in the Empyrean), should have attached itself to this last, feeble representative of a barbaric tradition of Germanic power.

Although circumstance drew him into the cockpit of Italian politics, it is not as a politician or political commentator that Dante interests us chiefly, but as the most superb exponent of medieval ideas. Dante had the ideas of the era at his fingertips; he was a superhuman amateur who mastered a dozen disciplines. The *Divine Comedy* is the work of a man driven by a lifelong need to make sense of the world, who has, at great cost, succeeded. For this reason, the *Divine Comedy* is a textbook of medieval attitudes.

The physical world in which the poem is set, for example, is an extremely careful and accurate picture of the universe as it was conceived by medieval man before the Copernican revolution. The earth is at the center; the moon, planets, sun and stars move in fixed orbits around it, and the angelic and celestial regions lie beyond. This attractively unified world picture was not merely of physical importance, for the

ascent from earth to heaven was both a physical and a spiritual ascent.

As a young poet and scholar, Dante had already opened himself to the most advanced philosophical influences of his day. The resultant paradox in his intellectual make-up—which was the paradox of contemporary European civilization as well—was that Christian faith was combined with an intense admiration for pagan classical writings. In choosing Virgil as his guide for the journey through Hell and Purgatory, Dante was acknowledging the value of natural reason, unillumined by Christian revelation, as it was used by the noblest pagans. It would be difficult to say whether the general scheme of the *Divine Comedy* owed more to the Christian story of Christ's descent to Hell and ascent to Heaven, or to the descent into Hell that is the central episode in Virgil's *Aeneid*. During the thirteenth century Christian thought had been nearly overwhelmed by the effects of a renewed acquaintance with the writings of Aristotle, which covered, in a masterly fashion, nearly every aspect of natural knowledge—physics, biology, politics, ethics, logic and so on—and made a very deep impression on Europe's foremost scholars. When Dante looked for rational explanations of perennial problems (such as the influence of the stars or the origins of political life), he turned to the writings of the philosophers of Paris, notably Albert the Great or St. Thomas Aquinas, or to the pagan philosophers themselves, carefully choosing arguments from their works for his own synthesis.

Dante's house in Florence.

The thirteenth century had also seen astonishing innovations in religious life, chiefly associated with the creation of the new orders of friars. St. Francis and his followers, who founded the Franciscan order about the time the Magna Carta was sealed, aimed to live a life of utter poverty, in imitation of the life of Christ and his apostles. The Franciscans rejected conventional worldliness, not by retreating to the isolation of a monastery but by living humbly among the common people. The friars did not make much of a mark outside the universities in northern Europe, but in Italy they became as much a part of the texture of life as Wesley's successors were to be in industrial England. In Dante's day, many of the Franciscans were revolutionary critics of the Church, hunted and persecuted by the ecclesiastical authorities. Dante sided with these radicals, who provided him with his vision of an apostolic Church, truly devoted to the original purposes of Christianity, and set against the Church of Boniface VIII—which, in Dante's view, had "fallen into the mire" in attempting the impossible combination of spiritual functions with political power.

The *Divine Comedy* did not reflect a generally accepted thirteenth-century philosophical, political and religious synthesis—precisely because no such synthesis existed. Its inclusiveness is quite personal, the result of Dante's incomparably wide sympathies. The souls whom the author has placed in the Heaven of the Sun, for example, include not only the great orthodox doctors of the Church, but also Siger of Brabant and Joachim of Fiore—who were commonly regarded as dangerous heretics. Thus, the *Divine Comedy* makes an excellent introduction to thirteenth-century thought, but it does not really reflect the temper of the age.

Unlike the impersonal analyses of contemporary scholastics, the *Divine Comedy* is a highly personal work of art, and—despite Dante's hatred of the Florentines—it is also a product of that city, not of the cloister. It cannot help but remind us of Michelangelo's Sistine ceiling—a similar attempt to make sense out of everything that the Christian and the pagan worlds offered. The desire to achieve such a synthesis was one of the central and recurrent aims of Florentine Renaissance minds. Dante Alighieri's *Divine Comedy* was the first attempt to create that synthesis, and, because every educated Florentine knew Dante's work intimately, it became the constant inspiration for the others.   G. A. HOLMES

Warfare dominated Europe after 1320. Edward I pursued an imperialist policy designed to bring the whole of Britain under his sway, and the success of his Scottish campaigns led to a firm alliance between France and Scotland that persisted until 1560. The intervention of Welsh princes in English politics reached its peak during the Barons' War. Llewelyn the Great was recognized as Prince of Wales and overlord of the Welsh magnates under the Treaty of Shrewsbury in 1267. But he refused to pledge his fealty to the new King of England and in 1277 Edward was forced to invade North Wales.

Scotland's vacant throne

When Alexander III of Scotland died in 1286, his granddaughter, a young Norwegian princess, succeeded to the throne. It was Edward's hope that his son Edward of Carnarvon would marry her and thus unite the two crowns, but the "Maid of Norway" died on her journey to Scotland in 1290, leaving ten claimants to the vacant throne. To avoid civil war, the Scots accepted Edward's adjudication that John Balliol should succeed the princess. Balliol's nobles soon deprived him of power and formed an alliance with Philip IV of France, with whom England was currently at war over conflicting claims to Gascony, a region in southwestern France. Edward led an army north in 1296 to subdue the Scots, and at his orders the sacred Stone of Scone, on which Scottish kings were customarily crowned, was removed to Westminster Abbey. Once Edward's armies withdrew, there was a series of popular risings in Scotland. The rebels, ably led by William Wallace, threw off the English yoke. Scotland's independence was short-lived, however: Wallace was defeated at Falkirk in 1298, and forced to flee to France. In 1304 Edward resumed his Scottish campaign and Wallace was captured and executed.

Robert Bruce, the grandson of one of the claimants of 1290, put spirit into the Scots' revolt—and was crowned King of Scotland in 1306. Edward I died shortly thereafter, on the eve of yet another expedition against the rebels, and in the next few years Bruce reconquered most of his kingdom, regaining all the castles garrisoned by the English except Stirling. When Stirling also fell, Edward II

at last stirred himself to lead a great army against Bruce. On June 24, 1314, at Bannockburn, a few miles south of Stirling, the Scots won a decisive victory, assuring their independence.

The disaster of English arms at Bannockburn left the worthless Edward II at the mercy of his barons, but after the fall of Thomas of Lancaster in 1322, none of them were able to dominate the government. The baronial opposition, which had originated with an attack on the King's favorite, Piers Gaveston, concentrated in the later

The Battle of Crécy where the English won a great victory.

stages of Edward's reign on the removal of the new favorites, Hugh Despenser and his son. Queen Isabella, accompanied by Edward, her eldest son, departed for her native France, where she allied herself with the exiled Roger Mortimer, Earl of March. In 1326 they landed in England to avenge Lancaster's death; the Despensers were slain, Edward II was imprisoned and his son was recognized as king by Parliament. A year later the deposed monarch was cruelly murdered in Berkeley Castle and power passed to Isabella and her paramour Mortimer.

Edward III

Edward III was only seventeen when he dismissed Mortimer, excluded his mother from state affairs and became the effective ruler of England. Energetic, and eager to shine on the battlefield as well as on the tournament ground, Edward soon became the most popular of all medieval English kings, a warrior who led his people to national glory. Although the English monarch's long-range ambition was to enlarge the English duchies in France, he

first avenged the English humiliation at Bannockburn by defeating the Scots at Halidon Hill near Berwick in 1333. Edward restored Balliol to the throne and insisted on the cession of considerable territory. Robert Bruce's young son David, the rightful king, escaped to the French coast, where Philip VI openly took his part.

The Hundred Years' War

The perennial cause of friction between England and France was the anomalous position of Gascony, the last Continental fief of the English kings. Edward III refused to abandon his patrimony, and the successors of St. Louis continued to agitate for the expulsion of the English from southwestern France. From this conflict arose the Hundred Years' War, which lasted, truces notwithstanding, from 1337 to 1453.

At the time of Charles the Fair's death in 1328, successive Capetian kings had provided a direct male heir to the French throne for three and a half centuries; Charles failed to do so, and the Crown passed to a cousin, Philip of Valois, the nephew of Philip IV. Within a decade Edward III claimed the French Crown as the son of Charles IV's sister —and Philip VI retaliated by confiscating Gascony. Edward secured alliances with the Flemish princes and with the Emperor, while Philip recruited Italian mercenaries. The English heralds delivered a challenge to Philip to appoint a day for the battle, but Philip, who had been warned by the renowned astrologist Robert of Sicily not to engage the

English army while Edward was in command, stalled.

Edward invaded Normandy in the summer of 1346. His army marched up the left bank of the Seine from Rouen toward Paris, where Philip had amassed a great army to defend his capital. The English were forced to retreat, closely pursued by the confident French. At Crécy, however, Edward won a decisive victory; using tactics learned in the wars with Wales and Scotland, English archers equipped with longbows slew the French cavalry. The sixteen-year-old Prince of Wales, who commanded the vanguard, was accoutered in the black armor that was to give him the chivalrous name "The Black Prince." The victory at Crécy won immediate fame for English soldiers; the flower of French aristocracy had been cheated of what seemed like certain victory by English yeomen armed with the weapons of Robin Hood.

Philip's Scottish allies, who invaded England in 1346, were defeated at Neville's Cross, and David II, who was promptly captured in the fighting, was not ransomed until eleven years later. Edward next laid siege to Calais, which held out—largely through the determination of its governor, Jean de Vienne—for over a year before it was finally starved into surrendering. The King agreed to spare the town, provided that its leaders would come before him barefoot and with ropes around their necks to present him with the keys to the city. The lives of the six valiant burghers who volunteered for the humiliating task were spared through the intervention of Queen

Edward III with the burghers of defeated Calais.

John II of France, who was taken as a prisoner to London.

Philippa, and before long Calais became the leading town for the English wool trade—a function that it continued to perform until the French recaptured the city in 1558.

Battle of Poitiers

John II, who succeeded his father Philip IV in 1350, was forced to debase French coinage to pay for his coronation at Reims, and in the following year he was forced to issue no less than eighteen ordinances announcing further devaluations. John was eager to achieve a chivalrous victory over the Black Prince, and he led an immense French army against him in Gascony. In a pitched battle at Poitiers John very nearly achieved his goal; the French fought desperately, but they failed to appreciate that the English were employing virtually the same tactics that they had used at Crécy. John's force lost the day when Gascon troops circled around behind the French and attacked them from the rear. The French monarch, his son and his ally, the King of Bohemia, were all captured, and many of his chief nobles were killed.

John was transported to London in 1356 and his son, the future Charles V, became regent. The most powerful individual in France at this time was Etienne Marcel, provost of the Paris merchants, who dominated the meetings of the Estates-General that were called in 1357 to stabilize the country's finances.

The Jacqueries

At this juncture a group known as the "Jacqueries" emerged on the French political scene. The movement took its name from the derisive nickname, "Jacques Bonhomme," that the French nobility had given to the peasants because of their patience in enduring all oppressions —such as crippling feudal dues.

The cry "Death to a gentleman!" was raised, and the peasants began to arm themselves. Atrocities occurred throughout the country. Marcel tried to use the Jacqueries to assist him in reducing the power and prestige of the nobles, only to be murdered himself on July 31, 1358, as he was about to welcome Charles of Navarre to Paris. The Dauphin then returned to Paris, suppressed the uprising and prepared to sue for peace with England. Edward III had failed to take Chartres when the French refused to fight a pitched battle against him, and both countries were exhausted. A peace treaty was signed at Bretigny near Chartres. By the terms of the treaty Edward abandoned his claims to the French Crown, contenting himself with the Duchy of Aquitaine and its dependencies, Calais, Ponthieu and Guisnes. The French agreed to pay three million gold crowns for King John's ransom. Yet the Peace of Bretigny was no more than a truce; Frenchmen everywhere echoed the words of the citizens of La Rochelle: "We will acknowledge the English with our lips, but never with our hearts." During the first stage of the Hundred Years' War the ideal of chivalry came to dominate Western society. It had its own unwritten codes of behavior, its own orders of knighthood (such as Edward III's Order of the Garter), and its own literature. In essence, chivalry implied that responsibility went hand in hand with privilege. It inculcated an ideal of social service that was both unpaid and unservile—service of the weak (especially womenfolk) by the strong, of the poor by the wealthy, and of the lowly by those of high estate.

The German succession

War was the norm in Europe during the fourteenth century. Germany was the scene of periodic strife between the Hapsburg antiking and the Bavarian Emperor Louis IV. Pope John XXII declared Louis deposed in 1327, and his act led to a violent pamphlet war between the Pope and two adversaries, Marsiglio of Padua and William of Occam, both of whom supported the deposed Emperor against the Avignonese Pope. It was only through a papal alliance that another candidate, Charles IV of Luxemburg, finally succeeded in obtaining his election as Holy Roman Emperor in 1347.

Revolt in Rome

On Whitsunday, 1347, Cola di Rienzi, an innkeepr's son who had become a notary, led a revolution against the nobles of Rome. Marching into the capital, Rienzi summoned a parliament, abolished senatorships and had himself proclaimed tribune and liberator of the Holy Roman Republic. Rienzi, a dictator with extravagant ambitions, sought to bring the whole of Italy under his sway—not by conquest (as Robert of Sicily had attempted) but through the consent of the people. Representatives of various municipalities assembled at Rome to celebrate the "Feast of Italian Unity" and Rienzi declared that Rome would establish a new "imperium" in the West, giving voice to the dreams of Dante and Petrarch, Pope Clement VI urged

The city of Rome, from a gold seal of Ludwig of Bavaria.

the exiled Roman patricians at Avignon to depose Rienzi, but the tribune, aided by a Hungarian army, defeated the expatriates' troops. Yet at the end of the year Rienzi abdicated and asked Emperor Charles IV for protection. He was tried and condemned at Avignon but his life was spared.

Granada

The Moorish kingdom of Granada managed to maintain a vigorous independent existence despite internal factions and envious neighbors. Under the Nasride dynasty the fortified palace of the Alhambra —named for the Arabic adjective that described the color of its reddish, sun-dried bricks—slowly rose on the plateau of Monte de la Asabica in Granada.

The Hanseatic League

The consolidation of the Hanseatic League and the kingdoms of Poland and Bohemia occurred in this same period. The absence of a firm government in Hamburg, Lubeck and the seaports of northeastern Germany allowed those ports to acquire independent status, and they soon drew together to form an association (*Hansa*) for mutual security and the protection of their trading rights. They enjoyed extensive privileges in various countries —in England, for example, members of the Hanseatic League paid lower customs rates than other aliens. The Hansa towns first formed into a league in 1344, and those governments that would not accept their monopoly on Baltic trade found themselves cut off from supplies of naval timber.

Casimir III of Poland

In Poland, Casimir the Great's prudent foreign policy not only saved his kingdom from partition, but increased its stature. He gained from Bohemia the right to a free hand in Silesia and made a satisfactory peace with the Teutonic Knights—thus providing Poland with defensible frontiers. Casimir codified the law, reformed the administration and encouraged trade (notably by granting the Jews privileges). Having no direct heir, he decreed that his throne should pass to his nephew, Louis I of Hungary, upon his death.

By the time he ascended the Polish throne in 1370, Louis had already built up a reputation as soldier, autocrat and patron of learning. He had avenged the murder of his brother Andrew, consort of Queen Joanna of Naples, by overrunning that kingdom in 1347, but the Pope had refused to sanction his coronation. His long struggle against Venice, which lasted from 1345 to 1358, brought him control of many towns on the Dalmatian coast.

Meanwhile, in Buda, Cracow, Granada, the Hansa cities, Paris, London, and Florence, the Black Death was taking a heavy toll.

The Black Death

By 1345 the shipping lanes between Europe and the Levant were regularly plied by merchant vessels carrying cargoes of spices, silks, fine porcelains—and plague. Rats on board those ships harbored fleas on their hides, and those fleas in turn harbored Pasteurella pestis, *the bacillus that causes bubonic plague, in their stomachs. Within a decade after the first outbreak of plague in Europe, some 33,000,000 people—roughly one-third of the Continent's population—had succumbed to the dread disease. Medieval physicians were powerless to check the plague's spread, and clerics convinced their followers that the disease was divine retribution for unnamed sins. By the time the plague had run its course, it had decimated Europe and doomed its feudal social structure.*

The sailing vessels that plied the trade routes linking fourteenth-century Europe and the Levant were invariably rat-infested—and those rats were usually flea-infested. As a result, sailors, dockworkers and port dwellers of the era frequently developed severe skin infections, worms and typhus. Flea-borne diseases rode the caravan routes and shipping lanes in the early 1300s, and minor epidemics were common.

Within the stomach of each flea lurked *Pasteurella pestis,* the bacillus that causes bubonic plague. Infection followed these host rats westward: by 1346 the plague was rampant in Asia Minor and by early 1348 it had reached Sicily and the mainland of Europe.

To fourteenth-century Europeans, the Black Death—as the first great epidemic was later called—was a God-sent punishment for their sins. The plague itself was occasionally said to be visible—as a cloud of mist or a pall of black smoke—but it remained mysterious in its origins and its workings. Doctors were powerless to control it. They prescribed a variety of arcane treatments for its prevention and cure, but most physicians had as little confidence in the efficacy of their prescriptions as did their patients. That mutual lack of confidence was more than justified; it would have required powers of diagnosis far beyond the range of the medieval doctor for him to identify the three lethal strands of pure plague—bubonic, pulmonary and septicemic. Indeed it is only within the last few decades that techniques have been evolved to check and stamp out such an epidemic.

Once launched on the mainland, the plague spread with awesome speed. It must have seemed to contemporary Europeans that nothing would stop the disease until the last man had died. Indeed, the only medical mystery that remains today is why the bubonic plague did *not* consume the whole population.

Villages in the third category were all but impossible to find in Italy, the first country on the Continent to be overwhelmed by the Black Death. Florence, one of the greatest cities of Europe, possessed somewhere between ninety and a hundred thousand inhabitants in 1348. Of these, according to one contemporary chronicler, "not one in ten was left alive" when the plague had run its course. In a memorable description of the plague contained in the prologue to the *Decameron*, Boccaccio claims that a hundred thousand Florentines died during the epidemic. Such statements were not intended to be taken as precise estimates; rather they were hyperbolic expressions by eye witnesses of the enormity of their experience—as meaningless statistically as an assertion made by the Pope's advisers that the Black Death cost the lives of 42,836,486 people throughout the world.

From Italy, the plague spread both overland and, on shipboard, along the European coastline. On land, where the advance of the disease was governed by the motion of rats or infected men, the progress was laborious. It is noteworthy, for instance, that the Black Death reached Moscow from the Crimea by way of Italy, France, England, and the Hanseatic ports—not by moving overland. Germany, on the other hand, was assailed principally by land, as the plague moved up the Mosel valley, through Bavaria and through the Balkans.

The fearful suffering was made worse by the ferocious persecution of the Jews that accompanied it. Medieval men felt a desperate need to blame his tribulations on some scapegoat, and the Jews were a convenient minority group, already unpopular for economic and social reasons. A few unfortunates were tortured into confessing that they had poisoned local wells, and instantly the whole race was inculpated. In Germany the Black Death also produced the Flagellant Crusades. In an attempt to take upon themselves the sins of the world, long processions of penitents literally whipped themselves into a frenzy at services held in every town they visited.

Marseille seems to have been the first French town to be infected. The plague soon reached Avignon,

Boccaccio, whose *Decameron* describes the horror which the Black Death aroused, by Andrea del Castagno.

Opposite Death Riding Triumphant, from Palermo Cathedral.

A military operation in the West Country

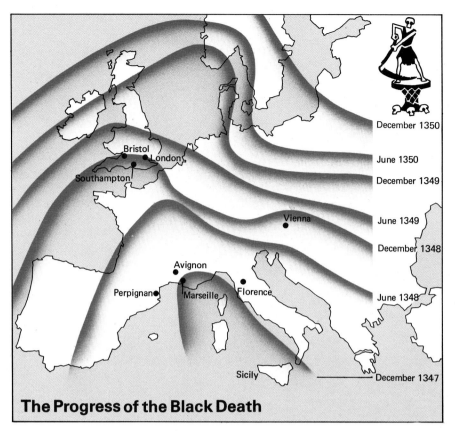

The Progress of the Black Death

December 1350
June 1350
December 1349
June 1349
December 1348
June 1348
December 1347

Bristol
London
Southampton
Vienna
Avignon
Perpignan
Marseille
Florence
Sicily

where it spared Pope Clement VI—who retreated to his chamber and took refuge between two enormous fires—but treated the populace with particular severity. The Pope's immunity was not exceptional, however. Although many men of importance perished throughout Europe, the rich—who could flee the cities and take shelter in their spacious and relatively hygienic manors—suffered conspicuously less than their poorer contemporaries.

In France, as elsewhere in Europe, little pinpoints of reliable data about the plague's course stand out from the mists of uncertainty and vagueness. In Perpignan, for instance, records show that, out of 125 scribes and legists active before the Black Death, only 44 survived; seven of the town's eight doctors and sixteen of its eighteen barbers and surgeons also disappeared.

The first case of bubonic plague in England almost certainly occurred at Melcombe Regis in Dorset in June or July of 1348. Other ports, however, vie for the doubtful honor of being the first victim, and Bristol and Southampton must certainly have been infected within a few weeks of the outbreak of the epidemic. It is possible to visualize the plague's spread, in the first months, as a kind of military operation: the initial attack on the Dorset ports, followed by a bold thrust across the country to the north coast, seaborne landings at scattered ports to outflank the defense, slow mopping-up operations in Devon and

View of a city by Amrogio Lorinzetti; the plague, brought by boat, from the East spread rapidly due to crowded and unhygenic living conditions.

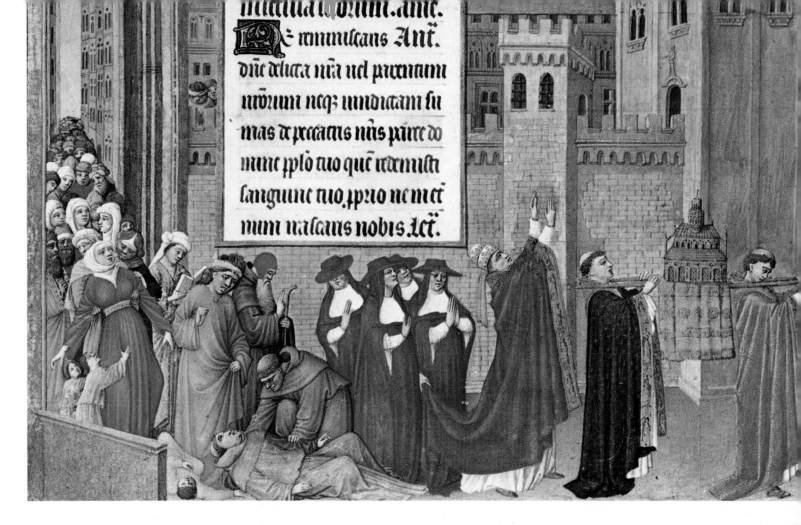

Cornwall, and then a final thrust up the Thames valley towards London. After March, 1349, the campaign analogy can no longer be pursued; the disease poured forward in a hundred different directions and sprang up simultaneously in a hundred different spots. By the end of 1350, virtually every village in England, Scotland, and Wales had suffered casualties.

It is possible to chart the progress of the Black Death in England with greater accuracy than elsewhere because of a wealth of manorial and ecclesiastical records. It is, of course, dangerous to argue that because only twenty-five per cent of the beneficed clergy died in the deanery of Henley, while forty-three per cent died in the deanery of Oxford, the same ratio applied to the general population in those areas. There is, however, enough evidence to establish a general pattern: East Anglia and the West Country were probably the worst afflicted areas; London, where the Black Death raged throughout the whole of 1349, seems to have lost between twenty and thirty thousand people out of a total population of some seventy thousand—a stark figure, although modest in comparison with the lurid estimates of contemporary chroniclers and some nineteenth-century historians.

By December, 1350, the epidemic had blanketed the whole of Europe—and by December of the following year it was virtually at an end. Certain areas—Bohemia, large sections of Poland, a mysterious pocket between France, Germany and the Low Countries, and tracts in the Pyrenees—had largely escaped the effects of the plague.

Attempting to establish any overall estimate of mortality is hazardous and speculative. There is a better chance of doing so in England than elsewhere, yet even in England's case calculations differ widely and must be hedged around with a multitude of qualifications. Reliable sources have estimated that England's mid-century population of 2,500,000 to 4,000,000 persons had been reduced by 50 per cent by 1400. As a rule of thumb, the statement that "roughly 33 per cent of the population of Europe died of the plague before it had run its course" is reasonably reliable. That figure could conceivably have been as high as 45 per cent or as low as 23 per

The Church's pleas for forgiveness and an end for the plague are ignored as Death strikes a friar during a papal procession; from the *Tres Riches Heures du Duc de Berry.*

Medical knowledge was as powerless as religion to help victims of the Black Death.

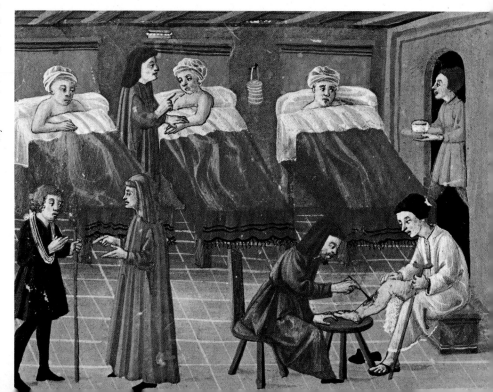

The social structure of Europe shattered

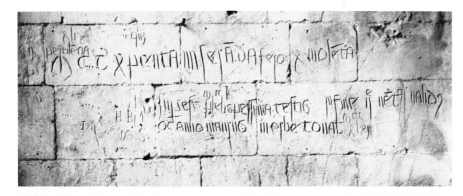

cent—but those are certainly the outside limits.

It is impossible to eliminate one-third of a continent's population over a period of some four years without desperately dislocating that continent's economy and social structure. In Europe in the mid-fourteenth century, that blow was buffered by the fact that the Continent was suffering from over-population—or rather from a surplus population that current agricultural techniques could neither feed nor employ. Vast economic expansion in the thirteenth century had already given way to mild recession, and the population of Europe in 1345 was probably only slightly above what it had been in 1300—that is, in the neighborhood of 100 million persons.

Chronic underemployment remained widespread, however, until the plague struck. The sudden disappearance of roughly one-third of the labor force inevitably altered the relationship between employer and employee, and radically modified the relationship between landlord and tenant. To maintain his available labor supply, or to bribe reinforcements away from neighboring employers, the manorial lord was now frequently forced to pay greatly increased wages. To ensure that his cottages were occupied, he had to accept reduced rents or modified labor services.

In theory, the movement of labor was controlled; tenants should not have been able to dictate terms to their masters. But in the chaos produced by the plague, such regulations could not be enforced. Economic realities asserted themselves within this feudal framework: prices of manufactured products soared in England, as canvas, iron, and salt all more than doubled in cost between 1347 and 1350. At the same time, livestock—such as cows, sheep and oxen—fell disastrously in value. The result was that the typical landlord was paying more for his purchases, getting less for his farm-produce, and less as rent for his cottages, and was at the same time being forced to give higher wages for whatever labor he could secure. Most found themselves in grave economic straits. A common remedy was to reduce the extent of the land that a landlord farmed himself, and to

Top "Miserable . . . wild . . . distracted, the dregs of a people alone survive to witness." Graffiti on the walls of England's Ashwell Church, dating back to 1350, show the horror that the living continued to feel when the plague was over.

A doctor protects himself with a pomander and by burning herbs as he takes the pulse of a plague victim.

Burying plague victims at Tournai, Belgium.

rent vacant tenements, and this profoundly affected the structure of rural society.

Thus the Black Death created striking modifications in the social structure of the European countryside. Its influence upon the Church was perhaps even more dramatic, however. Among the lower ranks of the clerical hierarchy particularly it is almost literally true to say that anyone who did his duty conscientiously had barely one chance in ten of survival. Where the most infectious, pulmonary form of the disease was in question, continued contact with the sick was almost sure to prove fatal. In such circumstances, only a priest who shirked his responsibilities could reasonably hope to see out the epidemic; in England and Germany—and probably in the other countries of Europe as well—roughly half the clergy proved that they knew how to do their duty. But even though the clerics suffered more severely than the laity, they somehow contrived to leave their contemporaries with the impression that they were behaving with something less than nobility. The reputation of the Church fell almost as rapidly as the death roll of priests mounted. By 1351 the Catholic Church in Europe had been stripped of its ablest members.

G.M.Trevelyan has claimed that the Black Death was as significant a phenomenon as the Industrial Revolution, and that the latter was actually less striking in its effect because it was not, like the plague, "a fortuitous obstruction fallen across the river of life and temporarily diverting it." "The year of the Black Death" wrote Friedell, even more emphatically, "was . . . the year of the conception of modern man."

Today one feels less certain that the years of the Black Death were in fact so marked a watershed. For one thing, it should never be forgotten that the plague of 1348 was only the first of a series of epidemics that sputtered throughout Europe until the beginning of the eighteenth century. Bubonic plague returned to England in 1361, 1368–69, 1371, 1375, 1390 and 1405.

In addition, it is hard to identify with precision any major trend that was initiated by the Black Death, rather than simply reinforced by it. The substitution of wages and cash rent for labor services was certainly given striking impetus by the depredations of the plague, but this was a process that was already far advanced in some areas before 1347— and the next half century by no means witnessed continued and uninterrupted progress toward the disappearance of the feudal relationship. It was unquestionably easier for a tenant to desert his manor during the immediate aftermath of the Black Death, but that right had already been tacitly conceded by many landlords during the years of surplus labor that preceded the plague. The dearth of available manpower that followed the plague often made it more, not less difficult for the peasant to choose his place of work and move his home. Even in such fields as architecture—where it has often been accepted as dogma that the shortage of skilled workmen after the

Above left Flagellants try to drive off the plague by whipping themselves.

Above Our Lady of Mercy protects the faithful while plague strikes down its victims with arrows.

The birth of Perpendicular architecture

plague led to the substitution of the Perpendicular for the Decorated architectural style—the seeds of change had actually been sown long before the first workman died. The transept and choir of Gloucester Cathedral—the very cradle of the Perpendicular style—were completed as early as 1332.

The Black Death may not have been a conspicuous innovator of new trends, but its influence on the second half of the fourteenth century was nonetheless considerable. For one thing, the position of the tenant was permanently strengthened in relation both to his landlord and to the wage scale, which never fell back to the rates prevailing before the plague. The Black Death was the most significant among the factors contributing to the turmoil that marked the end of the fourteenth century. The insurrections of the Jacquerie in 1358 and of Tuchins in 1381, the rising of the weavers in Ghent in 1379, the Peasants' Revolt in England in 1381, all arose from social and economic conditions that would have existed even if *Pasteurella pestis* had never left its home in Central Asia. But it is highly unlikely that conditions in Europe would have reached a point of desperation as rapidly as they did if the plague had not occurred. The Peasants' Revolt, for example, was at least in part a reaction to the Black Death. Attempts by labor-hungry landlords to wrest from their tenants many of the rights that the latter had won over the preceding decades did much to create a climate of discontent in England.

The real "contribution" made by the Black Death was far less precise. By the second half of the fourteenth century, the disintegration of the manorial system was already far advanced. The Black Death aided the process immeasurably by exacerbating

existing grievances, heightening contradictions and making economic nonsense of a situation that previously had seemed outmoded but still viable. It is not even absolutely certain that the plague "caused" the Peasants' Revolt or the similar uprisings in other countries. It cannot even be said that, but for the epidemic, the Revolt would have taken a substantially different form. What can be asserted is that

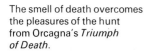

if there had been no Black Death, bitterness would never have risen by 1381 to the level that it did.

In the same way, it can be argued that although the Black Death did not "cause" the Reformation, it did create the circumstances that made such ecclesiastical reform possible. "The plague not only depopulates and kills," wrote Neibuhr, "it gnaws [at] the moral stamina and frequently destroys it entirely." Paradoxically, the decades that followed the plague saw not only a decline in the prestige and spiritual authority of the Church, but also the growth of a new, radical, questioning religious fervor, based upon disillusion and even despair. In Italy, those decades marked the great period of the Fraticelli, Franciscan rebels who once had been denounced as heretics by the Pope and now deemed the Pope himself a heretic. In England that era was the age of Wycliffe and of Lollardy, a period of new and aggressive anti-clericalism that drew its strength from the discontent and doubts of the people at large. The age was one of spiritual unrest, or pertinent questioning of the value and conduct of the Church, and of disrespect for established idols.

Such a spirit would have been abroad even if bubonic plague had never visited the shores of Europe. The Black Death can hardly be made responsible for the growth of doubts about the doctrine of the Transubstantiation—but it did create a state of mind in which doctrines and dogmas were more easily doubted. Wycliffe was a child of the Black Death in the sense that he belonged to a generation that had suffered terribly and learned through its sufferings to question the premises on which the Church and society were based. The Church itself became a victim of the Black Death; large numbers

St. Roch, the plague saint.

of its dedicated ministers perished, and its reputation and authority began to decay. The Reformation was inevitable, but it might not have come so quickly and so violently if the walls of establishment religion had not first been undermined and outflanked by the visitation of the plague.

Can it truthfully be said, then, that "the year of the Black Death was the year of the conception of modern man?" Such colorful generalizations must be viewed with suspicion; eras seldom end and new generations rarely begin with such convenient tidiness. However, the Black Death—especially when considered as a series of epidemics rather than an isolated phenomenon—did unquestionably hasten the decline of values and the breaking down of behavior patterns that had stood firm over many centuries. It opened men's minds, dispelled their illusions and awoke their doubts. It played a crucial role in the phenomenon that can be most conveniently described as "the ending of the Middle Ages."

PHILIP ZIEGLER

A German *Pestblätte* for protection against the Black Death.

After Louis II's deposition in 1346, the German princes chose Charles of Bohemia, the Pope's candidate, to be the next Holy Roman Emperor. Charles had been brought up at the French court, where he met Clement VI and earned himself the nickname "the priest's Emperor." True to Clement's wishes, he repealed his predecessor's anti-papal legislation and undertook not to interfere in Italian affairs. Indeed, the principal event of Charles IV's reign was the publishing of the *Golden Bull*. The effect of that papal decree, which was promulgated at the Diet of Metz in 1356, was to devalue imperial power, leaving the government of Germany in the hands of the electors.

The establishment of a poorly-conceived imperial electoral college during the preceding century had resulted in "double elections," anti-kings and civil wars. The new constitution fixed the number of electors at seven. They included the Archbishops of Mainz, Trier and Cologne, the King of Bohemia, the Count Palatine of the Rhine, the Duke of Saxony and the Margrave of Brandenburg. The Pope was excluded from German politics—and although Innocent IV protested, he was forced to acquiesce. Even more significant was the fact that the other German princes had been deprived of any say in the choice of their Emperor.

Thus the successor of Charlemagne had become in effect an elective president, dependent upon three spiritual and four temporal rulers. As a result a later Holy Roman Emperor would describe Charles IV as "the stepfather of the Empire, but the father of Bohemia" —for as the electors had hoped, Charles concentrated his efforts and attention on his native duchy. During his reign, Charles acquired

Lower Lusatia and Brandenburg and in 1348 founded Prague University, the first seat of learning in Central Europe. On his death in 1378, his son Wenceslas inherited both Bohemia and the Empire.

The Avignon Papacy

The popes at Avignon found that their expenses increased considerably during their exile, for they were obliged to finance a series of wars in Italy to safeguard the remnants of papal territorial possessions there. To gain the revenues necessary for those campaigns, the fiscal machinery of the Church had to be overhauled throughout Europe. New dues such as annates and clerical tenths were imposed, and Avignon became the center of an intricate network for controlling appointments. All the Western states were in the process of developing new administrative and financial machinery at this time, but the papacy set the pace. More money was raised than had seemed possible, and the residence at Avignon grew in splendor; the cardinals, who were growing in importance under the reorganized Curia, lived in greater luxury than their predecessors at Rome ever had.

All the Avignon popes were born in the south of France, and Frenchmen dominated the College of Cardinals (113 out of the 134 were French). In these circumstances there was no chance of a Pope's being able to act as mediator in the Hundred Years' War.

Many contemporary rulers urged the Pope to return to Rome, among them Emperor Charles IV himself. Catherine of Siena, who encouraged Gregory XI to consider the matter impartially, reminded him that "it is more needful for you to win back souls than to recover

your earthly possessions." Gregory summoned up his courage and entered Rome in 1377, but his life was in constant danger. Upon his death a year later, Charles IV tried his utmost to ensure the election of a pope who was not French, and while the conclave of cardinals met in the Vatican, the Roman crowd outside chanted "We want a Roman, or at least an Italian." Urban VI, who was elected by the conclave, was both an Italian and indisputably anti-French. The French cardinals withdrew from Rome to Naples, declared Urban deposed and chose the Bishop of Cambrai as anti-pope.

Charles died before he could alert Christendom to the dangers of two rival popes. The Great Schism —a line of Italian popes at Rome and a rival succession of French popes at Avignon—lasted for forty years, and the scandal was only ended by the Council of Constance. The Schism literally split Christendom, for France, her ally Scotland, Spain and Naples supported Avignon, while the Emperor, England and the northern kingdoms supported Rome.

Rivalry between Venice and Genoa

In Eastern waters the struggle between Venice and Genoa continued. The Genoese admiral Luciano Doria sailed into the Adriatic, defeated the Venetian Vittorio Pisano at Pola in Istria and blockaded Venice. The city, which was dependent upon imported food, was threatened with starvation. With the Genoese fleet already inside the lagoons, Venice's days as a great sea power seemed numbered. Suddenly Pisano seized the channel leading from the lagoons to the sea. His masterly stroke turned the tables on the Genoese, who suddenly found themselves threatened with starvation. In June, 1380, the Genoese surrendered. Genoa never recovered and Venice became undisputed master of the Levantine trade.

The Ottoman Empire

The westward expansion of the Ottoman Empire became a matter of grave concern for the nations of Central Europe when, in 1345, Turkish troops crossed into Europe and settled on the Gallipoli Peninsula. When the city of Adrianople fell in 1360, the Turks made it

A portrait of the poet Petrarch by Andrea del Castagno.

their capital. In that same year the corps of Janissaries—the spearhead of both army and government—was organized and those warriors soon conquered much of Bulgaria and Macedonia and began raiding eastern Greece and Albania.

Petrarch

If Wycliffe was "the Morning Star of the Reformation," Petrarch (1304-74) was most certainly the Morning Star of the Renaissance. As a young man this remarkable Florentine spurned a legal career in order to devote himself to humane letters. He turned to the classics as an escape from his own age, which he found repellent. At age twenty-two, Petrarch took minor orders. The benefices found for Petrarch by the Colonna family supported his activities and enabled him to travel widely.

There were two sides to this remarkable man: he was both an independent scholar, who assembled a library of classical authors and wrote about Cicero and St. Augustine, and a noted vernacular poet, who made public his love for Laura in the matchless lyrical verse of the *Canzoniere*. Several colleagues openly criticized Petrarch's Italian verses—implying that it was vulgar to write poetry in colloquial language —and occasionally students caught reading the *Canzoniere* were disciplined. Petrarch's vindication came in 1341, when he was awarded

Emperor Charles IV with his son and Charles V of France at a state banquet.

the poet's crown by the Senator of Rome. Classical authors would no longer be revered for their every utterance; Petrarch had questioned the deadweight of authority with a fresh mind, and his work had a powerful influence in the revival of classical scholarship.

Boccaccio

One of Petrarch's last compositions was a Latin version of Boccaccio's story of Griselda. Giovanni Boccaccio (1313–75) was a born storyteller whose *Decameron* followed the path

The Alcazar at Seville, begun by the Moors and finished by Peter the Cruel of Aragon.

of the authors of earlier romances. He was the father of Italian prose and, perhaps, the first author to gain fame during his own lifetime as a result of his writings alone. He was not a politician like Dante or a civil servant like Chaucer, but a professional author. He spent his idle hours with Maria, the illegitimate daughter of Robert, King of Naples, and she served as his model for Fiammetta, the presiding genius of the feasts that form the setting for the *Decameron*.

Charles V of France

In France, Charles v (1364–80) showed himself to be a progressive statesman. He was determined to seize control of the financial machinery that had been set up by the Estates-General and to use the increased revenue provided by the salt and the hearth taxes for reform

and consolidation, and also for the formation of a professional army.

Spanish Civil War

Growing conflict between the Castillian supporters of Peter the Cruel (1350–69) and those of his step-brother, Henry of Trastamara, ultimately led to a civil war that was to involve both France and England. French "free companies" commanded by Bertrand du Guesclin forced Peter into exile at Bordeaux, a region ruled by the Black Prince. The Prince, sympathetic to Peter's cause, invaded Castille and defeated the pretender and his French allies at the battle of Najera in 1367. Peter was restored to the throne, but he soon fell out with the English and Henry returned to Castille in 1369 to reign undisputed. The sole legacy of Peter's reign was the completion of the Alcazar at Seville, the palace begun in 1181 during Moorish rule.

Second phase of the Hundred Years' War

In 1369 nobles of the Court of Armagnac in British-held Aquitaine appealed to Charles v to rid them of the Black Prince, and when the Prince refused to appear in person at the king's court, the Hundred Years' War was resumed.

In his last months, the Black Prince promoted overdue reforms in the Good Parliament and secured the impeachment of Lords Lyons and Latimer for war-profiteering. John of Gaunt, Edward's fourth son and the outstanding political figure in England, made his Palace of the Savoy into the finest residence in England with his wealth from the wars. Gaunt almost certainly aimed at succeeding to the throne.

The Black Prince's ten-year-old son Richard II came to the throne in 1377 and John of Gaunt ruled England as regent.

Wycliffe and Church reform

Gaunt's circle included two of the most remarkable Englishmen of the Middle Ages, John Wycliffe and Geoffrey Chaucer. Wycliffe was rector of Butterworth, a parsonage in Gaunt's patronage, but he spent most of his life at Oxford, where he dominated university life. He found the prosperous Church completely out of touch with the great changes that were taking place in the

structure of society; on all sides men were crying out for Church reform, yet the smallest change was prevented by the innate conservatism of the institution itself. The Oxford don provided his own remedy for a decaying faith by gathering together a band of "poor preachers," scholars who spent their free time preaching the Gospel in market places and on village greens, as the friars had in their heyday. Wycliffe studied the era of primitive Christianity in the *Acts of the Apostles* and in Paul's epistles. By contrast, the fourteenth-century Church, with its rival popes living in great splendor at Avignon and Rome and its English bishops too occupied with state affairs for pastoral work, seemed to have overreached itself. Wycliffe preached a return to Biblical simplicity with an enthusiasm that was to prove infectious. One of his greatest achievements was to inspire a translation of the Bible—known as "The Lollard Bible"—into the English tongue. Wycliffe's views on the sacraments brought about his downfall. He attacked the practice of auricular confession and denied the orthodox doctrine of transubstantiation in the Mass, and his enemies—who had tried unsuccessfully to bring him to trial in 1376—found their chance to do so during the Peasant's Revolt. Like Luther in the 1520s, Wycliffe was dis-

credited by the popular movement.

Geoffrey Chaucer (*c.* 1340–1400), the first English poet of consequence, was a Londoner who spent

King Richard II of England from the Wilton Dyptich.

his life as a diplomat and later as a customs officer in the King's service. His first major work, *Troilus and Creseyde*, which embroidered upon the ancient tale of Troy in the medieval tradition, was largely based on Boccaccio's *Il Filostrato*. Chaucer came into his own with *The Canterbury Tales*, a verse *Decameron* about English pilgrims. All English society except the aristocracy was faithfully observed in the *Tales*, which described such deftly-drawn characters as the Knight, the Man of Law, the Franklin, and the Wife of Bath.

Chaucer reciting *Troilus and Creseyde*.

Wat Tyler "Captures" London

For decades English peasants had been forced to contend with residual feudalism, intermittent warfare, spiraling taxes and recurrent plague. In late May of 1381, the oppressed peasants of Kent and Essex rose in simultaneous, spontaneous rebellion against the Crown. An army of incensed tenant farmers marched on London in early June of that year, and King Richard II's helpless ministers took refuge in the Tower. The apparently doomed government was saved by the fourteen-year-old King's bravura: crying "Sirs, will you shoot your King?", Richard rode out to meet his assembled subjects. And by the time the Lord Mayor of London had rallied a force to "rescue" the King, Richard had made peace with the peasants. His actions averted civil war but they could not stem the popular tide; similar risings erupted across Europe in the next decade as peasants everywhere demanded a voice in their government.

Domestic scene from *The Occupations of the Months*.

Opposite Richard II, whose courage destroyed the Peasants' Revolt.

At the end of May, 1381, some villagers at Brentwood in Essex roughhoused a tax collector. There was nothing unusual in their action: the age was a turbulent one in which disputes led readily to violence, even among respectable members of the community. A visit from some awe-inspiring officer of the law was usually sufficient to quell any local disorder. But in the early summer of 1381 the usual did not happen.

No less a person than the chief justice of the King's Bench went down to Essex to hold an inquiry and punish the Brentwood rowdies. The justice found himself surrounded by an armed multitude who drove him off after making him swear on the Bible never to come their way again. Manhandling a tax collector was one thing; mishandling a royal justice was quite another—and infinitely more serious. However, instead of taking to the woods as outlaws or fleeing the country, the villagers appealed for the support of their neighbors, and insurrection spread rapidly throughout the county.

These events appear to have taken the government by surprise, although they were simply the sudden boiling over of an already seething mass of discontent that had been brewing in the countryside for several months. Now that some had openly defied authority, countless peasants left their homesteads and took to the roads. Dissidents in Kent made their way to Maidstone, and there chose as their leader Wat Tyler.

Nothing is known for certain of Tyler's origins or background. Some said that he was a highway robber, others that he was an artisan from Deptford who had slain a tax collector for insulting his daughter. It was reported at various times that he was a disbanded soldier from the war in France, and that he was the wayward younger son of a respectable Kentish family. It is clear from the way Tyler impressed himself upon contemporaries and chroniclers—and hence on posterity—that he had a strong personality and a gift for leadership. Yet Wat Tyler was never anything more than the leader of the rebels of Kent. There was no single "Peasants' Revolt" with a single leader, but rather a number of uprisings, each with a separate identity and separate leader (if it had any leader at all). What gave Tyler prominence, and turned his share in the revolt into a dramatic political event, was the decision made by the men of Kent to combine with those of Essex, on the other side of the Thames, and march on London. On June 11, these two great peasant armies began to converge on the capital.

When the news filtered through to the King's ministers at London, disbelief gave way to despair. The revolt was the culmination of a decade of troubles. The war against France had faltered ever since the Black Prince, heir to the throne, had contracted a recurrent fever. The Prince died in 1376. His aged father, King Edward III, followed him the next year and was succeeded on the throne by a ten-year-old grandson, Richard II. Aristocratic factions competed for control of the government and for the spoils of office.

When the war had begun back in 1337, the English economy was booming, with a rising population that made even the cultivation of marginal land profitable. But the boom was already weakening when, in 1348, the bottom was knocked out of the economy by the arrival of the Black Death. Competition for increasingly scarce labor pushed up wages. Landless laborers, hitherto the lowest stratum of the village community, were suddenly quite well off, for they could offer their services to the highest bidder. Some of those who had steady jobs on a yearly contract gave them up to work for higher daily wage rates somewhere else.

Above A bullock-drawn plough from the Lutrell Psalter.

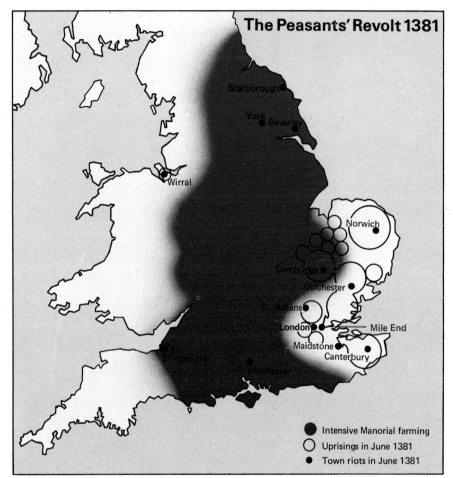

The Peasants' Revolt 1381

Scarborough
York
Beverley
Wirral
Norwich
Cambridge
Colchester
St. Albans
London — Mile End
Maidstone
Bridgewater
Canterbury
Winchester

● Intensive Manorial farming
○ Uprisings in June 1381
● Town riots in June 1381

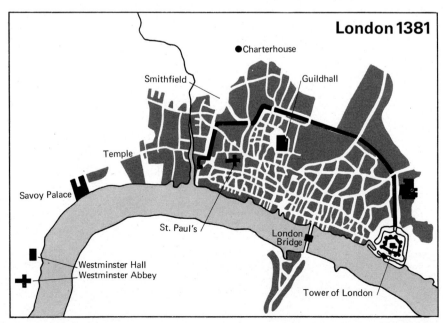

London 1381

● Charterhouse
Smithfield
Guildhall
Temple
Savoy Palace
St. Paul's
London Bridge
Westminster Hall
Westminster Abbey
Tower of London

The more established peasants on the other hand —those who held land and paid for it in rents and labor services to their landlord—found themselves in an invidious position. Caught in an economic squeeze, the landlords raised rents while exacting every ounce of old-fashioned labor services (which did not have to be paid for, and were hence much more valuable than they had been when labor was cheap).

It was this economic crisis that made Parliament all the more reluctant to grant taxes—and all the more ready to believe that the men who controlled the government in the King's name were incompetent and spend-thrift. The situation was becoming desperate and the Commons very truculent, when, in January, 1380, the Archbishop of Canterbury, Simon Sudbury, a fair-minded man and a sound administrator, offered to take over as Chancellor. With another prominent churchman, Robert Hales, the prior of the Knights Hospitaler, acting as treasurer, there was a fair prospect that the country would at least be governed honestly.

Unfortunately, Parliament failed to provide Sudbury and Hales with a proper revenue; instead of a tax graduated according to people's ability to pay, the Commons would agree only to the levy of a flat-rate poll tax—of one shilling per head of the population over sixteen years of age. This was both inadequate and iniquitous.

For some reason, the government did not attempt to disperse the rebels who gathered outside London on June 11. It probably hoped that the peasant armies would break up of their own accord when they became weary and short of food—but the rebels proved to be much better organized and better disciplined than anyone had anticipated. By the evening of Wednesday, June 12, the men of Essex had reached the outskirts of London and had camped at Mile End. The main body of the Kentishmen encamped at Blackheath, while an advance guard pushed on to the south suburbs. The only bridge across the Thames was closed against them, but many sympathizers from London crossed over by boat to join the rebels, who broke open two prisons at Southwark and sacked the Archbishop's palace at Lambeth. The King and his ministers, gathered at the Tower of London, caught sight of flames in the distance and knew for certain that the uprising was serious. They could not make much sense of it, however, and sent envoys to ask the rebels' purpose; the peasants replied that they were loyal subjects of the King who wished to ask him to take action about

"All men were created equal"

the misgovernment of the realm by John of Gaunt.

That night at Blackheath, a priest named John Ball preached a now famous sermon to the assembled multitudes. In the beginning, he said, all men were created equal, and it was only the contrivances of the wicked that had reduced some men to servitude. Englishmen now had the chance, if they would seize it, of casting off the yoke that they had borne so long, and winning the freedom they had always desired.

Early the next morning, the fourteen-year-old King attempted to speak to the rebels from a boat lying on the river at Gravesend, while his listeners crowded the banks. They clamored for him to come ashore, but his ministers took fright when the rebels abused them as "traitors," and made the rowers pull away. As the royal party retreated to the Tower, the rebels poured into the city. It proved impossible to defend the gates against the insurgents, who had many supporters among the urban proletariat, and the houses and property of unpopular ministers, foreigners, and lawyers (against whom the rebels showed a special animosity) went up in flames.

That night the young King held council in the Tower. Opinions were divided: some were for an immediate show of force; others said that attempts should first be made to calm the mob down by negotiation. Siding with the latter, King Richard had it proclaimed throughout the city that everyone should come to meet him the following morning, June 14, beyond the city boundary at Mile End. Part of the plan was to draw the rebels away from the Tower, allowing unpopular ministers a chance to escape, but the plan misfired when some of the rebels remained on watch.

The Mile End meeting went well. The rebels were courteous and the King conciliatory. He agreed to free everyone from the burdens of serfdom, and set his clerks to work preparing charters. As to the alleged traitors, he said that the rebels could do as they wished with them—but only after their guilt had been proved by due process of law. (Meanwhile, some of the rebels had decided to settle this matter for themselves. While the King was at Mile End,

they broke into the ill-guarded Tower, dragged out Archbishop Sudbury and Robert Hales, and beheaded them on Tower Hill.)

Some of the rebels were satisfied with the Mile End meeting and the execution of "traitors" and began to disperse; but many remained, including the more militant leaders of the Essexmen and the Kentishmen who followed Tyler. Later on that Friday, June 14, the rebellion degenerated into a reign of terror, and attacks on property gave way to the slaughter of anyone the mob disliked. In an effort to regain control of the situation—by dividing peasant protest from the passions of the London mob—King Richard called another meeting for Saturday at the Smithfield cattle market, just outside the city wall.

Riding up to the King at Smithfield, Tyler added several new and impossible demands to those made at Mile End. He insisted that all men should be equal, and admit no lordship save that of the King, that the estates of the Church should be confiscated and distributed to the laity, and that all bishoprics should be abolished save one. The King kept up a show of sympathy, but Tyler's studied insolence provoked a member of the royal party to denounce him as a notorious highwayman and thief. Tyler drew a dagger and lunged at the enraged noble. The mayor of London, William Walworth, intercepted Tyler and struck him down from his horse, and one of the King's squires ran a sword through the rebel leader.

The peasants let out a great cry and strung their bows, but Richard rode toward them crying, "Sirs, will you shoot your King? I will be your leader, follow me." For one perilous moment the peasants hesitated—and then followed Richard out to the field of Clarkenwell. Mayor Walworth hurried back into the city to raise every armed man who could be trusted—but when he and his party returned to rescue the King, they found him talking at ease with the rebels. Richard would not allow force to be used, but granted the peasants his pardon and sent them away to their homes.

Events in London provided the most dramatic story, but risings elsewhere were no less important. There were disturbances at York, Scarborough, Beverley, and Winchester—although whether these were anything more than town riots of a kind familiar in the fourteenth century is difficult to say. At towns in eastern England, however, there was clear evidence of opposition to merchant oligarchies and monastic landlords. At St. Albans the townsmen forced the abbot to grant them the sort of municipal self-government that towns of comparable size elsewhere had long before achieved, and at Bury St. Edmunds there was a violent assault on the abbey that owned the town lands.

Meanwhile, the royal government had taken the offensive. Proclamations announced the death of Tyler, repudiated concessions extorted by force, and called on local officials to establish order. Dismay among the peasants in Essex revived insurrection—but this time the government was prepared, and the rebel forces were cut down by troops at Billericay.

A thief at work.

Below left Feeding the barnyard cock—and sparrows.

The head of Archbishop Simon of Sudbury, from Sudbury Parish Church, Suffolk.

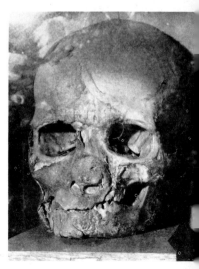

Rebellion: the only resort for the unenfranchised

Peasants reap corn under the direction of a reeve.

Rebel leader John Ball leads his "army" into London. The banners are those of England and St. George.

Judicial commissions were set up to search out and punish offenders, and a hundred or more were executed before the government relented and banned capital punishment. In the Parliament of November, 1381, a general amnesty was granted to all except 287 named offenders who had committed serious crimes.

Any account of the peasant uprisings of 1381 must attempt to explain why they were concentrated in eastern England. If peasant misery, provoked to rebellion by an iniquitous tax, were the only cause, it is surprising that there were no risings in midland England, where the manorial economy was most strictly organized and the burdens of serfdom most severe. Peculiarly, Kent, the center of rebellion, was the one part of England where there was little if any servile tenure; it was a county inhabited by both peasant smallholders and numerous wage laborers, and it was one of the few places where the Statute of Laborers was enforced effectively. Freeholders were common in East Anglia, but there were also many serfs—tied to the soil and obliged to render services and special payments to a landlord. Unlike the great estates of midland England, the manors there tended to be small—too small to be economic-

ally viable agricultural units—and most lords allowed the peasants to farm the tenements in their own way. Some landlords had freed their serfs, relying instead on rents, but others retained their legal hold over the peasants in order to exploit their labor as well as their prosperity.

It was this contrast between free and unfree, between the good fortune of some and the ill luck of others, that apparently lay behind the discontent in East Anglia. Moreover, both there and in Kent there was a distinctive social custom; when a peasant died, his holding was divided equally among all his sons. This policy had subdivided and ultimately impoverished peasant holdings. The Black Death was therefore a blessing in disguise, for it gave the survivors new opportunities for prosperity, provided they were prepared to work hard and build up a little capital to invest in vacant holdings. Too often, however, those opportunities were whittled away by exacting landlords; savings were reduced by rising rents, and hard-won capital drained away in unfair taxes. Thus, the basic cause of the Peasants' Revolt was mounting frustration—the poll tax was simply the last straw. England's peasantry resorted to evasion, and rebelled against pertinacious attempts to collect the infamous head-tax.

On the whole, the rebels were remarkably moderate in their demands. They were simply seeking a fair deal—all they asked for at Mile End was abolishment of the remaining burdens of serfdom. Instead of demanding an end to rents, they merely asked for the reasonable rent of fourpence an acre. And instead of seeking an end to taxation, they asked only for the sort of taxes "which our forefathers knew and accepted."

Fearful monastic chroniclers made much of the element of communistic equality revealed by Wat Tyler at Smithfield, but there is little evidence that such sentiments were widespread. The peasants were rebels against the iniquities of an economic system, not revolutionaries attempting to overthrow it. Indeed, nothing is more remarkable in the English rebellion of 1381—in contrast to contemporary peasant uprisings on the Continent—than the infrequency of attacks upon landlords themselves. There was astonishingly little bloodshed during the English rising—until the rebellion began to degenerate into anarchy. Even then, most of the bloodletting was in the towns, where personal animosities were sharper. The houses of the gentry were invaded and plundered (probably for food as much as for anything else), and their manorial accounts and legal records destroyed, but the gentry and their families were unharmed. Those individuals who suffered did so because they were the agents of central or local government, or because they were lawyers. The hostility shown toward lawyers is particularly significant—it was they who were taken as the chief symbols of obstruction to free enterprise and self-help, rather than the landlords, who were considered victims of economic circumstance.

The nobles and gentry could voice their discontent in Parliament, but rebellion was the only pos-

sible resort for the unenfranchised. The rebels voiced no demand—at least no articulate demand—for a share in Parliament or government, but the political consciousness of the rebellion was strikingly manifest. Admittedly, that consciousness was crude and shallow: the rebels demanded the heads of supposed traitors—but in murdering Sudbury and Hales, they murdered men who were honestly, if feebly, trying to improve the situation. Sudbury and Hales became the scapegoats for a decade of political ineptitude. Many of the gentry would have sympathized with the rebels' disdain for the ruling clique. But in the rebels' unswerving loyalty to King Richard and their insistent claim that they were "his true Commons," they were criticizing the failure of the knights and burgesses, as well as the magnates in Parliament, to serve the country properly. It was a forcible reminder that the upper classes could no longer treat political affairs as if they alone were concerned.

In their distrust of central government, and in their hankering after what they fondly imagined were the good old days in matters of rents and taxes, the rebels were manifesting a very conservative form of discontent—a discontent that fastened upon mismanagement rather than upon the structure of society. In demanding the abolition of restraints upon peasant free enterprise, the rebels were, of course, asking for economic change—but their actions do not indicate that they wanted social re-

volution. Thus, John Ball's famous sermon concentrated more on democratic freedom than on socialist equality, and in this way may be said fairly to reflect the aspirations of his listeners.

Those who rose in rebellion achieved little for themselves, but they did for the first time reveal the power and determination of the lower orders. The story, garbled and simplified in the telling, of how Wat Tyler "captured" London remained to fortify the courage of individual peasants and frighten the ruling classes. Some of the consequences were unfortunate: upper-class fears manifested themselves in a renewed insistence on order and conformity, new ideas were made synonymous with subversion, and criticism—such as Wycliffe's criticism of the Church —was driven underground. But beneath that show of upper-class solidarity, change went on nevertheless. There was a tacit understanding that the clock could not be put back, or the lower classes disregarded, and as economic developments made peasant free enterprise seem good sense, landlords relaxed their insistence on ancient customs and found more acceptable ways of exploiting their tenants' prosperity. English peasants eventually gained their freedom—without having to resort again to armed rebellion. Perhaps this was because they had not made the mistake of asking for too much or waging a class war. On the Continent of Europe, the story was a different and far more bitter one.

W. L. WARREN

A double view of the Revolt: on the left Wat Tyler is killed while Richard II looks on; on the right Richard addresses the mob.

Henry V and his English archers defeat the

The Peasants' Revolt in England was paralleled by risings in France and Flanders. Languedoc rose in protest against the rapacious Duke of Anjou, who quashed the insurrection at Montpellier and then sent two hundred men to the stake, two hundred to the gallows and two hundred to the block, while depriving 1,800 others of their property. When new taxes were proclaimed in Paris in 1382, men stormed the Hotel-de-Ville, armed themselves with mallets and made a bid for control of the city.

France after Charles V

These outbreaks and the manner of their suppression owed much to the early death of Charles v. The monarch's death in 1380 left his young son Charles vi (1380–1422) and his kingdom at the mercy of "The Princes of the Lillies," as the royal dukes of Anjou, Berry and Burgundy were called. The Princes, who had intervened in the rebellion in Flanders, defeated the Flemings in a pitched battle at Roosebeke on November 27, 1382, and crushed resistance in Ghent.

When the Count of Flanders died in 1384, his son-in-law, Philip the Bold of Burgundy, inherited his lands. The death of the Duke of Anjou later that same year left Philip in a position of enormous power in France. In 1388, however, Charles vi reached his majority. He restored his father's councilors and then turned to his brother Louis of Orleans.

In 1392 Charles had an attack of insanity and, as his malady became gradually permanent, the government passed to Philip the Bold of Burgundy. When Philip died in 1404, his son John the Fearless made a bid for the throne, but he was opposed by the mad king's licentious brother, Louis of Orleans, with whom Queen Isabella was openly living. Each mustered armies, fortified his Paris residence and prepared for civil war. It appeared that disaster had been averted in November, 1407, when the Duke of Berry brought Burgundy to the bedside of the ailing Orleans—but three days later Orleans was assassinated on Burgundy's orders.

The foundation of New College

Within five years of Wycliffe's death, Oxford University entered on a new phase of its existence: William of Wykeham's scholars moved from their temporary quarters to the new buildings of St. Mary College of Winchester, familiarly known as New College. Wykeham, Bishop of Winchester and Lord Chancellor, designed his college to house a warden, seventy poor scholars, ten chaplains and sixteen choristers—and to ensure that his benefaction was not wasted, he established a grammar school at Winchester where boys were given instruction in Latin (an essential preliminary to the university course). After a two-year probation at New College, those students qualified as perpetual fellows. Statutes minutely regulated the lives of Wykeham's scholars, who were the first in Europe to have study rooms to themselves. The buildings, no less than the statutes, were planned by Wykeham with great care and set the standard for collegiate buildings in England for centuries to come.

John Huss

Through Richard ii's marriage to Anne of Bohemia, a close connection had developed between Prague and Oxford universities, and numerous Bohemian students had come to Oxford to hear Wycliffe lecture and had returned with copies of his works. John Huss (1369–1414) was too young to have sat at the doctor's feet, yet he became Wycliffe's greatest convert.

After 1401 Huss was recognized as the leading figure at Prague University and the leader of the

John Huss, condemned as a heretic by the Council of Constance, and burnt.

Slav Party in the Empire. He was thought to be a natural choice to lead a nationalist movement in the wake of the anti-German risings of the previous decade. The contingent of German scholars at Prague succeeded in condemning Huss' views, but King Wenceslas, who needed the Slavs' support in his efforts to end the Great Schism, overturned the Germans' ruling and changed the constitution of the University to make the Slavs supreme. The Germans accordingly withdrew and formed a rival school in Leipzig. In 1409 Huss again became rector at Prague, and a year later the archbishop held an inquiry into his doctrines and pronounced him a heretic. The city of Prague rose in protest and was itself placed under an interdict.

Relying on a safe-conduct issued by the Emperor, Huss obeyed the Pope's summons and journeyed to the Council of Constance. Upon his arrival Huss, who had come to debate with the cardinals, found himself on trial for heresy. He was condemned not for heresy, but for refusing to abjure: "I may not offend God and my conscience by saying that I hold heresies that I have never held," he maintained—and on July 6, 1415, Huss was burned at the stake.

Bohemia was in an uproar over Huss' betrayal by the Emperor Sigismund, and Hussite doctrines became the central plank in the Slav Party's program. The Slavs refused to recognize Sigismund as their king, and Pope Martin v, whose election at Constance had officially ended the Great Schism, proclaimed a crusade against them in 1420. Under the resolute leadership of John Ziska and an extremist named Procup, the Slavs defeated every German army sent into

New College and Wadham College, Oxford, with doctors and scholars.

French at the Battle of Agincourt

Bohemia. Finally at the Council of Basel (1431–35) the Hussites accepted a compromise: under the *Compactata*, Bohemians and Moravians were permitted to receive both kinds of Communion, provided that the sacraments were administered only by ordained priests. Free preaching was to be tolerated so long as the bishops' authority was recognized. These arrangements satisfied the majority of the Hussites, and Sigismund entered Prague in 1435. The memory of Huss had been vindicated.

The Cathedral at Prague. Prague was a center of discontent until the Czech people were given partial independence.

Council of Pisa

Heresy was only one of the problems facing the Church at the beginning of the fifteenth century. In past centuries ecclesiastical crises had been overcome through a series of general councils, each of which was summoned by a reigning pope. But with rival popes at Avignon and Rome, this method was out of the question. Instead, a council was summoned over the heads of both popes. Paris University persuaded Charles VI of France to withdraw his support of Benedict at Avignon and, with the additional support of the Emperor and Henry IV, Charles convened the Council of Pisa in 1409. At this gathering, which was attended by ecclesiastics from all over Europe, both popes were deposed. The conclave then elected a Franciscan as Alexander V, and upon Alexander's early death settled on an Italian clerical

The Emperor Sigismund, the leading spirit at the Council of Constance.

brigand, who became John XXIII.

The two deposed popes refused to resign, however, and a threefold division of the Church replaced the Schism. Pisa had failed to end the Schism and, more importantly, it had failed on the issue of Church reform, the matter foremost in the minds of the Paris theologians.

End of the Great Schism

In 1414, the Emperor forced John XXIII to convoke the Council of Constance. Sigismund of Hungary presided over this three-year-long enclave, which was attended by princes as well as prelates. Pope John, who came to Constance hoping to exploit the divisions of the Council, was deposed by the Emperor and Gregory XII in Rome resigned. Shortly thereafter the Avignonese pope, Benedict XIII, was abandoned by his supporters, leaving the field free for the election of Odo Colonna as Pope Martin V in 1417. The Great Schism was at last ended.

Portuguese independence

In Portugal John I, illegitimate son of Pedro I, succeeded to the throne in 1385 after leading a popular revolt to drive the Queen Regent and her daughter Beatrice from the country. At the time of the coup, Beatrice was betrothed to John, Prince of Castile—and the Castilians promptly invaded Portugal and besieged Lisbon, only to be decisively defeated at the battle of Aljubarrota in August, 1385. After centuries of insecurity, the independence of Portugal from Castile was finally assured. As a further

guarantee, John I signed the Treaty of Windsor in 1386. That agreement, by which Portugal and England became permanent allies, was secured when John married the daughter of John of Gaunt. (John of Portugal's remarkable son, Prince Henry the Navigator, encouraged voyages of exploration eastward around Africa, and set the Western powers on the course of much more extensive discoveries.)

Far East

There were significant changes in the Far East during this period. A Shogun named Yoshimitsu ended the civil war between northern and southern Japan in 1392 and brought the country under firmer rule than it had ever known. His mission over, Yoshimitsu resigned his shogunate to his son and retired to an estate near Kyoto. There he built the Golden Pavilion, to which he attracted a remarkable group of artists and dramatists. In neighboring China, a revolutionary monk named Chu Yüan-chang (1368–98) founded the Ming dynasty and, after seizing Nanking, built up an army powerful enough to expel the Mongols from his homeland.

In Persia, the Mongol vizier Timur the Great (or Tamerlane, 1369–1405) seized power in his native Samarkand and soon overran Khorasan, Afghanistan and Kurdistan. He defeated the Mongol Golden Horde in 1391, conquered Mesopotamia and, in 1397, invaded India, devastating the kingdome of Delhi. Timur defeated the Ottoman Turks at Ankara in 1402 and was planning a campaign against China in the months before his death.

English victory in France

Like Edward III, Henry V was primarily a soldier. With Parliament's blessing he revived the English claim to the French throne and landed an army at Harfleur in Normandy in the summer of 1415. After the port surrendered, the English monarch marched north along the coast, where he eventually encountered a considerable French army encamped between the villages of Agincourt and Tramecourt. There, on October 25, English archers wrought havoc upon the French cavalry. Henry proceeded in triumph to Calais and then returned home. Two years later he led

a second expedition to France, this time with the intention of systematically extending his conquest of Normandy. In 1419 the fortress of Rouen, last stronghold of the French army, surrendered. Through Burgundian pressure the French finally came to terms.

The Treaty of Troyes, signed in 1420, virtually ceded France to Henry V. By its terms he was to marry Catherine, daughter of the insane Charles VI, to govern France as regent during his father-in-law's life, and thereafter to succeed him as king. Paris and the north rejoiced at these arrangements but in southern France the Dauphin continued to be recognized as the true heir. As the thirty-eight-year-old English ruler prepared to embark upon a third expedition to France, he suddenly died, leaving an infant of nine months to succeed him as Henry VI.

The English Parliament appointed the infant King's uncle John, Duke of Bedford, as Protector of England, but when Bedford also became Regent of France, power in England passed to his brother Humphrey, Duke of Gloucester. Difficulties with England's Burgundian allies and dissension in the Council between Gloucester and Cardinal Beaufort hindered Bedford's progress in the field. It was not until 1428 that he was ready to launch an attack on the territory south of the Loire that had openly declared its preference for the uncrowned Charles VII. Bedford opened his campaign with the siege of Orleans, the gateway to the south, but the city, and with it the Valois cause, was miraculously saved by Joan of Arc, the "Maid of Orleans."

A monument to Pope Martin V in St. John Lateran, Rome.

The Maid of Orleans

The peasants of southern France believed that she was a saint, and followed her into impossible battle; the English insisted that she was a witch, and ultimately burned her at the stake. Footsoldier and foe alike were certain that some supernatural force guided the peasant girl from Lorraine who called herself Joan of Arc. No mere mortal could have rallied the vanquished troops of the deposed Dauphin as the Maid had done—nor could any commander alive have led such a motley force against the English siege troops that surrounded Orleans and routed them in less than a week as the Maid had done. Joan's "voices" saved France and restored the Dauphin to the throne, but they doomed her in the process. As she went to the stake on May 30, 1431, a penitent onlooker exclaimed "We have burned a saint!"

On February 12, 1429, a French army led by Jean d'Orleans, natural half-brother of the King's cousin, Charles d'Orleans, was ignominiously routed by a mere supply train of the English army. The Bastard of Orleans' humiliating defeat left the King despondent, the court stunned and the French citizenry thoroughly discouraged. It seemed that nothing could halt the English army's advance; Orleans, cornerstone of the kingdom and the gateway to central France, appeared doomed. The country braced itself to face the final English onslaught—but as it did, word began to spread through the French countryside of an extraordinary girl from Lorraine who claimed that she brought the King help from God.

Like most of Europe, fifteenth-century France was still suffering from the aftereffects of the Black Death, and according to contemporary chroniclers Charles VII's kingdom had not yet recovered its former strength. In France as elsewhere, there had been a rash of popular risings following in the wake of the plague, and these recurrent civil disturbances had further undermined the precarious French monarchy. France, therefore, was unprepared to counter the English invasion when it came; the young Dauphin's troops could offer only token resistance to the invasion launched by their former allies.

In 1340, nearly a century earlier, the King of England had openly proclaimed himself King of France. Intermittent fighting had ensued, but by the end of the century peace had been re-established. In 1392 the unhappy King Charles VI of France had become so unbalanced that he could no longer rule his kingdom effectively. Like the regular reappearances of the plague, Charles' insanity recurred intermittently after 1392, but the internal weaknesses of his kingdom did not become fully evident until the night of November 23, 1407. On that fateful night the King's brother, Louis d'Orleans, was assassinated by John the Fearless, Duke of Burgundy. In the political vacuum created by Charles' incapacity, the royal princes engaged in a bitter struggle for power—their feuding soon developed into civil war.

In an attempt to restore order to the faction-torn country, several rival claimants asserted their uniformly dubious claims to Charles' throne. Among them was King Henry V, scion of the Lancaster dynasty, which had recently seized the English throne from the last Plantagenet, Richard II. On August 14, 1415, Henry V disembarked on the beach of Saint-Adresse near Le Havre. Less than three months later his small expeditionary force brought an imposing French army to its knees on the field of Agincourt. In a battle that almost defies description, the English lost some four or five hundred men, the French almost 7,000. The nobility of France was decimated. Thousands fell on the battlefield and nearly fifteen hundred others were taken prisoner and transported to England. Among the captives was Charles d'Orleans, leader of the "Armagnacs" and foremost opponent of Henry V's French ally, John the Fearless, Duke of Burgundy. (After Agincourt, Henry's "Burgundian cousin" made it clear that his interests enlisted him on the side of the victorious young King of England.)

Henry began the methodical reconquest of Normandy, an ancient English possession, in 1417, and a year later Paris was delivered into the hands of the English and their Burgundian allies. The luckless Charles VI of France became a mere puppet and his son, the Dauphin Charles, barely escaped a Burgundian plot to take him prisoner. The Dauphin attempted to secure support for his projected campaign against the English through negotiations with Henry's wavering ally John the Fearless, whose immense territories stretched from Burgundy to the North Sea. On September 10, 1419, the two met on the bridge at Montereau, a village located at the junction of the Yonne and Seine rivers in northern France. The interview—and the Dauphin's ambitions—were cut short when one of the Dauphin's overzealous followers assassinated the Duke of Burgundy. The Duke's murder drove his son Philip

Joan and her banner; a marginal drawing from the *Register* of Parlement.

Opposite Joan of Arc; a symbolic painting from Antoine du Four's *Lives of Famous Women.*

The Dauphin—known as the King of Bourges

Charles VII, the weak Dauphin whom Joan made King of France; by Jean Fouquet.

the Fair into firmer alliance with England, and the Dauphin was obliged to abandon Paris and take refuge south of the Loire.

The notorious Treaty of Troyes, signed on May 21, 1420, officially recognized England's claims to the French Crown. Henry V sealed the pact by marrying Catherine, daughter of Charles VI of France, and the French Crown was officially entailed upon him. The Dauphin was formally excluded from the succession, and his mother, Queen Isabella of Bavaria, further discredited his candidacy by encouraging suspicions about his legitimacy. The University of Paris, which had played a major part in drawing up the Treaty of Troyes, warmly welcomed the handsome young English King, and a gold coin, struck by Henry to win the confidence of the French merchants, was symbolically named *le salut*—the salvation.

Two years later a brace of events occurred that no one had foreseen: Henry, who was in the prime of life, died suddenly on August 31, 1422—and two months later, on October 21, Charles VI followed him. The succession was left to two rival claimants, the Dauphin Charles and Henry and Catherine's nine-month-old son, the infant Henry VI. In accordance with the provisions of the Treaty of Troyes, the Crown of France rightfully belonged to the infant King. To secure Henry VI's claim, his uncle, the Duke of Bedford, assumed the title of Regent of France, subdued Normandy and the Ile-de-France and established the court at Paris. Disowned by his mother, the Dauphin could lay claim to no more than the southern half of France, and he became known by the derisive title of King of Bourges.

In 1428 Bedford judged that his hegemony north of the Loire was sufficiently well-established and he undertook a major offensive against the Loire-side city of Orleans. Bedford's target was a city of primary strategic importance, for it controlled the roads to the south. Its capture would enable the Regent to link up northern France with the English fiefdom of Guienne (Aquitaine) in the southwest of France.

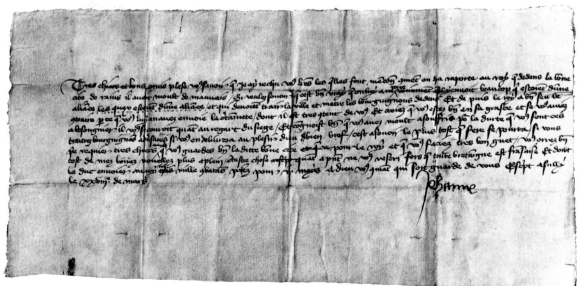

A letter from Joan to the people of Reims, March 12, 1430.

Joan of Arc at the court of Charles VII.

Directly controlled by English
Burgundian territory
Anglo-Burgundian territory
Lands loyal to Anglo-Burgundian alliance
Controlled by French monarchy
Fiefs of France
new French territory

France 1420

Rouen
Paris Reims
BRITTANY
ANJOU BERRY
BURGUNDY

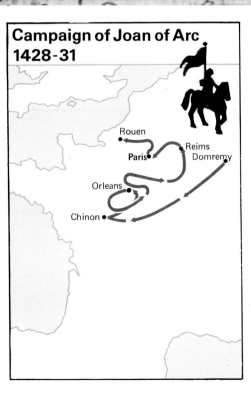

Campaign of Joan of Arc 1428-31

Rouen
Paris Reims
Domremy
Orleans
Chinon

France 1453

Rouen Reims
Paris
BRITTANY
ANJOU
BURGUNDY

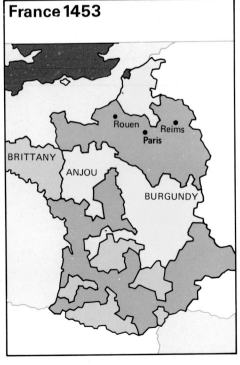

"You shall be crowned King at Reims"

John, Duke of Bedford, leader of the English army in France, from the *Bedford Hours*.

Philip the Good, Duke of Burgundy, England's major French ally.

Below The castle of Chinon, commanding the confluence of the Loire and the Indre, captured from the English by Joan.

The siege of Orleans, therefore, was mounted with deliberation. Bedford's commanders, employing a strategy that had proven effective ten years before at Rouen, encircled the town with a temporary barricade to prevent egress. The population, completely surrounded by allied troops and undermined by famine, could expect no help from the Dauphin, who was without resources, without initiative and moreover without much confidence in his own cause. It was at this point that the peasant girl from Lorraine first sought an audience with the Dauphin.

After keeping Joan waiting for two days, the King finally consented to receive her. By all accounts, the peasant maid's first words to her sovereign renewed the Dauphin's flagging hopes: "Fair Dauphin, I am called Joan the Maid. The King of Heaven sends you word by me. You shall be crowned and consecrated King in the city of Reims, and are to be the viceroy of the King of Heaven, who is King in France." Furnished with arms and a small company of men—all that the Dauphin's utmost efforts could raise—Joan set out for Orleans, and on April 29, 1429, she succeeded in getting a relief convoy into the beleaguered city. She entered to the tumultuous acclaim of the townspeople, who "felt as if the siege were already raised," according to an eyewitness.

Astonishing as Joan's feat was, it was less dramatic than the events that followed. To the astonishment of the Dauphin's supporters and the stupefaction of

The coronation of Charles VII at Reims.

Below Joan leads the French attack on Paris.

Bottom The capture of Joan of Arc by Burgundian troops at Compiègne.

the allies, the siege of Orleans was raised after only three engagements. On Wednesday, May 4, the English fortifications at Saint-Loup were taken and the Loire-side gate to the city was liberated. On May 6, a skirmish took place on the opposite bank of the Loire—and when it was over, the English had lost the fortifications of Les Augustins. A day later the fortifications of Tourelles—which guarded the approach to the city's main bridge—were also taken. The left bank of the Loire was now open; Orleans had been relieved.

Realizing that his cause was lost, the English commander raised the siege a day later, on May 8, 1429. Joan forbade her men to pursue the enemy or to engage in further combat, for May 8 was a Sunday—a day of truce. The brief campaign was over; in less than eight days, a city invested for more than six months had been liberated.

The Dauphin and his advisers were uncertain as to the best way in which to utilize their unanticipated victory. Their quandary produced a temporary lull in the campaign, and Joan was forced to intervene. She urged Charles to advance upon Reims, where, the maid insisted, he would receive the consecration of his kingship.

From a strategic point of view, the march to Reims—deep within the Anglo-Burgundian zone—was extraordinarily daring, and it was undertaken in circumstances of the utmost improbability. The first English fortifications on the Dauphin's invasion route had to be taken by storm, but Joan's troops were equal to the task: Jargeau fell on June 10, Meung on June 15, and Beaugency two days later. The first decisive encounter of the campaign took place on Saturday, June 18, when the French King's army clashed with a force led by Bedford's commanders Talbot and Falstaff. The unpremeditated engagement was a stunning victory for the Dauphin: the English lost two thousand men and Talbot was captured, while French losses were negligible. (Some

"We have burned a Saint"

Witches on their broomsticks; Joan was accused of witchcraft as well as heresy.

contemporary chroniclers speak of two French deaths, others of three.) Continuing northward virtually without opposition, Charles reached Reims and was crowned there on Sunday, July 17.

Such a reversal of circumstances was all but unparalleled in the annals of history and it is not surprising that the highly superstitious English at once suspected that their opponents had been aided by supernatural forces. In a letter written at the end of July, 1429, Bedford himself called Joan "a hound of the Evil One," and the University of Paris was not slow to express a similar view. A year later Joan was captured by a Burgundian force at Compiègne, and while the spineless Dauphin stood by, the Maid of Orleans was ransomed by the English, imprisoned and subjected to a farcical ecclesiastical trial at Rouen. In the course of that inquest, the simple dignity of Joan's replies disconcerted the most able of her interrogators, and their charge of sorcery could not be made to stick. In the end, it was on the very minor charge of wearing men's clothing that the chief prosecutor, Pierre Cauchon, succeeded in having Joan condemned. Cauchon, a member of the University of Paris who had been made a bishop for his active part in drafting the Treaty of Troyes, ordered the Maid's death.

Before she was led to the stake on May 30, 1431, Joan repudiated the confession that had been tormented out of her, and as the flames leaped around her an observer exclaimed, "We have burned a saint!" Less than two years after the coronation ceremony at Reims, the hostility of the English, the opposition of the universities and, above all, the defection of her associates had conspired to martyr the Maid of Lorraine. The Dauphin, now Charles VII, hastened to dissociate himself from the peasant girl to whom he owed his crown, and truth about the trial and condemnation of Joan of Arc was not established until almost twenty years later.

On November 10, 1449, eighteen years and six months after Joan's death, French troops entered Rouen, freeing the city after thirty years of English occupation. During those years the resumption of Anglo-French hostilities had turned to Charles' advantage: in 1430 the Duke of Burgundy had been forced to surrender Compiègne, and in 1435 he had been obliged to sign a separate peace treaty with his cousin Charles. A year later Arthur de Richement, the Constable of France, entered the liberated city of Paris, and within a decade tentative overtures of peace were being made. That new atmosphere of amicability was officially acknowledged through the marriage in 1444 of Henry VI and Margaret of Anjou, a close relation of King Charles. Years of foreign domination had made the French citizenry aware of their own aspirations, however, and in 1449 a popular insurrection drove the English governor from Rouen and forced the King of France to renew military activity in the region. It is noteworthy that one of the first things that Charles did after he recovered Rouen was to order an inquiry into the matter of Joan of Arc.

Lawyers and judges at Joan's trial.

The results of that inquiry, which was based upon the transcript of the trial and the testimony of surviving witnesses, seemed to justify another, lengthier investigation, and a second inquiry—this time a full ecclesiastical one—took place in 1452. Not until three years later, after a trial authorized by Pope Calixtus III, was Joan finally cleared of the charge of heresy. On July 7, 1456, the martyred Maid was solemnly rehabilitated.

In the course of their long conflict, France and England established their reciprocal independence and achieved internal unification. By 1456, England was ready to assert her insular destiny and France was ready to undertake the development of a centralized monarchy. Elsewhere in Europe, other nations began to assert their autonomy. Each sought to establish for itself a precarious national equilibrium, one that could survive the personal ambitions of individual princes and the economic rivalries of their subjects.

At a time of such confusion and uncertainty, the career of Joan of Arc had a remarkably decisive impact upon the course of European history. In much the same spirit as the townspeople of Orleans—who once welcomed her as a heroine and a saint—historians and the general public alike acknowledge Joan of Arc's exceptional contribution to world history.   REGINE PERNOUD

The burning of Joan at Rouen.

Left Pope Calixtus II who rehabilitated Joan, thirty years after her death.

Cosimo de' Medici finances armies and

The English assumed that the "spell" cast by the sorceress of Orleans had been lifted when she was executed, and they anticipated that their conquest of France would swiftly follow. As an essential preliminary to recovering England's Continental holdings—and to discredit the illicit coronation of Charles VII at Reims—Cardinal Beaufort crowned the child Henry VI in Paris in December, 1431. Within a year the strained alliance between England and Philip, Duke of Burgundy, began to founder.

At the same time, intrigues initiated by Humphrey, Duke of Gloucester, were undermining Bedford's authority at home and he was forced to return to England. France rallied in his absence: English influence in northern France was soon confined to Normandy and Paris. Despite Bedford's courageous leadership, the second campaign was a disaster and Philip, deciding to abandon the English alliance, summoned a general peace congress at Arras. Philip then agreed to recognize Charles VII as King of France in return for the cession of several Somme towns held by Charles' supporters. Charles in turn acknowledged Philip's sovereignty. The terms of the *entente* humiliated Charles, who soon broke the spirit of the agreement. Philip had expected to become Charles' principal councilor and greatest feudatory, but the French King remained deeply suspicious of him.

The Congress of Arras offered England the whole of Normandy and extensions to the Duchy of Gascony if she would agree to sign a treaty recognizing Charles VII as King of an attenuated France. Bedford, ever hopeful that the fortunes of war would shift in his favor, refused the Congress' terms. When Bedford died a year later, English authority in France crumbled, and Charles entered Paris. Almost at once he had to face a rebellion led by the great nobles—Brittany, Alençon and Bourbon—who supported the Dauphin (the future Louis XI). The English took advantage of French dissension to reconquer Harfleur, but the Duke of York, the English regent in Normandy, failed to exploit his success, and French troops reconquered most of Gascony. By 1444 both sides were too exhausted to pursue the fighting, and a truce was signed at Tours. The truce led to the marriage of Henry VI and Margaret, daughter of the Duke of Anjou.

France captures Bordeaux

Five years later England was on the verge of civil war, while France had broken the brief truce and reclaimed the whole of Normandy. Fighting resumed, and Charles VII's military reforms soon began to tell: the French soldiers were much better disciplined and more effectively led than their opponents —and they were determined to rid their homeland of foreign troops. Bordeaux fell in June, 1451, but the town's inhabitants—who had been privileged subjects of the King of England for decades—had little love for French taxes and military obligations, and the following year they invited the English army to take over the town. Margaret of

The chapel of King's College, Cambridge, founded by King Henry VI.

Anjou then instructed John Talbot, Earl of Shrewsbury, to bring the whole province under English rule. A massive French army counterattacked in the spring of 1453, and in July of that year Castillon was besieged. Chanting their war cry "Talbot, Talbot, St. George," the British garrison marched out to attack the French camp, but in a day of heavy hand-to-hand fighting they were overwhelmed. Talbot himself was slain and his men fled.

Charles VII was able to enter Bordeaux in triumph on October 19, 1453—an event that marked the effective end of the Hundred Years' War. It had taken a century of almost constant warfare to convince England's kings that it was

not feasible for them to administer dominions in France. The English were, however, permitted to retain only Calais and a few neighboring towns. Charles VII, "le Bien Servi," had indeed fulfilled the prophecies of Joan of Arc, the heretical peasant girl from Domremy.

Henry VI of England

Henry VI was an unhappy child who grew up amid the incessant rivalry between Humphrey, Duke of Gloucester, leader of the war party, and Cardinal Beaufort and his brothers (the legitimized descendants of Gaunt), who were anxious for peace. He had no talent for government and longed to withdraw from the world. (His piety found expression in his foundations at Eton and King's College, Cambridge.) Gloucester's wife, in the full knowledge that her husband was next in the line of succession, attempted to practice witchcraft on the King in 1441.

The unpopularity of the match that Cardinal Beaufort had arranged between Henry VI and the high-spirited Margaret of Anjou, coupled with the reverses in France, reflected on Beaufort and weakened the prestige of the Crown. With the deaths of both the Cardinal and his old rival, Duke Humphrey (who spent his last days in prison as a suspected traitor), power passed to the Duke of Suffolk. Parliament promptly laid the disasters in France at his door and impeached him for maladministration and corruption. The weakling King turned on his favorite minister:

Suffolk was banished in 1450 and was assassinated at Calais.

Violence continued to dominate domestic politics in England. In 1450, in what was known as Cade's Rebellion, 30,000 men from Kent and Sussex marched on London to demand the head of Lord Chancellor Say and the restoration of Richard of York to the Council. Government had effectively broken down throughout the realm.

Philip the Good of Burgundy

Under Philip the Good (1419–67), Burgundy was consolidated as a powerful "middle kingdom," between France and Germany. With Flanders and Artois—which Philip inherited—as a nucleus, the Prince forced one of his cousins to surrender her lands in Holland, Zeeland, Hainault and Friesland. He annexed Brabant upon the death of another cousin. Philip achieved his design of centralizing the government of this collection of provinces by compelling the vigorous municipalities in each region to submit to his rule. For years Ghent opposed him, but he crushed its independence in 1453. Though the Treaty of Arras had not brought him the national influence that he had anticipated, Philip remained a ruler to be reckoned with. His court set new standards in ceremony and etiquette—many of which were adapted by future kings of France and England. He established the Order of the Golden Fleece in honor of a mistress whose tresses "had been the object of many pleasantries."

The library at Oxford founded by Duke Humphrey.

Flemish Mysticism

The mid-fifteenth century was a period of intense interest in Flemish mysticism. It marked the second generation of the "New Devotion" movement, which stemmed from the work of Gerard Groot (d. 1384), a Carthusian monk who founded the houses of "the Brethren of the Common Life." The rule of the Brethren and their mystical theology provoked criticism — the Dominicans maintained that certain of their practices were heretical — but the Council of Constance approved their way of life. Thomas à Kempis (c. 1380–1471), trained to follow the ideals of Gerard Groot, was sent to the new Augustinian Convent of Mount St. Agnes at his native Kempen. To support the convent, he spent his days copying missals and devotional works. He wrote many edifying tracts and sermons, culminating in his *Imitation of Christ*, which reveals in the simplest language the life of the spirit. In the next several centuries, his treatise would be read and re-read more frequently, perhaps, than any other volume except the Bible.

The Flemish School

At different times both Hubert van Eyck and his brother Jan worked at the Burgundian court, developing a uniquely Flemish school of painting that was rich in detail and color. Much of their work reflected the splendor of Philip the Bold's court, yet their religious paintings demonstrated a depth of feeling that forms a counterpart to the writings of Thomas à Kempis. The van Eycks' finest achievement, on which each in turn lavished his genius, was the large and complex polyptych of the *Adoration of the Lamb* in the Church of St. Bavon in Ghent. Jan, the younger brother, developed a novel technique of painting in oils with varnish that helped to preserve his brilliant colors for posterity.

Cosimo de' Medici and Florence

The fortunes of the Medici Bank had long been linked with papal finances, and Giovanni de' Medici (d. 1429) reaped enormous profits from the Council of Constance. Four years after Giovanni's death, his son Cosimo urged the powerful Albizzi family of Florence to wage

Prince Henry the Navigator, who tried to reach Japan by sailing eastward.

war against Lucca. When the Florentines came off badly in the campaign, Cosimo joined the populace in decrying the war — and was exiled for his duplicity. The Albizzi soon found that they had killed the goose that laid the golden egg, however, for the Medici Bank alone could provide the funds that were necessary to finance their government. In September, 1434, the newly elected signory of Florence ordered Cosimo's recall.

Cosimo de' Medici succeeded in banishing all possible rivals to his authority. Although he never took the title of prince, Florence was his city and until his death in 1464 he ruled it through a series of docile administrators. Cosimo, who ruthlessly suppressed conspiracies in 1444 and again in 1457–58, took considerable care to appear as the friend of the peasant and the artisan. He used his considerable wealth as a parton of art and letters, encouraged Marsilio Ficino and other philosophers and supervised a great collection of manuscripts; his library was the first private library ever opened to the public. He built the Church of St. Lorenzo, enlarged St. Mark's, and supported Donatello and Ghiberti.

Artists and scholars living in Italy during the middle of the fifteenth century enjoyed the richest patronage in history. The Medici in Florence and the Sforzas in Milan vied with each other and with successive popes for the services of Italy's greatest artists. Architects and artists were commissioned to beautify palaces and churches, and poets were paid to sing their praises.

Naples and Sicily united

As successor to the amorous Joanna II, the last of the Angevins in Italy,

Alfonso the Magnanimous, King of Aragon, acquired Naples in 1435 — thus reuniting the crowns of Naples and Sicily. He made Naples the hub of his Aragonese empire in the Mediterranean and turned his court into a remarkable center of art and humanism.

Prince Henry the Navigator

Prince Henry the Navigator founded a new school of seamanship at his residence in the Portuguese capital of Algarve. His aim was to establish a sea route to the East that outflanked the Moslem world. To achieve that aim, Henry harnessed the crusading zeal of the medieval world to the enterprise of discovery. Each year his expeditions penetrated farther down the west coast of Africa. By the time of Prince Henry's death in 1460, Portuguese navigators had explored the Senegal and Gambia rivers and the Cape Verde Islands — and had brought gold and slaves home to Lisbon. The European world had entered a new era of discoveries.

Council of Basel

A reformist party at the Council of Basel succeeded in asserting that it was heresy for a pope to contradict the decrees issued by a general council. Pope Eugenius IV (1431–47) took immediate exception to the Council's decree, and divisions hardened concerning negotiations for reunion with the Greek Church. In 1434 a revolutionary movement in Rome drove Eugenius to Florence, where he remained for nine years under Cosimo de' Medici's protection. The despotic Cardinal Vitelloschi ruled as Eugenius' viceroy for several years, only to be murdered by another cardinal. In an effort to break up the anti-papal Council of Basel, Eugenius convened a council at Florence in 1438, but the prelates at Basel refused to adjourn until their mission had been accomplished.

The stock of the papacy had rarely been lower than it was at the mid-point of the fifteenth century. Lorenzo Valla had recently proved that the Donation of Constantine, the document on which the papacy's claim to lands around Rome was based, was a forgery. In France a national synod had endorsed the Pragmatic Sanction of Bourges, a document embodying many of the

anti-papal reforms decreed at the Council of Basel. In addition, the Sanction limited the revenues that the papacy could collect in France. A year later, Germany followed suit: the Diet of Mainz drew up a similar Pragmatic Sanction that abolished payment of annates and papal provisions to benefices in the Empire. The decline in respect for the papacy was eventually reversed by the skillful diplomacy of Aeneas Sylvius Piccolomini (the future Pius II). The Concordat of Vienna negotiated by Piccolomini and signed in 1448 by the new Emperor Frederick III, won back Germany for the Pope.

The Orthodox Church

John VIII, Emperor at Constantinople, traveled to Italy in 1439 to

Frederick III giving the future Pius II the poet's crown.

discuss the basis for a reunion of the Eastern and Western Churches. Before departing he accepted the Pope's conditions for ending the schism between Byzantium and Rome that had persisted since 1054. John and his successor found it impossible to enforce the union in the face of popular resistance, however, and Orthodox bishops in lands conquered by the Turks continued to regard the Sultan with greater respect than the Roman Pope.

Nicholas V (1447–55), perhaps the greatest pope of the fifteenth century, was a Tuscan scholar who planned to make Rome the imperial capital of art and literature and wanted to harness the Renaissance to the services of the Church. Coincidentally, Nicholas' chief antagonist, the Sultan Mahomet II (1451–81), was also a patron of learning and the arts.

Le siege du grant turc auec ij. de ses pncipaulx coseilles
Le siege du capiteine gnal de la turquie

The Fall of Constantinople 1453

*The Eastern Roman Empire had endured for eleven centuries, but now it was reduced to little
more than the city of Constantinople itself. Another Constantine—the last to sit on the Byzantine
throne—ruled the decaying city and nervously watched the Ottoman Turks inexorably
advancing from the east. Eastern and Western Christendom were split over doctrinal disputes—
and there would be no help coming from Europe. Overtures to the Turkish Sultan were
dramatically rebuffed; Constantine's ambassadors of peace were beheaded as they arrived.
On Easter Monday, 1453, the Sultan's advance guard was sighted and the gates to the city
were closed. The Greeks heroically resisted the Turkish siege, but it could have only one
outcome. As the Turkish victors streamed into the fallen city, they were witnessing the end of one
long and brilliant chapter in man's history—and the beginning of another.*

The traveler from the West, seeing Contantinople for the first time during the early decades of the fifteenth century, would have been saddened—even possibly horrified—by what lay before him. Brought up on tales of this golden metropolis—second only to Rome itself in splendor, and seat of an Empire that had lasted more than a thousand years and could boast the longest chain of unbroken monarchy in the history of Christendom—the traveler would have found instead a crumbling ruin of a city, half-deserted and shot through with despair. "Its inhabitants are few," wrote Pedro Tafur, a young Spaniard who arrived in 1437. "They are not well-clad, but miserable and poor, showing the hardship of their lot . . . The Emperor's palace must have been very magnificent, but now is in such a state that both it and the city reveal the evils which the people have suffered and still endure . . . Inside, the building is badly maintained, except for those parts where the Emperor, the Empress and their attendants live, and even these are cramped for space. The Emperor's state is as splendid as ever, for nothing is omitted from the ancient ceremonies; but, properly regarded, he is like a Bishop without a See."

Tafur's description was accurate; the once-glorious Empire of the East, which had formerly stretched from Italy to the borders of Mesopotamia, now extended little farther than the walls of Constantinople itself. For centuries the Empire had stood as a bulwark against the tide of Islam, allowing Christianity time to put down deep roots in Eastern Europe—and even after the loss of the Anatolian heartland to the Seljuk Turks in the eleventh century, the Empire had remained rich, powerful and—ostensibly—prosperous. The quays of Constantinople were crowded with the shipping of three continents, and merchants from every land and clime thronged its bazaars. City wharves and warehouses overflowed with silks and spices, ivory and gold, while beneath the mosiac-encrusted cupolas of its thousand churches lay some of the holiest relics of Christianity.

Constantinople's prosperity aroused increasing envy and cupidity among Western Crusaders throughout the twelfth century, and it was perhaps inevitable that they should make their own bid for control of the Greek metropolis. The seizure of the city, on Good Friday, 1204, by that exercise in unmitigated piracy still ludicrously known as the Fourth Crusade, stripped Constantinople of its treasures and condemned it to fifty-five years of misrule by Frankish thugs occupying the throne of the Byzantine emperors. The city was left weak, desperately impoverished and well-nigh naked to its enemies.

Not long after Michael VIII Palaeologus rode back into his shattered capital in 1259, a new dynasty sprang up in the Turkish-held lands across the Bosphorus: the house of Osman—or, as we now prefer to call them, the Ottomans.

Under Osman and his successors, Turkish conquests came swiftly. By 1340 virtually all of Asia Minor was in their hands; in the next twenty-five years they crossed the Dardanelles, set up their capital at Adrianople (modern Edirne) and made themselves masters of western Thrace. Their victory at Kosovo in southern Yugoslavia in 1389 won them Serbia and the Balkans. By that time the Byzantine Emperor, surrounded by enemies, plagued by palace revolutions, his morale further shaken by the Black Death, had been forced to acknowledge the Turkish Sultan as his overlord. Only one hope now remained: a grand Christian alliance to deliver the Empire and save Europe—while there was still time—from the Moslem invader.

The possibility of such an alliance was dim. The Eastern and Western Churches had long been in schism, and it seemed unlikely that the Pope would declare a Crusade for the rescue of schismatics who did not even recognize his primacy. The Catholic princes of the West, blind as ever to political realities, tended to look on the Turkish conquests as divine retribution for those who had rejected the Christian

A janissary by Giovanni
Bellini : the janissaries were
a corps of highly trained
troops from Christian families
who formed an elite corps in
the Sultan's army.

Opposite The siege of
Constantinople by the Turks,
showing Turkish boats being
dragged across land behind
the suburb of Pera : from the
*Voyage d'outremer de
Bertandon de la Bronuiere.*

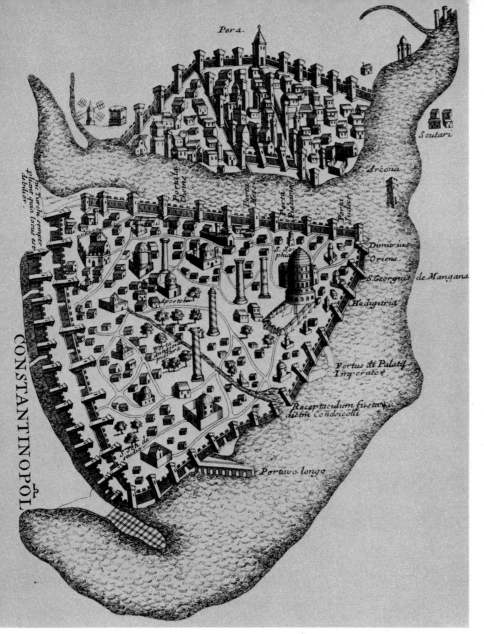

The city of Constantinople.

II had given proof of a character to be respected and feared. An intellectual who spoke six languages —including excellent Latin and Greek—he was by nature introverted and morose, almost pathologically secretive and possessed of a streak of cruelty that terrified his subordinates. From childhood Mehmet had hated all Christians, and as he grew older this hatred had been transformed into a single, burning idea: to capture Constantinople. Now that he was Emperor, he intended to lose no time in realizing that ambition.

When the Greek ambassadors came to congratulate him on his accession, however, the young Sultan affirmed his peaceable intentions and blandly promised to respect Byzantine territory. But within a matter of months he had summoned architects and masons from all over his dominions, and on April 15, 1452, the first stones were laid in the construction of a great castle on the European side of the Bosphorus, a few miles north of Constantinople, where the straits are at their narrowest. Neighboring churches and monasteries were razed to provide building materials, and just four and a half months later, on the last day of August, the fortress—now known as Rumeli Hisar—was completed. Constantine sent ambassadors to ask Mehmet his intentions, although he must have known them only too well. Mehmet's answer was clear: as each ambassador arrived, he was immediately beheaded.

And still Europe would not understand. The Pope was genuinely concerned, but could stir no enthusiasm for a relief expedition; the Western Empire was a broken reed. In November a Venetian ship that refused to stop when hailed from Rumeli Hisar was sunk by Turkish cannon, its crew was decapitated and its captain publicly impaled—but the Most Serene Republic, which was doing good business in Ottoman ports and had no wish to become involved in an expensive war, chose to ignore the incident. Genoa took a similar line. The whole district of Pera to the east of the Golden Horn was a Genoese colony whose best hope of preservation seemed to lie in coming to an agreement with the Turks rather than in taking up arms against them. France and England were still exhausted after the Hundred Years' War, and England was further handicapped by a King, Henry VI, whose apparent saintliness was insufficient to conceal his undoubted imbecility. From all the other monarchies of Europe the response was equally unpromising. By March of 1453, when the immense Ottoman army—well over a hundred thousand strong—began to move from Adrianople toward the Bosphorus, it was clear that the city's survival was going to depend on its inhabitants alone.

The Emperor now ordered a hasty census of all able-bodied men—including monks—who were capable of bearing arms. The results were even worse than he had feared: after nine successive visitations of the Black Death in less than a century, Constantinople had lost some 40 per cent of its already dwindling population. There were, however, more than a thousand foreign residents of the city, including almost the entire Venetian community, who pledged

Truth. Was Constantinople worth a Mass? Its Emperor thought so; and in 1439, at Florence, the emissaries of John VIII Palaeologus accepted papal authority. In theory the Churches were now reunited, but in practice the schism survived. "Better the Sultan's turban than the Cardinal's hat," declared the Byzantine minister Lucas Notaras—and the majority of his compatriots agreed with him. When John died in 1448, he left his brother Constantine an embittered and divided city.

We know very little about this last and most tragic of all the Byzantine emperors. At the time of his accession he was forty-four. Although no reliable portraits have come down to us, he seems to have been tall and rather swarthy—a little unimaginative, perhaps, but straightforward and absolutely honest, an able administrator and, above all, a brave soldier. It was just as well. Before Constantine had been three years on the throne, the Turkish Sultan, Murad II, died of apoplexy at Adrianople. By the standards of his time, Murad had been a peaceable ruler, prepared to live on friendly terms with his Christian subjects. His successor was a young man of a very different stamp.

Though still only twenty-one, already Mehmet

A mighty three-fold rampart

their support—and these had recently been joined by a Genoese contingent led by a famous soldier of fortune, Giovanni Giustiniani Longo. Disgusted by the apathy of his government, Giustiniani raised a private army of seven hundred on his own. Constantine gave them an enthusiastic welcome, but even with foreign reinforcements he had less than seven thousand men to defend fourteen miles of walls.

Those walls were for the most part in excellent repair. The ramparts that ran along the Golden Horn needed little defending, since the harbor could be closed by stretching a chain across its mouth from Acropolis Point, the southern tip of the Horn, to the shores of Pera on the north. The Marmara walls, south of the city, rose straight out of the sea and were protected by treacherous shoals—making them equally inaccessible. The weight of the Turkish attack therefore was expected to come from the landward side. Here a great three-fold rampart ran for some four miles in an unbroken line across the neck of the peninsula on which the city stood, joining the imperial palace at Blachernae in the north with the Marmara walls at Studion in the south. It was, and still is, a magnificent fortification—and it had never been breached since its construction by the Emperor Theodosius, one thousand and six years before.

On Easter Monday, 1453, the advance guard of Mehmet's army was sighted by the Byzantine lookouts. At once the Emperor ordered all the gates to the city closed, the bridges across the moats destroyed and the boom laid across the Golden Horn. Within three days, the Turkish army was drawn up along the whole length of the land walls. At the center was the red and gold tent of the Sultan himself, surrounded by his picked corps of Janissaries. The defenders saw for the first time what they would have to face—and on the following day they felt it. Mehmet

prided himself on his cannon—a comparatively new weapon, which he planned to use on an unprecedented scale. Three had already been employed to considerable effect from Rumeli Hisar, but the Sultan had brought several others from Adrianople. These had been specially made for him by a renegade Hungarian engineer, and included one twenty-seven-foot-long monster, capable of hurling cannonballs weighing half a ton for a mile or more. But the walls held against the bombardment.

The walls of Constantinople.

Rumeli Hisar, which controls the Bosphorus. Built by Mehmet in 1452, this was the first sign that he intended to capture the city.

When Christ deserted Constantinople

At sea, too, the long battle had begun. The Ottoman navy had sailed up through the Dardanelles and the Sea of Marmara, and now lay at the entrance to the Bosphorus, about a mile away from the mouth of the Horn. Mehmet's navy was not doing well. Repeated efforts to force the boom had been beaten back by an effective combination of arrows and "Greek fire," an incendiary invented by the Byzantines that burned on the surface of the water. And on April 20, three Genoese galleys and an imperial transport had actually managed to smash their way through the enemy and, under cover of darkness, had slipped into the harbor.

This reverse infuriated Mehmet. He immediately ordered the speeding-up of a plan he had formulated during the first days of the siege: the construction of a huge causeway up the valley that led from the Bosphorus shore, over the hill of Pera, behind the Genoese colony and down again to the waters of the Horn. On Saturday, April 22, Constantinople witnessed what was possibly the most extraordinary scene in all its history, as countless teams of oxen dragged some seventy ships on wheeled cradles over

Constantine VIII Palaeologus the penultimate Byzantine Emperor: from the *Journey of the Magi* by Benozzo Gozzoli.

a two-hundred foot ridge and then slowly lowered them down the other side into the harbor. The Greeks' amazement must have been darkened by despair—they could no longer rely on a safe anchorage for their fleet. Yet, more important, they now had another ten miles of wall to defend. The Genoese colony of Pera, whose benevolent neutrality had hitherto been an invaluable source of information on Turkish movements, was surrounded.

Another month went by, during which food supplies began to run short. The defenders struggled valiantly on, but the walls were beginning to crumble under the incessant pounding of the cannon, and Constantine was finding it increasingly difficult to maintain his subjects' morale. Then, on May 23, came a last, shattering blow to Christian hopes. During the preceding winters, the Venetians in the city had sent an urgent appeal to their republic, begging Venice to intervene on Constantine's behalf. At last in early May, they had secretly dispatched their fastest brigantine to look for the relief expedition. The ship had searched the Aegean, but found no trace of an Italian fleet. The crew, knowing that their return to Constantinople meant almost certain death, had nevertheless insisted on doing so. The Emperor wept as he thanked them. Only Christ, he murmured, could save the city now.

To many, however, it seemed that Christ too had deserted Constantinople. On May 24 the moon went into eclipse, and while the city's holiest icon was being carried in procession through the streets it suddenly slipped from its platform. Hardly had it been replaced when a hailstorm burst over the capital—a storm of such fury that the whole procession had to be abandoned. And the next day men awoke to find Constantinople shrouded in a dense fog—a phenomenon unheard of at the end of May.

Five months earlier, a service of reunion with Rome had been held in Hagia Sophia, and since that time the church had been avoided by the Orthodox faithful. But now, in this final hour of trial, doctrinal differences were forgotten. On the evening of May 28, when it was plain that Mehmet was preparing for his final assault on the land walls, the Emperor joined his people in the great church where, with Orthodox and Roman priests officiating side by side, the Christian liturgy was celebrated for the last time in Constantinople.

At half-past one in the morning the Sultan gave his order to attack. The sudden noise, bursting out of the stillness, was immediately answered by all the bells of the city, rallying every able-bodied defender to the walls. Though each man must have known that the cause was lost, all still fought magnificently; two successive Turkish charges, the first by the irregular *bashi-bazouks*, the next by a wave of fanatical Anatolians, were driven back—and a third, by Mehmet's own regiment of Janissaries, fought hand-to-hand for an hour or more without making any appreciable headway. Suddenly Giustiniani fell, mortally wounded. Seeing their leader carried from the walls, the Genoese soldiers panicked and fled, leaving the Greeks to face the enemy alone.

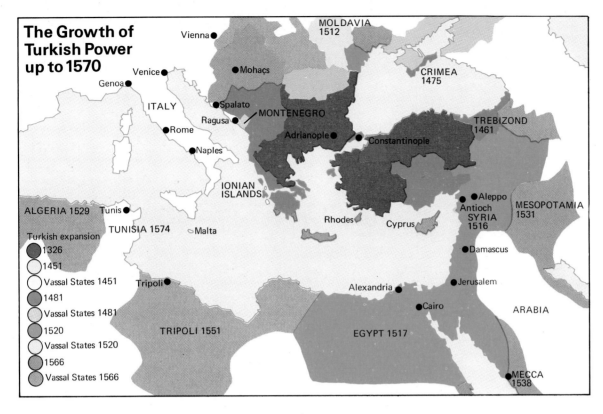

The Growth of Turkish Power up to 1570

MOLDAVIA 1512

Vienna

Venice

Genoa

Mohács

Spalato

ITALY

Ragusa

MONTENEGRO

Rome

Adrianople

Constantinople

Naples

CRIMEA 1475

TREBIZOND 1461

IONIAN ISLANDS

ALGERIA 1529

Tunis

TUNISIA 1574

Malta

Rhodes

Cyprus

Aleppo

Antioch

SYRIA 1516

MESOPOTAMIA 1531

Turkish expansion
- 1326
- 1451
- Vassal States 1451
- 1481
- Vassal States 1481
- 1520
- Vassal States 1520
- 1566
- Vassal States 1566

Tripoli

Damascus

Alexandria

Jerusalem

Cairo

ARABIA

TRIPOLI 1551

EGYPT 1517

MECCA 1538

Almost simultaneously came another, even greater catastrophe. At the northern end of the walls, where they joined the imperial palace, was a tiny postern gate, through which the defenders had been making occasional sorties to harry the Ottoman flank. By some mischance the gate had been left unbarred; the Turks fell upon it and burst through.

The Byzantine Empire was finished. The Emperor, seeing that all hope was gone, seized his sword and ran to where the fighting was thickest. He was never seen alive again. Much later, his body was identified among the piles of corpses. It had no head, but on its feet were purple buskins, embroidered with the imperial eagles of Byzantium.

As the victorious Turks streamed across the walls and through the streets, the massacre and carnage became appalling. Moslem tradition permitted three days of rapine and looting after the storming of a city, but the Sultan restricted his soldiers to one. He himself seems to have been strangely calm and subdued in the hours of his supreme triumph. Not till late afternoon did he enter Constantinople. He rode slowly to Hagia Sophia where, before the high altar, he touched his turban to the ground in thanksgiving.

Thus the Byzantine Empire gave place to the Ottoman. The news of its fall was received with horror among the peoples of the West, who suddenly felt profoundly guilty—as well they might. For it was Western Europe, with its Fourth Crusade, that had inflicted the first mortal wound upon the Eastern Empire; the Turks had merely administered the *coup de grâce*. Even at the end, the Christian princes, by firm and concerted action, might have delayed the inevitable; but they did not choose to do so. Instead, they argued and prevaricated—and while Europe dithered, Byzantium died. The Empire's life had been long, brilliant and glorious.

Taken as an isolated event, Constantinople's fall was not a matter of as much direct political significance to Europe in general as was at one time believed. Many of the great developments for which the city has been wholly or partly credited—events that mark the end of the Middle Ages—were already under way. Explorers and navigators had long since begun seeking out and mapping new trade routes to the Indies. In Italy the Renaissance had run half its course, and Byzantine scholars there had been revealing the mysteries of Greek culture for fifty years and more. Nor can it be argued that Mehmet's victory opened up Europe to Turkish invasion, for the Turks had already gained a European foothold.

For the Greeks and Turks, however, the events of May 29, 1453, are still annually commemorated—by the former as their greatest tragedy, by the latter as their most shining triumph. And it is right and proper that they should, for on that day the histories of both peoples were radically changed. The Greeks entered upon nearly four centuries of subjugation, during which their Church provided the only focus for their national aspirations. The Turks, for their part, saw the defeat of their arch-enemy as the confirmation of their European Empire.

After five centuries, the rest of us can afford to take a dispassionate view. We can applaud the way the new capital soared, phoenix-like, from the ashes of the old, and we can accept the events here related as just another proof that the dominions of this world, even that of God's vice-regent on earth, cannot last forever. But we too owe a debt to Byzantium—which preserved and cherished the Greek spirit for a thousand years while Western Europe was groping its way through the Dark Ages, and which somehow combined that spirit with a new religious awareness, to form a technique of expressing spiritual values in visual terms that is without parallel in Christian art. When Constantinople fell, the world was diminished.

JOHN JULIUS NORWICH

Sultan Mehmet II, conqueror of Constantinople, by Giovanni Bellini.

"A horse, a horse, my kingdom for a horse,"

The fall of Constantinople enabled Mehmet the Conqueror to press his attack on Eastern Europe. Believing that he was a modern Alexander, the Sultan led his troops into Bosnia, Albania and Serbia, where John Hunyadi's heroic defense of Belgrade in 1456 finally checked the Turkish advance. (Hunyadi's troops had been aroused by a nationalist crusade preached by John, the friar of Capistrano.) The Peloponnesus fell to the invaders, ending the rule of the Palaeologi in Greece, and in 1461 the Turks conquered the Empire of Trebizond, the last independent Greek state still in existence.

Mehmet's troops then turned their attention to the Genoese and Venetian stations in the Aegean, and an alarmed Pope Pius II (1458–64) urged the rulers of Christendom to join him in the mightiest of all crusades. In the years before he took holy orders, Pius had charmed the courts of Europe with his brilliant verses and his witty, immoral plays. Emperor Frederick III had crowned him poet laureate of Germany. But now, "forsaking Venus and Bacchus," he preached the moral duty of fighting the Turks. Only Hungary and Venice heeded his words and, as an example to the rest, Pius himself took up the Cross. Curiously, neither his crusading zeal nor his sudden death moved the conscience of the West.

The Turkish fleet soon wrested Scutari and Euboea from the Venetians and by 1478 their raiders had reached the outskirts of Venice. The desperate Republic signed a peace treaty with Mehmet in 1479, surrendering most of their posts in Albania and undertaking to pay a yearly tribute for the privilege of trading in the Levant. Mahomet's forces attacked southern Italy, raided Styria and Carinthia, and besieged Rhodes, which was held by the Knights of St. John. It was only Mehmet's death in 1481 (and the ensuing dispute over his successor) that saved the Balkans and Italy. Renewed attacks were launched in 1512, which led to the conquest of Syria and Egypt under Selim I.

Greek Scholarship revived

The Greek scholars who fled to Italy and Central Europe as the Sultan's armies advanced into their homeland brought with them precious manuscripts hitherto buried in the libraries of Byzantium. During the next half-century or so,

the study of all aspects of classical Greek culture was revolutionized. The Humanist approach to art and letters—the fearless search for truth and beauty once limited to the civilization of Rome—gained a new dimension through the rediscovery of Greece. The Humanist outlook, which affected every aspect of life and questioned the very purpose of man's existence, was bound to lead to disputes with authority, especially the authority of the Church—the invention of printing made the results of that intellectual ferment known throughout the West.

Lorenzo the Magnificent

Under Cosimo de' Medici (d. 1464) the government of Florence passed

A bust of Lorenzo the Magnificent.

from an oligarchy to an autocracy. Lorenzo the Magnificent, who held the reins of power from 1478 to 1492, prided himself on being merely "a private citizen," although he made a princely marriage to Clarice Orsini. Lorenzo survived a 1478 plot in which his brother was assassinated, and skillfully used the occasion to increase both his position and his popularity. Greeted as the "savior of Florence" after concluding a favorable treaty with Naples, he effected a reform of the constitution and established the Council of Seventy, a body completely under his control. Lorenzo was respected throughout the peninsula for his masterful diplomacy—in his last years he effectively kept Italy at peace.

Lorenzo's regime appears liberal by comparison with the reigns of contemporary tyrants in Naples and Milan. The unscrupulous Ferdinand I, King of Naples (1453–94), struggled throughout his reign to preserve his doubtful title to the throne and to keep one step ahead of his barons' incessant intrigues. The history of the Sforza family of

Milan (1450–1500) is one of oppression, usurpation and assassination. Lodovico Sforza, who ousted his nephew from the duchy in 1479, remained insecure in spite of his ruthlessness, and his fears eventually involved all Italy in a war with the French. Curiously, despite such uncertain and oppressive political conditions, the Italian Renaissance flourished.

England after the Hundred Years' War

The defeat of the English army at Chatillon and the death of Commander Talbot in 1453 ended the fighting in the Hundred Years' War. Nothing but Calais remained of Eleanor of Aquitaine's inheritance. The Continental conflict was finally settled, but fighting soon resumed—this time in England itself. Richard, Duke of York and heir apparent to the weakling Henry VI, raised a private army, and in 1453, when Henry became temporarily insane, York was appointed protector. Henry recovered and Margaret produced an heir, but York was determined to fight for the throne.

Wars of the Roses

York's supporters defeated those of the Queen and Edmund Beaufort at St. Albans in 1455. The Wars of the Roses—a long series of short campaigns between Lancaster and York—had begun. Lack of "governance" and the utter breakdown of feudal society had made civil war inevitable, and the numerous soldiers of fortune who were returning from France (where they had been accustomed to the spoils of warfare as much as to the prowess of arms) took readily to the only profession they knew. Fundamentally, Richard of York stood for the restoration of law and order—and against the incapacity of the Crown.

Edward IV, by an unknown artist.

He received more support from the Commons than did his opponents, but most of the population remained indifferent to the strife.

York claimed the throne in 1460, but died soon thereafter at the Battle of Wakefield. His son Edward, Earl of March, then rallied the Yorkists to victory at Mortimer's Cross, marched south to join the Earl of Warwick (who was known as "the kingmaker"), and took the capital. At the age of nineteen, March became King Edward IV. He defended his title at Towton in Yorkshire, and Henry and Margaret fled to Scotland. The imbecile Henry was able to make a pathetic return to nominal kingship in October, 1470, when Warwick shifted his support to the Lancastrian camp, but his restoration was short-lived. On Easter Day, 1471, Edward IV won a decisive victory in the mist at Barnet—and with the subsequent defeat of Margaret's Welsh army at Tewkesbury and the brutal murder of Henry VI, Edward was at last secure on the throne.

For the next dozen years Edward IV proved himself a strong monarch, eschewing corruption and acting much as Sir John Fortescue had recommended in his tract, *The Governance of England*. But the legacy of treachery was not yet spent: Clarence, Edward's elder brother,

Henry VII, England's first Tudor king.

was executed in 1478 for plotting against the King; and when Edward died in 1483, his younger brother Richard dethroned Edward's son, Edward V (and probably ordered his—and his brother's—murder in the Tower). Richard III's days were numbered, however, and in 1485 Henry of Richmond—who represented the Beaufort-Lancastrian line through his mother, the widow of Owen Tudor—defeated the hunch-backed King on Bosworth Field.

cries King Richard

Elizabeth of York, wife of Henry VII.

Henry Tudor strengthened his doubtful claim to the throne by marrying Elizabeth of York, daughter of Edward IV, to form a union of the Red and White Roses that settled the disputed succession. The old feudal nobility had been decimated by years of internecine strife, and Henry VII was determined to maintain his supremacy.

France strengthened under Louis XI

In many ways, the first of the Tudors took as his model the French King Louis XI (1461–83). As a prince, Louis' taste for rebelliousness had led to his banishment to Dauphine, where he enjoyed the protection of the Duke of Burgundy. His vigorous administration of that principality proved invaluable training and earned Louis the nickname "The Spider" for his diplomatic cunning. There was no nonsense about him; he worshiped hard facts and spurned opinions. During his coronation banquet he amazed the courtiers by removing his uncomfortable crown, but they soon accustomed themselves to his ungainly figure, his coarse language and his penchant for ambling about the realm in shabby clothes and an old felt hat. Here was a Renaissance

Louis XI.

tyrant ruling by decree, who was very different from the princes of Italy. He frowned on the wearing of silk, considered gilding a wasteful luxury and lacked money for patronizing art—yet he felt that it was provident to keep the Church's good graces, and he showed himself to be a man of religion.

Louis' achievement lay in curbing the great feudatories of France, ending anarchy and freeing the country from intervention by England, Burgundy and Spain. He enlarged the frontiers of France, made it a unified kingdom (with the exception of Brittany and Lorraine) and brought it prosperity. Administration was overhauled and talented men of humble origin replaced the nobility in many governmental posts.

France conquers Burgundy

Charles the Bold (1467–77), son of Philip the Good of Burgundy, envisioned a kingdom that stretched from the North Sea to the Mediterranean, but Charles proved to be no match for Louis XI, who formed a coalition against him. By purchasing England's neutrality, Louis eliminated Charles' natural ally and negated the usefulness of the upstart's marriage to Margaret of York, Edward IV's sister. Charles curbed the city of Liège and successfully incorporated Gelderland, but he overreached himself in 1473 when he occupied Alsace-Lorraine and declared war on the Swiss cantons. In January, 1477, the Swiss pikemen vanquished the Burgundian cavalry at Nancy and Charles was slain. Louis immediately annexed the duchy of Burgundy proper and occupied Franche-Comte. Charles' Flemish possessions, fearing French annexation, compelled Charles' twenty-year-old daughter Mary to safeguard their local privileges under such humiliating terms that she gladly married Maximilian of Austria—and thereby inaugurated an era of Hapsburg domination of the Netherlands.

Hapsburg Empire

By the time that Frederick III, the second Hapsburg Emperor, was crowned by Nicholas V in Rome in 1452, he had already reigned for a dozen ineffectual years—and he was to survive for another forty-one. Upon his return from Italy,

the feud between Frederick and his brother Albert was renewed and the Emperor was eventually driven from Vienna. The imperial electors would have gladly deposed him—except that they were unable to agree upon a successor.

Frederick's son Maximilian took over the government in 1486—against the Emperor's will—and the deposed monarch retired to Linz to study astronomy, alchemy and botany. He was obsessed with a belief in the future greatness of his house, an obsession that was epitomized by his monogram A.E.I.O.U. (*Austriae est imperare orbi universo*). Frederick's vision became a reality in 1477 with Maximilian's marriage to Mary of Burgundy.

Matthias of Hungary

Matthias Hunyadi was elected King of Hungary in 1458 at the age of fifteen. In the aftermath of his elder brother's murder, the country was deeply divided and likely to fall to the Turks; few observers gave Matthias more than a few years as King, but he proved to be a good patriot, a competent soldier and an able administrator. He formed a regular army (known from the color of its armor as "The Black Brigade") created the Magyar Hussars, which became the best disciplined troops in Europe, and equipped his army and his fleet on the Danube with cannon. Thanks to his vigorous leadership the Turks failed to

conquer Hungary, the Czechs were expelled from the north of the kingdom and the Hapsburgs from the west. Matthias patronized artists, built up a great library and, in 1467, founded Pressburg University. His codification of the law in 1486 earned him the name "Matthias the Just."

The art of printing

Marco Polo's diaries, published at the end of the thirteenth century, were the first Western texts to note the existence of printed paper currency in China. At the time, the technique of printing was unknown in Europe. A century later, woodblocks were being used to reproduce playing cards and portraits of saints in Venice and in the Low Countries. The decisive step in the development of printing came with the invention of movable type around 1454. That discovery is generally attributed to John Gutenburg (*c.* 1400–68), a goldsmith.

The first Italian press was set up at Subiaco in 1466. By that time William Caxton, an English textile merchant who resided in Bruges and translated French romances as a hobby, had become fascinated by the new art. In 1477 he shipped a press home to England and set it up at Westminster. The first book that Caxton printed in England was *The Dictes and Sayengs of the Philosophers*, the first copy of which he presented to Edward IV.

Caxton presents a book to Edward VI.

Landfall at San Salvador

The patent from Spain's Catholic Kings gave the Genoese sea captain the mission to "discover and acquire islands and mainland in the Ocean Sea." When he set out across the unknown Atlantic, Christopher Columbus was seeking to establish the western route to Japan and China—the Cipangu and Cathay of Marco Polo's tales. Most men recognized that the earth was round ; from various sources one could calculate the distance to Japan as only 3,000 miles (it is actually 10,000 miles) ; and no one—least of all Columbus—suspected the presence of an intervening continent. Thus, the historic landfall of October, 1492, was not immediately recognized as the great discovery it was—and Columbus died believing he had reached the Orient. Columbus' error was soon detected, of course, and the impact of Europe on America—and America on Europe—was profound and enduring.

A ship, thought to be Columbus' *Santa Maria*

Opposite Christopher Columbus, the discoverer of America.

According to popular myth and many textbooks, Christopher Columbus, a Genoese in the service of the Spanish court, sailed with three ships from the River Odiel, crossed the Atlantic, and discovered America in 1492. In truth, Columbus' voyage revealed to contemporary Europe the existence of islands and a continent that were already inhabited —and had been for many centuries by peoples who had crossed the Pacific.

Of the people who first migrated to the Americas from Asia by crossing the Bering Strait, we know next to nothing. They were, no doubt, primitive hunters and gatherers who carried very little in the way of cultural baggage with them. They almost certainly developed their characteristic cultures independently in the Americas. They may, conceivably, have been reinforced by subsequent transpacific migrations, but there is no real evidence.

Thus, Columbus was not the first man to land in the Americas. In fact, he was not even the first European commander to land in the Americas: Icelanders and Greenlanders preceded him by nearly five hundred years, and it is possible that fishermen from English west-country ports, fishing off Newfoundland, may have sighted land before 1492. Columbus, then, did not discover a new world; he established contact between two worlds, both already old.

The significance of historical events, nevertheless, must be measured by their consequences. The discoveries of the Norsemen were all but forgotten by 1492, and those of the Bristol fishermen, genuine or not, got no publicity; but all Europe heard about Columbus. He made his voyage at a time when recently developed ships and navigating instruments made it possible to maintain contact with the discovered lands. His expedition was the first transatlantic voyage to have immediate, significant and permanent results; from that time, people, plants and animals flowed in a steady stream from the world of Europe to the world of America. Christopher

Columbus—not Leif the Lucky or some nameless fisherman from Bristol—made the voyage that brought the Americas firmly within the range of European action.

The precise objects of Columbus' first voyage have never been satisfactorily resolved. By the terms of his agreement with the Spanish monarchs, Columbus was to "discover and acquire islands and mainland in the Ocean Sea." This standard formula would obviously include the legendary island of Atlantis or Antilla, if such a place existed; but the phrase "islands and mainland" was almost certainly also understood to mean Cipangu and Cathay, the names by which Marco Polo had described Japan and North China some two centuries earlier.

In theory, at least, there was nothing fantastic about a proposal to reach eastern Asia by sailing west. Men recognized that the earth was round, and no one suspected an intervening continent; getting to Asia was a matter of winds, of currents and above all of distance. Could a ship, her crew and the stores she carried endure so far? Columbus apparently thought they could. What he proposed to do if he actually reached Cathay, he never explained. His ships were almost unarmed, carried few trade goods and no presents for princes. He bore a letter for the "Great Khan", but once Columbus arrived in what he believed to be the general neighborhood of Cathay, he made no serious attempt to find and enter its harbors. Instead, he wandered among the islands looking for gold and eventually, having lost his flagship, set sail for home.

Columbus returned to Spain in 1493, convinced that he had found outlying islands in the archipelago of which Japan was supposed to form a part —and such an archipelago is indicated on the German cartographer Martin Behaim's 1492 globe. Columbus supported his contention by combining Marco Polo's estimate of the east-west extent of Asia—which was an overestimate—and Polo's

COLOMBVS LYGVR·NO
ORBIS· REPTO

Insula hyspana

Woodcut of Columbus'
landing on what he thought
was the coast of Cathay.

A practicable western sea route to Asia not only promised an immensely valuable trade in silk and spices—it also evoked a wide range of cherished dreams.

Was Columbus to be believed? The King of Portugal and his advisers, who knew more about exploration than most people, apparently thought not. Had they believed Columbus, they could have made more diplomatic fuss than they did. They were already deeply committed to an attempt to reach India by the route around Africa, and so therefore had strong motives for discrediting Columbus. On the other hand, they also wanted to keep the Spaniards out of the eastern Atlantic, and were delighted to see them pursuing chimeras to the west. The Portuguese therefore kept their own counsel; they laid half-hearted claims to Columbus' discoveries, but made no trouble.

Columbus' arguments were not entirely implausible; they were supported by—or, with a little ingenuity, could be reconciled with—respectable and respected authorities. Columbus himself was a self-taught and extremely persuasive geographical theorist, a capable sea commander and a careful, although somewhat old-fashioned, navigator. He had also shown himself to be a hard-headed negotiator—to picture him as an impractical mystic is mere caricature.

Spain's regents, Ferdinand and Isabella, were sufficiently impressed by Columbus and his reports to undertake a considerable outlay in money and diplomatic effort. The Bull of Demarcation of 1493 assured them of papal support, and the Treaty of Tordesillas, signed by Spain and Portugal in 1494, guaranteed Portuguese acquiescence, at a price which—as later appeared—included the renunciation by Spain of both the eastern route to India and all claim to Brazil. Meanwhile, Columbus was sent off again with a powerful fleet and a numerous company to settle Hispaniola and its gold "mines"— and to pursue his search for Cipangu and Cathay.

Thus early, and as a result of Columbus' arguments, there appeared an ambiguity in Spanish colonial policy: were the new "Indies" to be developed as possessions, valuable in themselves—or were they to be treated as ports-of-call in a maritime drive to reach the commercial centres of the East? Columbus' insistence, after his second voyage, that Cuba was actually a promontory of mainland Cathay, deceived no one. Subsequent voyages—by Vespucci, by Columbus himself and by many lesser discoverers —revealed a landlocked Caribbean to the west of Cuba, and a great continental land mass to the south. Nowhere, on islands or mainland coast, were there kingdoms remotely resembling those described by Marco Polo or his fellow Venetian, Niccolo de' Conti.

The new territories had their attractions for settlers, however: free land, abundant labor, gold in the islands and on the Isthmus and pearls off Cumaná. And as the settlements grew, so did the revenue that accrued to the Crown. Maritime expeditions in search of Asia by a westward route, on

report of the distance from Japan to the Asian mainland—1,500 miles, another overestimate—with Ptolemy's estimate of the circumference of the earth, which was an underestimate. Columbus next assumed the length of an equatorial degree of longitude to be 10 per cent shorter than Ptolemy had taught— or 25 per cent shorter than the true figure. By this calculation, the westward journey from Spain to Japan was less than 3,000 nautical miles (the actual great circle distance is 10,000 nautical miles). Thus, according to Columbus' reasoning, Hispaniola and Cuba were near to where Japan ought to be, and the east coast of the mainland of Cathay was within reach. Columbus clung to this belief with passionate insistence to the end of his life.

Long-lived Christian legends—such as those of Prester John and of St. Thomas in India— appealed to those who sought an ideal of Christian perfection, now lost in Europe, that had existed long ago and might be found again, surviving far away.

The Westward search for the Orient

the other hand, were costly in lives and money—and for many years produced nothing but disappointment. There seemed to be no way of sailing round, or breaking through, the vast barrier that men now called "America." Spanish attempts to reach Cathay were consistently disastrous; meanwhile the Portuguese were fighting and trading in all parts of the Orient, and making Lisbon one of the greatest spice markets of Europe.

The events of 1519–21 posed this Asia-American dilemma in clear and unmistakable terms. In 1519 Magellan left Spain on his great voyage around the world, in the course of which he proved that an all-sea western route to Asia was feasible—but long, dangerous and scarcely economic. Magellan's expedition also revealed that the South Pacific was no mere gulf, but an ocean wider than the Atlantic.

In the same year that Magellan established a long-coveted Spanish outpost in the Moluccas, or Spice Island, Cortes set out from Cuba to conquer Mexico. The Aztec empire was unlike any the Spanish had encountered in the New World, and its immensely greater population, and sophisticated culture and economy made Mexico a prize that was seriously comparable with the kingdoms of the East. The riches of the Aztec nation invited systematic campaigns of conquest instead of random marauding.

Cortes hoped, in the Columbus tradition, to

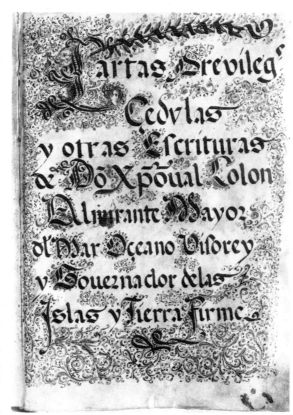

The beginning of the *Book of Privileges* granted to Columbus by Ferdinand and Isabella of Spain, and Columbus' coat-of-arms as Admiral of the Ocean.

Amerigo Vespucci, after whom the American continents are named.

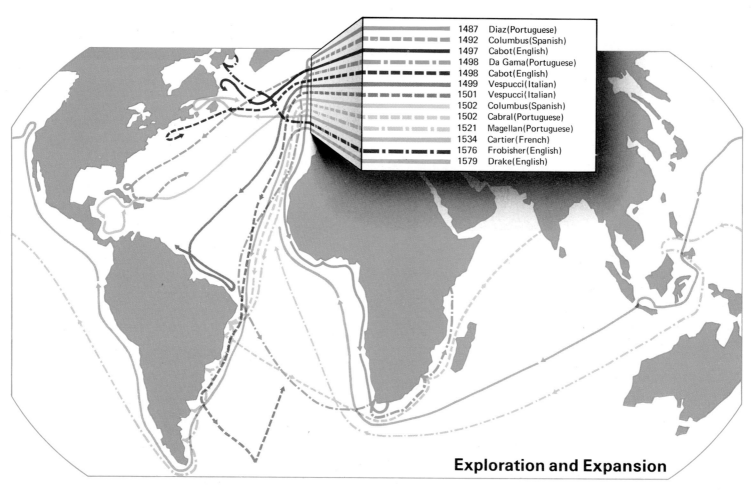

1487	Diaz (Portuguese)
1492	Columbus (Spanish)
1497	Cabot (English)
1498	Da Gama (Portuguese)
1498	Cabot (English)
1499	Vespucci (Italian)
1501	Vespucci (Italian)
1502	Columbus (Spanish)
1502	Cabral (Portuguese)
1521	Magellan (Portuguese)
1534	Cartier (French)
1576	Frobisher (English)
1579	Drake (English)

Exploration and Expansion

A mid-sixteenth-century Genoese map showing contemporary ideas of the world.

pursue the search for Eastern trade, in ships built on the Pacific coast. But in 1527—six years after Cortes delivered Mexico to Spain—Charles v decided to abandon Spain's claims to the Spicery. The distances and the hazards were too great, and the Portuguese were locally too strong. In 1529, by the Treaty of Saragossa, Charles sold out to the Portuguese.

Fresh developments in the "Indies" seemed to confirm the wisdom of his decision. During the 1530s, a second and greater native empire—the Inca, in Peru—was discovered, conquered and laid under tribute. In the 1540s, immensely productive silver veins were found both in Mexico and in Peru. Within a decade, streams of bullion were flowing into Spanish coffers, and the pepper profits of Portugal seemed insignificant by comparison. By mid-

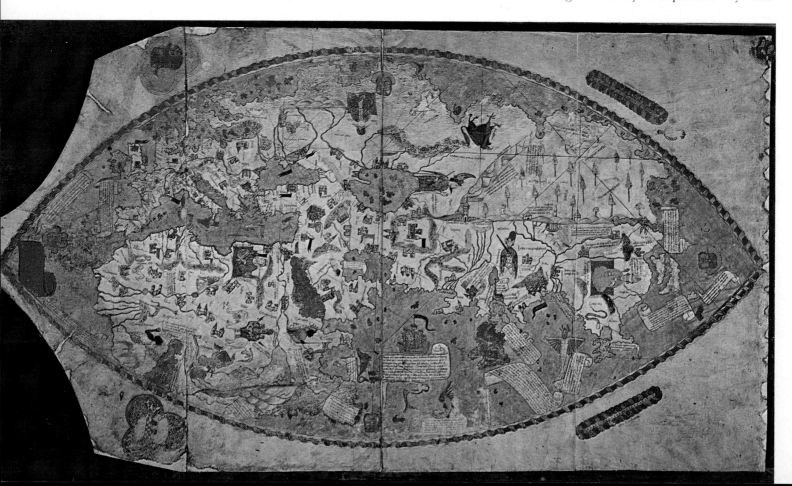

Silver and the search for Eldorado

encircling visions of Columbus and Cortes and other explorers.

In another and more general sense, the stories of the East and West Indies were also connected, for in the course of the seventeenth century, the Portuguese monopoly of European-Asian trade was invaded—and the volume of that trade greatly increased—by Dutch, English, French and other European trading companies. Since few European goods were salable in the East, the companies exported silver to pay for their purchases of spices, silks, calicoes and, later, coffee and tea. Much of this silver came directly or indirectly from America, and the impact of American silver upon the monetary and price systems of western Europe is well known: it made Spain, for a time, the economic envy and commercial terror of Europe. The use of American silver outside Europe is not as well known, and its effect is often overlooked. It is noteworthy, therefore, that throughout much of the seventeenth and all of the eighteenth centuries, Spanish or Mexican *piasters*, or pieces of eight, were the coins most commonly used and most readily accepted in business dealings between Asians and Europeans throughout the Orient. Piasters flowed to the East not only across the Pacific and through Manila, but also across the Atlantic and around Cape Horn, having played their part in European commerce on the way. Without this flow of silver, the successes of the various East

The Holy Roman Emperor, Charles V, whose economy depended on huge shipments of silver from the New World.

Ferdinand and Isabella, the Catholic Kings of Spain, entering Granada Cathedral.

century, the decision seemed final. Spain's overseas interest was to be concentrated on an empire of territorial dominion, tribute and mineral exploitation in the New World—not on an empire of commercial profit in Asia.

Spain's initial settlements in America had been outposts in the race to reach the East; Spain, in losing the race, gained an empire. Spheres of influence had been delimited, a sensible, strategic withdrawal had been made, and a fair compensation had been received. Yet the interwoven stories of the European colonization of the East and West Indies were not so easily separated. The Treaty of Saragossa, backed by Portuguese pugnacity, kept Spaniards away from the Moluccas, but the Portuguese made no particular protest when Miguel López de Legazpe landed in the Philippines in 1564 and seven years later founded Manila as a Spanish colony. Chinese junks and Portuguese ships from Macao were soon trading there, and Manila became a unique back door to the closed, self-sufficient, xenophobic half-world of late Ming dynasty China, linking a society in which silver was in high demand with one in which it was cheap and plentiful. The Spanish ships that carried silver from Acapulco to Manila returned with silk, porcelain, jewelry and drugs—some for sale in Mexico, some for transshipment to Peru (the source of much of the silver), some for re-export to Europe. At its height, the Manila trade equaled in value the official transatlantic trade of Seville. The Manila galleons maintained their hazardous but profitable sailing until 1815—a long-lasting reminder of the world-

Geographical knowledge enlarged

Opposite The Virgin of the Navigators, to whom sailors prayed for protection from the dangers of the sea.

India companies would have been difficult, perhaps impossible. Columbus and Cortes were intuitively right, in ways that they could not have dreamed of—for the exploitation of the New World was a necessary condition of the eastward spread of European trade and influence in the Old.

Silver was not the only New World product that altered the course of Old World history. European settlers used the apparently limitless land of the Americas to raise the products with which they were familiar—sugar, wheat, cattle—and in so doing vastly increased the world's supply of food. At the same time, traders brought native American crop plants to Europe, Africa and Asia, and some of these took root and spread. Potatoes, originally grown in a limited area in the high valleys of the Andes, became an indispensable staple throughout temperate Europe. Maize, which originated in Central America and spread both north and south in the centuries before Columbus' arrival, quickly established itself in southeastern Europe, West and Central Africa, and—perhaps most significantly of all—in China. It was an essential factor in the rapid growth of the Chinese population in the eighteenth century, particularly in inland provinces where rice could not flourish. Even the humble cassava, an insipid staple of the native peoples of northern South America and the Antilles, was carried to West Africa by slavers, where it became the chief food of millions of

natives. Thus, the establishment of transatlantic contacts—which in the Americas led to demographic catastrophe and the destruction of whole civilizations—made possible the support of immensely greater populations in Europe, Africa and Asia.

Along with new food crops, Europe acquired new luxuries and new social habits from America. Cacao—chocolate—had been a royal food and drink, a means of exchange, and the basis for social ritual in ancient Mexico. In seventeenth-century Europe, it became a fashionable fad, and Venezuelan planters made fortunes growing cacao beans in the eighteenth century for the European market.

Tobacco too had a profound impact on the Old World. An indigenous American plant, it was used by the natives in almost all the known ways—powdered as snuff, infused, and smoked in pipes, cigars, and cornhusk cigarettes. It made the circuit of the world within a century of Columbus' landfall, and aroused choruses of curiosity, enthusiasm or indignation wherever its use became prevalent. Vice or solace, drug or poison, it has probably made more men's fortunes than all the silver of the Indies.

The impact of all this upon the economic fortunes of Europe can hardly be exaggerated. It began to be felt within a few years of Columbus' first voyage. Moreover, the impact of discovery was not only economic, but intellectual and imaginative as well. In the space of a hundred years, European seamen achieved an enlargement of geographical knowledge that was unparalleled in its extent and in the speed of its discovery.

In addition, those explorers had encountered curious animals, unfamiliar plants, and strange natural phenomena in such variety that the purveyors of fabulous tales were suddenly unable to compete with the truthful narratives of sober adventurers. The knowledge they brought home, which was subsequently spread by the new device of printing, affected every aspect of European life and thought. Geographical exploration is the most empirical of all forms of scientific inquiry, the most dependent upon eyewitness experience. Practical navigators put the theories of revered authorities in cosmography to the test, and often proved them wrong. Inevitably, men of inquiring mind were encouraged to question, by observation and experiment, accepted authorities in other fields of knowledge. Unknown lands, and the social behavior of their supposedly simple inhabitants, caught the imagination of philosophers, poets and painters.

This new appreciation of the number and diversity of human societies led Europeans to look with fresh and critical eyes at their own society and institutions. Slowly, hesitantly, the idea grew in the minds of a few outstanding men, that there might be a new realm of learning and understanding beyond the horizon of the classics, ancient philosophy and the teachings of revealed religion. Magellan, contemplating the immensity of unknown oceans, prepared the way for Kepler, to whom the round earth itself was "of a most insignificant smallness, and a swift wanderer among the stars." J. H. PARRY

Cardinal Cisneros lands in Africa; the conquest of the New World and North Africa was seen in religious terms.

The thirty years between Columbus' discovery of America and Magellan's voyage around the globe were crowded with the achievements of other navigators. Columbus himself made three additional voyages, in the course of which he established a colony on Hispaniola and discovered Cuba, Puerto Rico, Jamaica and Trinidad. John Cabot, a Genoese living in England, persuaded Henry VII that he was capable of reaching "the Island of Brazil," and in 1497 he sailed westward under royal instructions "to discover and settle new lands across the Atlantic." Cabot's voyage was made in defiance of Pope Alexander's Bull of 1493, which reserved the new continents for Spain and Portugal. The intrepid Genoese reached Cape Breton Island and sailed south along the coast of Newfoundland. Cabot was convinced that he had found "the land of the Great Khan," but English commercial interest in Cabot's ventures faded as soon as it became clear that there was no spice trade in the region.

The Portuguese were more successful. Bartholomew Diaz rounded the Cape of Good Hope in 1487 during a storm which was so severe that Diaz' crew forced him to return immediately to Lisbon. A compatriot, Vasco da Gama, set out ten years later to retrace Diaz' steps and find a sea route to India. He reached Calicut on the Malabar Coast in May, 1498, and thus achieved, within the space of two generations, the ambitious scheme of Prince Henry the Navigator. A year after Vasco da Gama's return, Cabral assembled a fleet and established regular trade with Portugal's newly-discovered outposts. He sailed first to Brazil, where he stayed for ten days, and then made for the Cape of Good Hope and the Indian Ocean. He loaded his thirteen ships with pepper and other spices in Malabar and brought them safely home to Portugal. By 1503—thanks to the new sea route—the price of pepper in Lisbon had dropped to a fifth of what it was in Venice.

Spanish and Portuguese explorers in the New World continued to investigate the coasts, estuaries and islands of Central and South America. In 1501, a Spaniard named Amerigo Vespucci undertook a voyage for the King of Portugal which convinced him that the Brazilian coast was part of a "New World"—and not an outlying portion of Asia. The German geographer Martin Waldseemüller

proposed that the new continent should be named "America" after Amerigo Vespucci.

Two other feats round out these years of intensive discovery: on September 26, 1513, Balboa crossed the Isthmus of Panama and sighted the Pacific Ocean, and six years later Magellan circumnavigated the globe—a voyage that took him from Spain to Brazil, down the South American coast to the straits that now bear his name and into the Pacific. Although Magellan was killed in the Philippines, one ship from his fleet continued westward, and reached Spain in 1522.

Central Italy

The monarchs of Europe concentrated their attention on Italy during this era, for the cradle of the Renaissance remained a conglomeration of warring states that were ripe for plunder. The death of Lorenzo the Magnificent in Florence in 1492 removed from the Italian scene the one ruler capable of maintaining peace, and the election of Rodrigo Borgia, Lorenzo's longtime rival, as Pope in that same year virtually ensured that Italy would be plunged

Pope Alexander VI Borgia.

into turmoil. Pope Sixtus IV (d. 1484) had already weakened the papacy's moral authority by promoting his nephews in order to strengthen his territorial power. His successor, Innocent VIII, was a corrupt nonentity, and Cardinal Borgia's election as Alexander VI—achieved through wholesale bribery—opened the most scandalous chapter in papal history.

Alexander VI swiftly established Borgia rule in central Italy by securing sinecures for the seven children born him by a succession of mistresses. His second son, Cesare, became an archbishop at the age of sixteen and a cardinal two years later; his daughter Lucretia changed her husbands as policy dictated.

Poisoning became a standard political weapon as, by sheer ruthlessness, the head of the Church subdued the great houses of Orsini and Colonna in Rome. Moved by the murder of his son, the Duke of Gandia, Alexander appointed a committee of cardinals to plan reforms, beginning with the Curia itself. He soon thought better of the idea and abandoned it.

Living in great splendor at Rome as a secular monarch, the Pope spent a fortune patronizing the arts. Alexander decreed that the year 1500 was to be celebrated as a jubilee year of the Church, and the pilgrims who flocked to Rome—to be fleeced by papal collectors—saw for themselves the level to which the Church had been reduced by the House of Borgia.

Savonarola

The most outspoken critic of Alexander VI was Girolamo Savonarola (1452-98), the prior of San Marco in Florence. In sermon after sermon he denounced the corruption of the papacy, the shortcomings of Medici rule in Florence and the paganism of the Renaissance. When the Florentines banished Piero de' Medici in the aftermath of the French invasion of 1494, they turned to Savonarola. He refused an office in the Christian republic that he devised, but remained its guiding spirit nonetheless. The administration of justice was remodeled and poor-relief introduced.

Savonarola then demanded that the Augean stables of Rome be cleansed: he implored Alexander to call a general council to reform the Church, but his call went unheeded. The prior disobeyed a summons from the Pope and was excommunicated. Alexander persuaded the Signory of Florence to execute Savonarola.

Savonarola by Fra Bartolommeo.

Machiavelli

Niccolo Machiavelli (1469-1527), a Florentine who rose to become chief secretary of the republic, was led by his experiences in Renaissance politics to write *The Prince*, a manual of statecraft. Diplomatic missions had brought him into contact with Cesare Borgia, tyrant of the Romagna. Machiavelli admired Borgia's political realism without qualification—and indeed it is Cesare who is the hero of the

Bronzino's portrait of Machiavelli.

Florentine's book. *The Prince* taught rulers the means of maintaining themselves in power.

France invades Italy

After 1494, war became the norm on the Italian peninsula. Piero de' Medici, who had succeeded Lorenzo the Magnificent in Florence, signed a secret treaty with Ferdinand of Naples in 1492. The signatories planned to despoil Milan, which was ruled by Lodovico Sforza, and Sforza in self-defense invited Charles VIII of France to press his own claims to Naples. After Ferdinand's death in January, 1494, Charles prepared for war. Charles invaded Italy, marched on Florence and Rome and, in February, 1495, entered Naples.

Louis XII continues the Italian Wars

Upon Charles' death in 1498, his cousin the Duke of Orleans—last of the direct line of the House of Valois—succeeded him as Louis XII. After safeguarding his position within France by marrying Charles' widow, Anne of Brittany (thereby securing the duchy of Brittany for the Crown), Louis launched a second invasion of Italy. He laid claim to Milan as the grandson of Valentin Visconti, and with Spanish

whom all knowledge was his province

help he succeeded in driving Lodovico Sforza out of Milan in September, 1499. Lodovico briefly regained the duchy with the aid of Swiss and German mercenaries, but he was soon captured and taken to France as Louis' prisoner.

Louis XII next made a treaty with Ferdinand of Aragon for the partition of Naples, but the allies subsequently fell out over the division of the spoils, and Spain regained control of Naples in 1504. For another half-century the Italian peninsula remained a battleground of the great powers.

Ludovico Sforza by Leonardo.

Leonardo da Vinci

Leonardo da Vinci was perhaps the most characteristic of the giants of the Renaissance—a "universal man" who took all knowledge as his province. He combined superb artistic skill as a painter and sculptor with remarkable scientific insight—to a degree that no single man had ever achieved. Born at Vinci in the Arno Valley in 1452, he joined the artists' guild of St. Luke in Florence and trained under Verrocchio before moving to Milan, where his many-sided genius developed under

Leonardo's study for the Sforza monument.

The Recyell of the Historie of Troye, Bruges 1474.

the patronage of Lodovico Sforza. Leonardo made elaborate drawings for a bronze equestrian monument to Francesco Sforza, Lodovico's father, during this period. His project never advanced beyond the clay model stage.

After completing the *Virgin of the Rocks*, Leonardo painted the *Last Supper* on a wall of the refectory of the Convent of Santa Maria della Grazie at Milan. Working on the plaster in oil instead of fresco, Leonardo created an entirely original painting that became, for Christians the world over, the standard representation of Christ with his disciples. When Louis XII saw the finished work in 1499, he was so moved by it that he asked whether it could be removed from the wall and transported to France.

Throughout these years Leonardo filled his notebooks with meticulous drawings that showed his power as a creative thinker. Those sketches exemplified his acute observations of nature, his inventive genius and the extraordinary range of his interests. He drew daring flying machines, a helicopter which he developed from his studies of birds in flight, armored fighting vehicles and a submarine. He studied anatomy and optics and the formation of rocks, and his head was full of ideas

for constructing irrigation works and fortifications. In his paintings he put into practice his theories of perspective, light and shade that he had worked out in his journals.

For most of Leonardo's active life, Italy was the cockpit of war. Leonardo spent a season with Cesare Borgia in the Romagna as a military engineer, and in 1507 he was appointed painter and engineer-in-ordinary to the King of France. He ultimately settled in France.

Revival of classical scholarship

New printing presses were being opened each year in Italy, Germany, France, the Netherlands and England—and the most notable among them was the Aldine Press, established in Venice by Teobaldo Manuci. Before 1493 there were scarcely any Greek texts in print, other than Homer's ever-popular epics. Manuci therefore gathered together a band of distinguished scholars—his "Academy"—to advise him on the choice of texts and to edit them. Before he died in 1515, Manuci produced editions of twenty-eight Greek and Latin classics, notably the works of Aristotle in 1495 and the writings of Plato in 1513. His editions made the philosophy of ancient Greece available for the first time to Western scholars. After 1498 Manuci also printed octavo editions of the classics.

The revival of classical scholarship spread far beyond Italy. New universities sprang up at Aberdeen and Wittenberg, while Jesus, Christ's and St. John's colleges were established at Cambridge. Erasmus became Professor of Greek at Cambridge in 1511, and Lady Margaret Beaufort, the mother of Henry VII, founded professorships of divinity at Oxford that same year. In London the Humanist Dean Colet founded St. Paul's School and in Edinburgh the Scottish Parliament made schooling from the age of eight compulsory for the sons of "substantial householders."

Tudor power consolidated

Serious challenges to Henry VII's title were ended with the routing of the Yorkist supporters of the pretender Perkin Warbeck in 1497. The Tudor King consolidated his power by marrying his eldest son, Arthur to Catherine of Aragon and his daughters to the kings of Scotland and France. Two of those marriages had far-reaching effects: Margaret's marriage to James IV of Scotland in 1502 led to the eventual union of the two countries. And upon Arthur's sudden death, his brother Henry, new heir to the throne, was obliged to marry Catherine.

Maximilian strengthens the House of Hapsburg

Under the Emperor Maximilian I (1493–1518), the House of Hapsburg strengthened its hold on Germany by reforming imperial administration and extended its power in Europe through a series of dynastic marriages. In 1495, at the Diet of Worms, Maximilian abolished private warfare in the 240 principalities that comprised his Empire.

Through his marriage to the daughter of Charles the Bold of Burgundy, Maximilian acquired the Netherlands and the key city of Antwerp, and in 1496 he married his only son, Philip the Handsome, to Joanna of Castile. After the death of Isabella, Queen of Castile, in 1506, Philip and Joanna traveled to Valladolid to claim Castile from Ferdinand of Aragon.

Papacy defeats France

The renewal of the papacy owed much to Julius II (1503–13). As a soldier, he led an army against Perugia in 1506 and, with French aid, conquered Bologna. As a diplomat, he joined the League of Cambray, which had been organized for the express purpose of dismembering Venice and her holdings. With the French victory at Agnadello in 1509, Julius gained Rimini and Ravenna. He then sided with the Holy League to expel the French from Italy. The French recaptured Bologna in 1511 and destroyed Michelangelo's statue of Julius, but a year later Milan surrendered to the League and the Pope was called "Deliverer of Italy."

1512 Frescoes for Pope Julius

Insisting that he was a sculptor, not a painter, Michelangelo Buonarroti reluctantly mounted the scaffolding that his assistants had erected inside the Sistine Chapel and began the task of covering more than one thousand square yards of plaster with frescoes. For more than three years, from late in 1508 until 1512, Michelangelo labored under the Sistine's vaulted roof. Working almost singlehandedly, he covered the vast ceiling with some three hundred Biblical figures. The task was a staggering one, and took its toll: in a letter to a friend, Michelangelo complained in verse that "the brush endlessly dripping onto my face has coated it with a multi-colored paving." When he finished, the Florentine was, by his own description, "bent as a Syrian bow"—but his masterwork was lauded as a triumph of Renaissance art.

A portrait of Michelangelo by Jacopino del Conte.

Opposite Adam and Eve are dismissed from the Garden of Eden after eating of the fruit of the Tree of Knowledge of Good and Evil, one of Michelangelo's paintings from the Sistine Chapel.

When he yielded to Pope Julius II's insistent pleas and returned to Rome in 1508 to paint the frescoes on the vaulted ceiling of the Sistine Chapel, Michelangelo Buonarroti was accepting a unique and hazardous artistic challenge. The thirty-three-year-old Florentine was already recognized as the foremost sculptor of the age. His *Pietà* had been on display in St. Peter's in Rome for nearly a decade and his colossal *David* had dominated a central square in Michelangelo's native Florence for four years. And although he had worked on a number of paintings—including the *Doni Tondo* (the Holy Family) and the *Battle of Cascina*—Michelangelo had always preferred sculpture to painting. (Months later, when he was totally absorbed with his work in the Sistine Chapel, the artist complained "I am neither working in a pleasant environment, nor am I a painter").

After resolving a longstanding quarrel with Julius, Michelangelo returned to Rome in the spring of 1508. At that time the sculptor still hoped to be given permission to start work on the gigantic mausoleum that he and the Pope had planned several years earlier. Michelangelo intended to ornament Julius' tomb with a series of powerful figures—slaves, victories and prophets—and he had already begun work on several of those statues. But now the Pope had another scheme in mind; he wanted Michelangelo to paint the vaulted Vatican chapel named for Pope Sixtus IV. That ambitious project had been suggested to Julius by the treacherous Bramante, the architect in charge of the reconstruction of St. Peter's.

Bramante disliked Florentines in general and he was particularly jealous of Michelangelo. The latter's return to Rome acutely displeased the architect, and he did his best to provoke another quarrel between Michelangelo and the Pope by persuading Julius to ask the Florentine to paint the Sistine ceiling. The cunning architect suspected that Michelangelo would refuse, and he knew that the sculptor's refusal would exacerbate the already

precarious truce between the two men. If, on the other hand, Michelangelo accepted the commission, Bramante felt sure that he would botch it, since the project was alien to the sculptor's temperament. Such a failure would almost certainly force the Florentine artist to leave Rome—and Bramante had already arranged to have his friend and distant relation, Raphael, take over the work on the Sistine Chapel.

The professional risk that Michelangelo was taking in accepting Julius' offer was compounded by the fact that Raphael was just beginning to paint a series of frescoes in a number of smaller rooms in the Vatican. It was inevitable that the Florentine's Sistine frescoes would be compared with Raphael's *stanze*. Moreover, his work would have to compete with the scenes from the life of Moses and Christ—painted by the finest fresco artists of the *Quattrocento*—that already decorated the walls of the Sistine Chapel and were much admired.

Michelangelo had every reason to refuse the commission; instead, he accepted Julius' offer with apparent relish—and immediately set about complicating his task. He discarded the Pope's rather unpretentious plan to add the twelve apostles to the arch-stones of the vault while decorating the central section with grotesques, and he obtained Julius' permission to replace it with a far more ambitious composition consisting of three superimposed schemes. That revised design called for a series of panels depicting the Biblical story of *Genesis*. To them, Michelangelo planned to add portraits of Christ's blood ancestors, and the prophets and the sibyls who announced his coming on Earth. The third element of Michelangelo's composition was to be a series of *Ignudi* (nude youths), whose function was to provide a dynamic link between the Biblical scenes and the intermediate panels.

Not surprisingly, Michelangelo soon found himself faced with several significant problems. He arranged to have a number of his students come south from Florence to assist him, but he soon realized

The Temptations of Jesus: one of Botticelli's paintings in the Sistine Chapel.

A detail from Perugino's *Baptism of Christ* from the Sistine Chapel.

that they were not equal to the task. He sent some of them back to Florence and employed the others at menial tasks, while undertaking most of the painting himself. In addition, the already overtaxed artist was obliged to contend with the Pope's impatience to see the work finished and to deal with the ambitions of Raphael, who longed to take Michelangelo's place. Moreover, he ran into technical trouble, particularly with mildew. These dilemmas were minor ones, however; the artist's greatest problem was that he had to paint three hundred figures and roughly one thousand square yards of plastered surface while lying curled up under the ceiling. Michelangelo described the curious torture that he endured while carrying out his task in a poem to a friend:

> My stomach is thrust towards my chin,
> My beard curls up towards the sky,
> My head leans right over onto my back,
> My chest is like that of an old shrew,
> The brush endlessly dripping onto my face
> Has coated it with a multi-colored paving.
> My loins have retreated into my body,
> And my buttocks act as a counter-weight.
> I tread blindly without being able to see my feet,
> My skin stretches out in front of me
> And shrinks in folds behind.
> I am as bent as a Syrian bow.

Apart from anything else, Michelangelo's feat was one of sheer physical endurance. The Florentine began work on his frescoes at the end of 1508 or the beginning of 1509, and did not finish them until November of 1512.

Michelangelo's frank and generous character led him to adopt a totally different approach to fresco painting from that taken by his predecessors, who had sought to camouflage the shape and mass of the vaults they were painting. In contrast, Michelangelo deliberately emphasized the massive appearance of his figures by framing them with painted *trompe-l'oeil* architecture. Within those monumental structures, the artist created a vast, interlocking masterwork that so overwhelmed the other fine murals decorating the walls of the Chapel that they were completely forgotten.

The natural manner in which the human figures were portrayed, the high quality of the drawing, the use of perspective and the outstanding combination of coherence and movement embodied in Michelangelo's Sistine frescoes so enchanted contemporary critics that for centuries observers failed to realize that Michelangelo had shown himself to be a very fine colorist as well. Unfortunately, subsequent restorations—undertaken in 1565, 1625, 1710, 1903–5 and again in 1935–36—have dimmed the freshness of the original frescoes. During the eighteenth century, the panels were varnished with glue in a well-intentioned attempt at restoration that deadened the frescoes' colors. The accumulation of dust, the infiltration of water and the smoke from wax candles have also contributed to the ceiling's deterioration—to the extent that today they are darkened and cracked. Nevertheless, a careful

St. Peter's Montorio, Rome, designed by Bramante.

Chronology of the Renaissance

1300	Giotto working in Assisi
1304-21	Dante Alighieri publishes *Divine Comedy*
1348-51	Black Death devastates Europe
1360	Boccaccio publishes *Decameron*
1405	Aretino translates Plato
1416	Donatello casts statue of St. George
1420-43	Brunelleschi builds cupola of Florence Cathedral
1440	Nicholas of Cusa publishes *On Learned Ignorance*
1450	Gutenburg perfects moveable type
1452	Piero della Francesca paints murals at Arezzo
1452	Alberti publishes *On Architecture*
1469	Lorenzo di Medici becomes ruler of Florence
1478	Botticelli paints *Primavera*
1481-83	Leonardo paints *Virgin on the Rocks*
1480	Beginning of Spanish Inquisition
1492	Columbus discovers America
1494	Aldus Manuci prints first pocket books
1495	Leonardo paints *Last Supper*
1498	Execution of Savonarola
1506	Bramante begins to rebuild St. Peter's
1508	Michelangelo paints ceiling of Sistine Chapel
1509	Raphael paints frescoes in Vatican
1511	Erasmus publishes *In Praise of Folly*
1513	Machiavelli publishes *The Prince*
1514	Castiglione writes *The Book of the Courtier*
1518	Titian paints *The Assumption of the Virgin*
1533-35	Rabelais publishes *Gargantua* and *Pantagruel*
1534	Luther publishes German Bible
1543	Copernicus' book on Astronomy
1548	Council of Trent begins
1548	Tintoretto paints *The Miracle of the Slave*
1550	Vasari publishes *Lives of Painters*
1568	Mercator's world projection
1580	Montaigne publishes *Essais*

The *Pietà*. Michelangelo preferred sculpture to painting, and was reluctant to paint the Sistine Chapel for Pope Julius.

Medal of Pico della Mirandola, expressing the philosophy of love in the words "Beauty, Love and Pleasure."

examination of the Chapel ceiling reveals richly orchestrated colors that are a far cry from the stony, monotonous palette so often attributed to Michelangelo.

From the beginning, Michelangelo was faced with an esthetic and theological dilemma that was as great as any of his technical quandaries: his frescoes clearly had to relate both in theme and order to the two series on the lateral walls. Those works, painted by the great artists of the *Quattrocento*, represented the history of humanity *sub lege* (that is, under the law of Moses) and *sub gratia* (during the life of Christ). Michelangelo decided, therefore, to concentrate

mainly on the history of the world *ante legem* (before Moses received the Ten Commandments)—and he filled the center of the vault with nine great Biblical scenes. To illustrate the announcement of the coming of Christ through the ages Michelangelo added the ancestors of Jesus, starting with Abraham, and the soothsayers.

Michelangelo also had to take into consideration the fact that his predecessors, in accordance with an ancient Christian tradition, had started painting their frescoes from the altar and worked their way toward the main door. Consequently, the same chronological order had to be preserved in the ceiling

Love, Sacred and Profane by Titian.

The Fall of Man and Neoplatonism

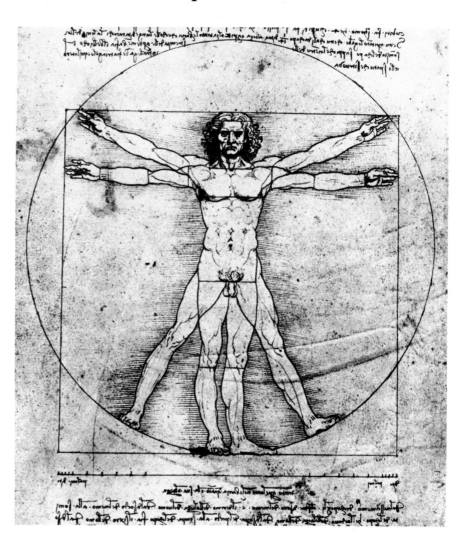

frescoes, which began with a scene depicting the first day of Creation (*God Dividing the Light from the Darkness*), painted above the altar, and ended with the *Drunkenness of Noah* at the far end of the Chapel.

That constant reference to the Scriptures lent a strong Christian flavor and religious fervor to the Sistine frescoes, one that is not apparent in Michelangelo's earlier works. The Christ of the St. Peter's *Pietà*, for example, is depicted as a kind of Apollo put to death, while the *David* looks more like a beautiful Greek youth than the ancestor of Jesus. The naked fauns lurking behind the Holy Family in the *Doni Tondo*, like the figures in the *Battle of the Centaurs*, Michelangelo's first work, reveal the esthetic and artistic influence of the Greeks and Romans—not the Bible—upon Michelangelo's early work. The paintings on the ceiling of the Sistine Chapel, on the other hand, are grounded in the concept of Original Sin and represent an impassioned call to the Redeemer.

The theme of the Fall of Man was not a uniquely Christian one, however, and Michelangelo's fervor may have been aroused as much by his Neoplatonic background as by his heightened Christian awareness. Indeed, Michelangelo spent his formative years in Florence at a time when Neoplatonism was rapidly becoming the favorite philosophy of the

Leonardo da Vinci's Vitruvian Man.

Above left A poem by Michelangelo, with a drawing of himself painting the Sistine Chapel.

The title page of Marsilio Ficino's treatise *On the Immortality of Souls*.

Michelangelo's
Universal Guide, from
the Sistine Chapel.

The Delphic Sybil.

The Flood.

intellectuals. He was profoundly influenced by that trend and at least one eminent scholar has called Michelangelo the only Renaissance artist "to adopt Neoplatonism in its entirety, and not just certain aspects of it."

It is, in fact, possible to interpret the Sistine frescoes in Platonic terms, starting from the main door instead of from the altar. According to that interpretation, the first scene to be observed, the *Drunkenness of Noah,* represents the imprisonment of the soul within the body and the fetters of an earthly existence. The next painting, the *Deluge,* symbolizes the despair of humanity enslaved by the passions of a mundane world, and the panel that follows it, the *Sacrifice of Noah,* reveals the moment when the soul first becomes aware of its own existence and tries to communicate with God by offering Him a gift. That awareness of self implies an awareness of sin—which is illustrated in the next painting, the *Fall of Adam and Eve.* When studied in inverse order, the other Biblical scenes on the ceiling—the *Creation of Eve,* the *Creation of Adam, God Dividing the Waters,*

The Soul rising to a final state of Grace

the *Creation of the Sun, Moon and the Planets*, and *God Dividing the Light from the Darkness*—illustrate the ascent of the human soul from earthly, material existence to a final state of grace.

Neoplatonism is one of the keys to understanding the apparent paganism of many Renaissance art works, for despite their outer charm and pagan worldliness, most of those works are grounded in ascetism. Indeed, an invitation to ascetism can be found at the core of Platonic philosophy. According to Neoplatonist doctrine, the soul can remember only God and can attain grace only by breaking the chains that bind man to the earth. Ficino's *Theologia platonica*, one of the classic books of the Renaissance, states that "the life of the body is a sickness of the dreaming, tortured soul. All our movements, actions and passions are nothing more than the twisting and turnings of sick people, the nightmares and delirium of the insane." It is essential, the author insists, to banish all temptations produced by the senses. "The desire of the senses, which draws us towards everything that is material, massive, dull and shapeless . . . is not love but merely a pointless, stupid hunger, degrading and hideous." That doctrine, which permeated the whole of the Renaissance, rejects all sensual pleasure but glorifies earthly beauty, which is seen as the first step up the "miraculous ladder" that ascends to God. Thus, Michelangelo's *Ignudi*, which created something or a stir when the Sistine ceiling was unveiled on August 14, 1511—and which led to the aforementioned accusations of paganism—were in fact symbols of truth and purity. (Michelangelo also expressed the Neoplatonic creed in one of his poems. "My eyes which are in love with beauty and my soul which is in love with salvation," he wrote, "can only ascend to heaven by the contemplation of all the beauty surrounding me.")

It is vitally important to appreciate the degree to which the Renaissance evolved its own philosophy of art—for if the Renaissance had not developed its uniquely "religious" and fundamentally optimistic conception of beauty, many superb works of art might never have been produced. Neoplatonism equated beauty and goodness with godliness. Its disciples maintained with absolute assurance that beauty was the "flower of goodness," and that it was through beauty that goodness was revealed to us. "We would not know the meaning of goodness," wrote Ficino, "nor would we seek it, since it is so well concealed, if we were not guided to it by the signs and marks of beauty and of love which accompanies it." Some fifty years later, in 1528, Castiglione took up the same theme in the *Cortigiano*:

It is very rare for an evil soul to inhabit a beautiful body. For outer beauty is the true sign of inner goodness . . . Beauty and goodness are more or less the same thing. This particularly applies to the beauty of the human body, whose main function, it seems to me, is to reflect the beauty of the soul. The latter, aware of the true beauty, which is that of God, glorifies and beautifies everything it touches.

In the light of these—and other—fervent declarations, it is not surprising that the Renaissance produced such poetic wealth and artistic originality. Or that Michelangelo produced such exuberant, inspiring, and fundamentally Christian frescoes for the ceiling of Julius' renovated Chapel.

JEAN DELUMEAU

The Creation of Man.

One of the *ignudi*, used for decoration at the corners of the main pictures.

Leo X, son of Lorenzo the Magnificent, by Raphael.

Pope Julius II envisioned Rome as the artistic capital of the world, but it was his successor, Leo x (1513–21), son of Lorenzo the Magnificent of Florence, who achieved Julius' vision. In doing so, Leo faced stiff competition from Europe's secular princes: Isabella D'Este of Mantua invited "the best painters in Italy" to decorate her palace, Francis I enticed Leonardo da Vinci to France and the Emperor Charles v appointed the Venetian, Titian, as his court painter.

Raphael, who was a generation younger than Leonardo and eight years younger than Michelangelo, received numerous papal commissions and rapidly became the leading exponent of the High Renaissance. While Michelangelo was completing the ceiling of the Sistine Chapel, Raphael was working on the frescoes in the Stanza della Segnatura at the Vatican and painting the *Sistine Madonna*.

A very different exemplar of High Italian culture was Ariosto's *Orlando Furioso*, which was published in 1516 after a dozen years of steady composition. That poetic romance, which dealt with the epic struggles of the Christians and the Saracens, had two secondary themes: Orlando's madness and his eventual cure, and the love between Ruggero and Badamante.

Three young kings

In England, France, Spain and Germany the old guard was changing, and the European scene was soon dominated by three youthful kings. Henry VIII succeeded his father in 1509 at the age of eighteen, and six years later the nineteen-year-old Duke of Angouleme

became Francis I of France. Charles of Ghent inherited the throne of a united Spain in 1516 when his grandfather Ferdinand I died, and in 1519 he succeeded his paternal grandfather, Maximilian I, as Holy Roman Emperor. Personal rivalries between these three young monarchs—each of whom looked upon himself as the embodiment of Renaissance chivalry—and the relations of each to the papacy were to dominate European politics for thirty years.

England joins the Holy League

Henry VIII entered Euorpean politics in 1511 when he joined Pope Julius' Holy League to drive the French out of Italy. The Royal Navy, reformed and consolidated at Henry's express wish, commanded the English Channel during this

Francis I of France by Clouet: after his victory at Marignano the defeat at Pavia shattered Francis' Italian hopes.

period and frequently put men ashore to burn French coastal villages. In 1513 Henry signed an offensive alliance with Spain that called for the invasion of France. The King led his army out to join the Emperor's troops, but in so doing he missed the only engagement of the short campaign. That clash, known as the Battle of the Spurs, took its name from the hasty retreat of the French cavalry.

Battle of Marignano

In the summer of his accession, Francis I set out for northern Italy with an army of 110,000 men. His immediate objective was to capture the Duchy of Milan, but he expected to subdue all Italy and sweep onward speedily to Constantinople. So he avoided a battle with the

Swiss by not using the orthodox route through the Mont Cenis Pass, marched into Italy and routed the Milanese at Villafranca. A few days later the Swiss infantry attacked Francis' camp at Marignano. They pressured the French relentlessly, but Gian Trivulzio, the French general, maintained his ground and when reinforcements arrived from Venice, the combined forces were able to defeat the Swiss mercenaries. The Battle of Marignano was the end of an epoch in European warfare—until that clash, Swiss troops had been invincible in battle.

One immediate result of Francis' first campaign was the signing of the Concordat of Bologna in 1516. The Concordat entitled Francis to appoint French bishops and abbeys. It freed the French Church from close papal control in return for the payment of annates to Rome—a system called the "Gallican Liberties," which were not abolished until the nineteenth century.

Charles V of Spain succeeds to the Hapsburg dominions

Before his death in January, 1519, Maximilian I readied his grandson, Charles I of Spain, for the Hapsburg succession. Francis I was determined to contest the election, and both Pope Leo x and Henry VIII initially pledged him their support (although the latter later announced that he would stand as a candidate himself). To insure Charles' election, his agents in Germany used vast sums of money—advanced them by the great German bankinghouse, the Fuggers of Augsburg—to influence the imperial electors. At the last moment the Pope abandoned his opposition to Charles and the seven electors—who were uniformly anxious to exclude Francis I from interfering in the Empire—elected Charles in June of 1519. Placing Spain in the care of his old tutor, Adrian of Utrecht, the Emperor-elect departed for the Netherlands—and on October 23, 1520, he was crowned at Aachen.

As the most powerful sovereign in the world, Charles v ruled the Empire, Spain, Sicily, Naples, Sardinia, the Netherlands, the Hapsburg dominions centering around Austria and most of the newly discovered continents across the Atlantic. The tension evoked by the prolonged election contest ultimately led to war, both with the French and within Germany itself.

The Field of the Cloth of Gold

The imperial election campaign postponed the long anticipated meeting between the kings of England and France, each of whom had sworn that he would not shave until he had seen the other. The arrangements for the meeting were in the hands of Thomas Wolsey, who had been both Lord Chancellor of England and a cardinal since 1515. Wolsey, who cast himself in the role of arbiter of Europe, devised the Peace of London, an agreement that he hoped to get England, France, the Empire, Spain and the papacy to sign. The Field of Cloth of Gold was intended as a "summit meeting" between the two kings to guarantee the peace of Europe. By the summer of 1518, 6,000 English workmen were busy preparing King Henry's quarters—including a huge banqueting hall—at Guisnes, and the French were no less active at Ardres. Midway between Guisnes and Ardres was the Val d'Or, the spot selected for the meeting. Pavilions and galleries had been erected nearby, overlooking a tournament ground.

More than 5,000 people accompanied Henry on his Channel crossing and rode with him to Val d'Or. The two kings, supported by the greatest nobles in their realms, rode to opposite edges of the field and then, as trumpets sounded, the sovereigns galloped forward to the appointed place and, still mounted, embraced three times.

Clement VII crowns Charles V as Emperor, by Vasari.

of the Reformation

The Field of Cloth of Gold where Henry VIII and Francis I met but could not agree.

Thus opened the Field of Cloth of Gold, a prelude to three weeks of jousting, banquets, dancing and pageantry that ended with a High Mass, celebrated in the open by Wolsey and sung to music especially composed by Robert Fairfax. Many contemporaries considered the program of events the Eighth Wonder of the World, for it enshrined the rebirth of chivalry. Most remarkable of all was the fact that the sovereigns of two countries that had been enemies from time immemorial should at last meet on such cordial terms. At the end of the festivities a treaty was signed that proposed marriage between the infant Mary Tudor and the Dauphin, and ended French interference in Scottish affairs. Both before and immediately after the Field of Cloth of Gold Henry VIII met with Charles V at Dover and Gravelines. There is no evidence to convict the English King of duplicity, however, for Charles found that he could not draw Henry into an alliance with him against France.

Erasmus of Rotterdam

Erasmus of Rotterdam (1466–1536), the greatest Christian Humanist of the age, sought to serve God by advancing knowledge. He had been ordained in 1492, but he soon found monastic life as uncongenial as he was later to find life at court. When he met John Colet at Oxford at the turn of the century, Erasmus promised to devote himself to studying theology. He sought out the best teachers of Greek in Europe and began to prepare for the task of editing the Greek text of the New Testament. Much of this work he undertook while lecturing at Cambridge, and his edition, with full notations, was published in Basel in 1516.

Erasmus profoundly hoped that once theologians had access to accurate editions of the Scriptures, religious contention would cease. Instead his efforts provoked further theological controversy, for his text showed Christendom that the Latin Vulgate was not infallible. It is in this sense that the adage, current in his own life-time, that "Erasmus laid the egg that Luther hatched," rings true. A return to scriptural evangelism spelled trouble for the Church.

Erasmus had not hesitated to ridicule medieval Scholasticism or lampoon popes and prelates in his *In Praise of Folly*, yet his loyalty to the Roman Church was never in question. He regarded Luther as a dangerous prophet and at the end of his life he wrote "I abhor the Evangelicists, because it is through them that literature is everywhere declining." It was as a man of letters, universally admired for his tolerance, wit and prodigious output, that Erasmus towered over his contemporaries. The breadth of his interests and the height of his scholarship are best seen in the great number of surviving letters that he wrote to such fellow Humanists as Sir Thomas More, to kings, popes and to a lively circle of friends. Apart from his editions of the Early Fathers and his work on the Latin New Testament, he produced two volumes of commentaries embodying his liberal philosophy — the *Adages* in 1500 and the *Colloquies* in 1524. Both were "best-sellers" and dominated teaching in schools and universities for a century.

Luther and the Reformation

In 1517 a papal hireling named Johann Tetzel came to Saxony to raise funds for the rebuilding of St. Peter's in Rome by selling papal indulgences. This practice—whereby a subscriber purchased the release of souls from purgatory and bought grace for himself with hard cash—was a time-honored instrument of Church finance. Tetzel, who went about his business with unprecedented effrontery, gravely provoked Martin Luther, and on October 31, 1517, Luther nailed his ninety-five *Theses*, denouncing the sale of indulgences, to the door of the palace church at Wittenberg. His action, the normal way of giving notice of a public disputation, was the beginning of the Continental Reformation that was to tear Germany apart.

Martin Luther (1483–1546) entered the Augustinian monastery of Erfurt at the age of twenty-two, but he soon transferred to Wittenberg to study Scripture. In 1512, while he was lecturing on the Epistle to the Romans, Luther discovered, in St. Paul's teachings, what he considered to be the key to all Christian doctrines: man's salvation by faith in Christ alone. Further consideration of Paul's writings led Luther to deny the sanctity of works. At this stage the monk had no intention of severing ties with the Church.

The posting of Luther's *Theses* brought matters to a head. Tetzel had recently proclaimed that it was through the grace of the indulgence that man was reconciled with God. He insisted that there was no need for repentance, provided a man paid what he could afford, and he assured his listeners that they could even buy the right to sin in the future. The idea that "everything might be done for money" was anathema to Luther, and he responded with the *Theses*. Complaints about his outburst reached Pope Leo X, and the ecclesiastical controversy that the Wittenberg monk stirred up soon expanded to include many more issues than merely the sale of indulgences.

Luther's act coalesced a general sentiment that had been gathering strength in sixteenth-century Europe, and many beliefs fused in the Reformation, which produced different results in each country.

Turkish expansion

Under Sultan Selim I (1512–20), the Turks renewed their westward advance. Following a struggle for the succession, Selim forced his father, Bayazid II, to abdicate and then turned upon his neighbor, the Shah of Persia, who had supported a rival contender for the Turkish throne. In 1514, Selim won a great victory at Chaldiron in the Euphrates Valley. He then overran Anatolia and Kurdistan, and would have penetrated deeper into Asia Minor except for the threat of Kansu, Sultan of Egypt. Selim returned to Syria, where he defeated Kansu through the skillful use of artillery. The towns accepted Selim's rule. But Egypt refused to accept Turkish suzerainty and Selim conquered it.

Moguls in India

One of the most remarkable monarchs of the age was Baber (1483–1530), founder of the Mogul dynasty

Erasmus of Rotterdam, humanist, intellectual and biblical scholar.

in India. At the age of twelve Baber succeeded to the throne of the tiny kingdom of Fergana in the mountains of Turkeshar. In ensuing years, he survived plots, mutinies and defeats in battle by courageous military leadership alone. In 1504 he led his army across the snow-capped Hindu Kush to capture Kabul, the capital of Afghanistan. As hope of regaining his captured kingdom faded, Baber found himself drawn to India, much as his ancestor Timur the Great had been in 1397. After preliminary raids on Lahore, he defeated Ibrahim, Emperor of Delhi at Panipat in 1526. By 1527 Baber was master of north India.

The Conquest of Mexico 1521

Like many a Spanish youth of his generation, Hernando Cortes was stirred by tales of the New World being explored and colonized by his countrymen. At the age of nineteen, he reached the Antilles; fifteen years later he was the wealthy proprietor of several estates in Cuba. But the rumors of fabulously rich kingdoms—always just beyond the next island or over the next mountain—were persistent, and early in 1519 Cortes set out at the head of an expedition to Mexico. By an incredible combination of luck, ingenuity and courage, Cortes and his small force overwhelmed the awesome Aztec empire. Horses and firearms—both unknown to the natives— were the keys to Cortes' success; and this easy triumph of European skill and technology over Indian brute force set the pattern for succeeding generations of conquerors—and foredoomed America's native population.

At the dawn of the sixteenth century, Western civilization stood on the threshold of a new age—an age of discovery and challenge, of bursting frontiers and distant, undreamed-of horizons that has had no parallel until our own day. America had been discovered, but the continent remained virtually unexplored.

The pattern was to change in 1519, with the appearance on those shores of a man of very different stamp from any who had gone before him. His name was Hernando Cortes and in less than three years—through a combination of brilliant leadership, superhuman courage and almost incredible good luck—he was to achieve the downfall of the Mexican empire and of its emperor Montezuma. His story is one of special significance, for it marks the first direct confrontation, in all their power and might, of the Old World and the New.

Cortes, the son of a humble country squire of Estremadura in southern Spain, had left home at the age of sixteen to seek his fortune. Three years later he arrived in Hispaniola. In the years that followed he acquired several large estates in Cuba and became, by local standards, a rich man.

Despite its pleasures, life in Cuba ultimately began to pall, and in 1518, Cortes talked, intrigued and bribed his way into the command of a new expedition to the west. On February 10 of the following year the expedition set sail. It had two main objectives, one material and one spiritual. The material one, as always, was gold—a subject never very far from the minds of the conquistadors. But the spiritual purpose was equally real and even more important; the conquistadors might be despoilers, but they were missionaries as well.

The Spanish commander's resources were small— eleven ships, carrying less than seven hundred men —but he possessed two secret weapons unknown to the American natives: firearms, including several small cannon, and sixteen horses. Cortes used both weapons in his first clash with the mainlanders. In a

battle fought near Tabasco in southeastern Mexico, terrified Maya Indians bravely stood their ground against the cannon, but the horses proved too much for them. At the outset they actually imagined horse and rider to be a single animal—some monstrous centaur bearing down upon them—and they soon fled. Cortes, striding over to a nearby tree, struck it a great blow with his sword and claimed the whole territory for Spain. The conquest of Mexico was under way.

The next morning, the Tabascans sent peace emissaries to the Spanish camp bearing rich gifts for their conquerors. Among these gifts was a young native maiden named Marina. This girl, whom Bernal Diaz describes as good-looking and intelligent, was probably the greatest godsend that Cortes ever received—not because she eventually became the conquistador's mistress and the mother of his child, but because she spoke both Mexican and Maya. Cortes already had a Spanish-Maya interpreter, so that from the moment Marina joined him, his language problems were at an end.

Other problems were only just beginning, however. The Spaniards' next landfall, some two hundred miles north of Tabasco, lay within the frontiers of the warlike Aztec empire of Montezuma.

When the Aztecs went to war they did so not to kill but to take prisoners for sacrifice—and they could never take enough. During the four-day consecration of the great temple at Tenochtitlan, no less than 80,000 victims met their deaths on the sacrificial altars. Throughout the carnage, the method of dispatch never varied: the victim's breast was ripped open with an obsidian knife and the still-palpitating heart was torn out and offered to the gods.

Among these gods was one named Quetzalcoatl, the Feathered Serpent. A recounting of his legend reveals a fantastic series of coincidences that makes the history of the conquest sound more like a fairy tale. Long ago—ran the legend—Quetzalcoatl had

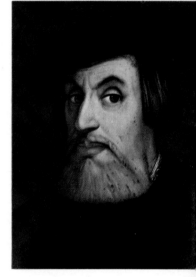

Hernando Cortes, the conqueror of Mexico; by N. Medellin.

Opposite Xochipilli, the Aztec god of poetry, music, theater and dancing.

A view from the *Florentine Codex*. In the background an Indian sights the Spanish ships; left, the Spaniards unload supplies; right, questioning an Indian.

Mask of the sun god, Tonatiun.

come down to earth in human from, white-skinned and black-bearded; then after twenty years he had sailed away to the east. It was said that he would return one day, dressed in black, to re-establish his rule. His homecoming would occur in a "One-reed Year," and would bring much tribulation and suffering in its train. According to the Aztec calendar, a "One-reed Year" fell only once in every fifty-two of our years. There had been one in 1415, and another in 1467; the next fell in 1519.

Thus, Montezuma had reason to be anxious even before he learned of the coming of Cortes—and when his spies reported sighting a band of mysterious strangers, led by a man with an unusually pale face and a black beard—and dressed in black from head to foot—the emperor's direst suspicions seemed confirmed.

Believing that there was a faint chance that "Quetzalcoatl" might be bribed not to come to the capital, Montezuma sent ambassadors down to the coast with propitiatory gifts. The move was a fatal one. These gifts, every one of which was of gold, convinced Cortes that he was indeed on the threshold of El Dorado; and he resolved to lead the puny force under his command against Montezuma's huge empire. Cortes knew that the authorities in Cuba would never countenance so dangerous an enterprise before he established a secure and independent colony on the mainland. Therefore, on the very spot where he had first received the Aztec ambassadors, the conquistador founded a new Spanish colony. In honor of his Good Friday landing he named the settlement Villa Rica de Vera Cruz—

the Rich Town of the True Cross—thus neatly reflecting the two preoccupations of the Spanish colonial mind—gold and the Gospel.

While preparations were being made for the great march to the interior, another group of Indian emissaries arrived at Vera Cruz. These friendly members of the Totonac tribe invited Cortes and his men to visit their city of Cempoala, twenty-odd miles to the northwest. Explaining that they had recently been conquered by the Aztecs and were presently being crushed by the savage tribute wrung from them by their hated overlords, the Totonacs asked to accompany the Spaniards on their campaign. Cortes accepted their invitation and agreed to take them with him on the condition that they give up their own predilection for human sacrifice and embrace the Cross.

Before setting forth, Cortes made a decision that, for sheer cold-blooded courage, must rank as one of the most remarkable of his life: he bribed a few of his sailors to puncture the hulls of his ships with holes and then, on the pretext that they were worm-eaten and unseaworthy, deliberately run them aground. Henceforth, whatever happened, there could be no retreat.

Thus, in August, 1519, this extraordinary young man set off without maps across an unknown country, against an empire of apparently limitless power, wealth and savagery, never knowing what lay beyond the next hill except that he would probably be encountering armies many times stronger than his and almost certainly hostile. On this trek, Cortes was accompanied by about five hundred Spanish musketeers (a sizable garrison had been left behind at Vera Cruz), thirteen horses, a few pieces of light artillery and perhaps a thousand Totonac irregulars.

Now there was hard fighting in store for them. The people of Tlaxcala, a town located roughly halfway between Vera Cruz and Tenochtitlan, rejected the Spaniards' peace overtures and put up an impassioned and heroic resistance. Only after three weeks and four major battles (in which they suffered immense losses) did the Tlaxcalans admit defeat and allow Cortes into their capital. Then, however, they too offered him their friendship—and proved as good as their word. Henceforth, they became his most trusted allies, and a large number of them accompanied Cortes on the next stage of his journey, which brought him to the holy city of Cholula.

Although the natives offered no overt opposition as the Spaniards entered Cholula, the conquistadors were immediately suspicious. Many of the streets had been barricaded, and piles of stones were visible on the rooftops. Most ominous of all, there were no women or children anywhere. It was the faithful Marina who first discovered the truth: the Cholulans intended to ambush Cortes' entire army the next day and to carry it off to Montezuma for sacrifice. Cortes laid his plans quickly but carefully. Early the following morning he gathered all the Cholulans he could muster within the Spanish stockade. Then, through Marina, he told them that he knew all that was in their hearts—and pronounced sentence. As he

A Temple "worse than any Spanish slaughterhouse"

did so, Spanish musketeers opened fire from the surrounding rooftops; by Cortes' own admission, more than 3,000 men died in the next two hours. It was a massacre, and he has been bitterly condemned for ordering it. Yet it is difficult to see what else Cortes could have done. He was not normally a bloodthirsty man—never once in the whole campaign did he resort to force unnecessarily.

The journey from Cholula to the capital—a fifty-mile-long march that led the conquistadors up between the twin volcanoes that guard the southeastern approaches to the city and over a pass 12,000 feet high—must have been the most grueling of all, On the other side of the pass, the road began to descend, and the Spaniards suddenly found themselves gazing down on a huge lake that sparkled in the sun. In the midst of that lake, linked to its shores by three slender causeways, was the city of Tenochtitlan.

On November 8, 1519, Hernando Cortes led four hundred tired and bedraggled soldiers along the southern causeway into the Aztec capital. Another, different procession approached from the opposite direction: the emperor himself, in his golden palanquin, was riding out to meet his god. The scene must have been a strange one.

The great Montezuma descended from his litter, and the other great chieftains supported him beneath a marvelously rich canopy of green feathers, decorated with gold, silver and pearls ... And there were other great lords who walked before the great Montezuma, laying down cloaks so that his feet should not touch the earth. Not one dared to raise his eyes towards him.

Dismounting from his horse, Cortes strode smiling toward the emperor—and now for the first time, the Old World and the New stood face to face.

This first encounter with Montezuma made a deep impression on the Spaniards—as did the emperor's address of welcome, in which he greeted Cortes as a king and a god, spoke of promises and prophecies and seemed virtually to be offering the Spanish leader the throne of Mexico. Despite Montezuma's effusive greeting, Cortes remained on his guard; although he was being treated as an honored guest, he had not forgotten that he was on an island fortress in a distant land, with only a handful of men and no lines of communication to the outside world. He followed Montezuma to a great palace that had been prepared for his reception.

At the age of fifty-two, Montezuma was tall and slim, with fine eyes and, as Bernal Diaz put it, "an expression that was at once tender and grave." In the weeks that followed, the Spaniards grew to love and respect the Aztec ruler, not only for his prodigious generosity but even more for his extraordinary natural grace and charm. Montezuma soon knew the conquistadors by name, and they in turn treated him in a manner befitting his rank. Cortes had, meanwhile, told Montezuma of his own Emperor, Charles v—the sovereign to whom the Aztecs were henceforth obliged to acknowledge their allegiance. They seemed to accept this condition readily enough; it was when the conversation turned

to religion that Montezuma's jaw seemed to tighten. Nonetheless, he willingly agreed to Cortes' request to be allowed to visit the great temple.

That visit was a nightmare that none of the members of Cortes' party ever forgot. "The walls of the shrines," wrote Bernal Diaz, "were so caked with blood, and the floor so bathed in it, that the stench was worse than that of any slaughterhouse in Spain." In the topmost sanctuary, before the idols, lay five human hearts, still warm and steaming; around the altar, their long hair matted with gore, stood the priests who performed the sacrifices and who afterwards ceremonially ate the limbs of their victims.

Montezuma, who seemed unable to comprehend his guests' revulsion, remained gentle and dignified amid those charnel horrors. Cortes saw that however ready the Aztec ruler might be to pay lip-service to the throne of Spain, he had no intention of forsaking his old gods. Somehow his authority would have to be undermined, while the Spaniards' own security was increased. Cortes therefore took a step that, in so precarious a position, few but he would have dared—he made Montezuma his hostage. As Cortes was careful to explain when he broke the news to Montezuma, the emperor was not a prisoner. His "captivity" would amount to nothing more than a change of residence; the day-to-day business of government would still be in the emperor's hands alone.

By the beginning of the year 1520 the conquest of Mexico might have seemed over. But suddenly Cortes' luck changed: the Spanish authorities in Cuba, infuriated by his insubordination and frantic with jealousy at his successes, dispatched a punitive expedition which Cortes destroyed.

Meanwhile, disaster had struck in the capital. In May, during an annual religious festival, Alvarado had suddenly suspected a plot against his garrison. Losing his head, he and his men had charged into the temple precinct, killing every Indian present.

An Aztec priest's knife, with a handle of wood set with mosaic.

Fighting in Tenochtitlán: Spanish cavalry and infantry with their Indian allies attack the temple.

yeqtla ti tetzavitl yn mal ques.

The death of Montezuma

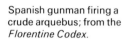

Spanish gunman firing a crude arquebus; from the *Florentine Codex.*

Right A friar describes the ceremonial of the province of Mexico to the Viceroy, De Mendoza, while native priests look on.

The title page of the *Codex Mendoza.*

More than a thousand natives, including the flower of the young Aztec nobility, were slaughtered, and within an hour the whole city was up in arms. Since that time the Spaniards had been blockaded in their palace. Thanks to Montezuma's intervention there had been no further bloodshed—but Montezuma's influence was waning. An opposition party, resolved to rid Mexico of the Spaniards once and for all, had arisen. And on the very evening that Cortes returned to the capital, a specially convened Aztec Council of State had deposed the emperor from his throne and selected his nephew Cuauhtémoc as his successor.

By morning the atmosphere had changed from passive sullenness to active hostility. For four days the Spaniards defended themselves as best they could against incessant Indian attacks, but on the fifth, seeing that the situation was hopeless, Cortes sent to Montezuma and asked him to negotiate a truce. The Spanish envoy found the ex-emperor sunk in despair. There was nothing he could do, he claimed—his friendship for Cortes had cost him his crown, and his people would no longer listen to him. He agreed to make one final effort, however, and for the last time he donned his robes of state and stepped out onto the terrace above the great square.

As Montezuma emerged, the howling mob below fell silent in a spontaneous surge of sympathy for the deposed monarch. Then, suddenly, a volley of stones was launched at the emperor. One of them struck Montezuma on the head, and he fell to the ground. The Spaniards carried him to his quarters, and Cortes himself hastened to the battered ruler's side. The wound did not seem particularly grave, but Montezuma had apparently lost the will to live. By nightfall he was dead.

Montezuma had been a noble and a tragic figure. He had foreseen, in a way that Cortes had not, that the fall of his empire was to be inevitable and total. Although mistaken in his belief that Cortes was a god, Montezuma could no more have prevented the conquest than if it had been divinely ordained.

His friendship with Cortes—for whose sake he ultimately gave both his throne and his life—was founded not on cowardice but on wisdom, for he had understood that violence could not prevail. Little more than a year after his death, Montezuma's premonitions were to be proved correct.

Cortes' last hope of remaining in the city perished with Montezuma. He knew that he must retreat—and fast. That night, when the crowds had dispersed, he and his soldiers slipped silently from their quarters and began their march along the western causeway (which was shorter than the southern one, and promised to be less well guarded). The Aztecs had not been deceived, however. The silence was suddenly shattered by the blast of a conch-shell trumpet. Suddenly the waters on each side of the causeway were alive with war-canoes, whose occupants showered arrows on the retreating Spaniards. In the chaos and carnage that followed, Cortes lost more than half his soldiers—many of whom died not from wounds but by drowning, weighed down by the pocketfuls of Aztec gold that they had been unable to resist carrying off with them. That dreadful night, June 30, 1520, was afterwards known as the *Noche Triste*—the Night of Sorrow.

Spanish sufferings did not end when what was left of the shattered column reached dry land. It was another two hundred miles and twelve agonizing days—during which the survivors were attacked by a huge Aztec army at Otumba and, miraculously, routed it—before they at last reached Tlaxcala and safety.

Few other commanders, after such a debâcle,

would have dreamed of continuing the campaign, but Cortes was still determined to re-enter the capital in triumph. He immediately set about the task of rebuilding his soldiers' strength and morale and collecting reinforcements. The *Noche Triste* had taught Cortes that he could never trust the causeways again. Therefore, at Tlaxcala, two hundred miles from the sea and 7,000 feet above it, he began to construct a fleet of thirteen shallow-draft brigantines, specially designed so that they could be dismantled into easily portable sections and reassembled on the shores of the lake surrounding Tenochtitlan. By Christmas all was ready; and on December 28 Cortes led some 550 Spaniards—roughly the same number as had accompanied him on his first expedition, but this time augmented by some 10,000 Indian allies and forty horses—back into the valley of Mexico. A base camp was set up at Texcoco, on the eastern shore of the lake, and while the brigantines were being prepared for action, the Spanish leader sent messages across the water to the new emperor, Cuauhtémoc, calling on him to surrender.

As Spanish strength had grown, so the Aztecs' had declined. Their capital had suddenly been struck by a new and dreadful scourge almost certainly introduced by the invaders—smallpox. Having no hereditary resistance to it, the Indians had perished by the thousands.

The final assault on the Aztec capital began in April, 1521. Victory proved far more elusive than the Spaniards had expected. The brigantines were invaluable, but they could not be everywhere at once, and attack after attack was driven back across the causeways. At last Cortes saw that there was only one solution—the slow, systematic annihilation of the city—and he therefore ordered his men to destroy the houses and the streets one by one, using the rubble to fill in the canals. The Aztecs fought on, but by the end of July the southern half of their city was a heap of ruins. The southern and western spearheads of the Spanish attack, led by Cortes and Alvarado respectively, met in the great marketplace of Tlatelolco. Bernal Diaz again described the scene:

On the way we passed through a small square, where there were wooden poles on which they had impaled the heads of many of our Spaniards whom they had killed and sacrificed during the recent battles. Their hair and beards had grown much longer than they were in life; which I never would have believed if I had not seen it.

Next to the marketplace was the high temple through which Montezuma had guided Cortes less than two years before. A party of Spaniards climbed to its top, set the shrines on fire, cast the idols down the steps and planted their banners. When the Aztecs saw the eagles of Spain fluttering from their highest pyramid, they knew that they had lost—yet the twenty-six-year-old Cuauhtémoc refused to surrender. Instead he made a valiant effort to escape to the mainland to continue his resistance from there, and it was only when the fastest of the brigantines overtook him that he finally gave himself up.

Bernal Diaz summed up the siege of Tenochtitlan:

During the whole ninety-three days of the siege there was the unceasing noise of their accursed drums and trumpets, and their melancholy battle-drums in the shrines and on the temple-towers. But after Cuauhtémoc's capture all of us soldiers became deaf—as if all the bells in a belfry had been ringing together and then suddenly stopped.

Thus, on the evening of August 13, 1521, the city of Tenochtitlan finally fell and with it fell the Aztec empire. Men still argue over the rights and wrongs of the conquest, some maintaining that imperialist aggression can never be condoned, others, insisting that Mexico was enriched by her Spanish colonial experience, and that Cortes was justified in eliminating the bloodiest civilization the world has known.

There is no statue of the conqueror in modern Mexico City, but in the Square of the Three Cultures, the spot where Cuauhtémoc acknowledged the end of his empire, a marble plaque provides what is perhaps the wisest epilogue of all:

It was neither a victory nor a defeat. It was the painful birth of that commingled people that is the Mexico of today.   JOHN JULIUS NORWICH

The death of the Aztec leader, Montezuma, from the *Codex Mendoza*.

Cardinal Wolsey falls from power as Henry

The entry of Hadrian VI to Rome, a detail from his tomb.

Optimists in Europe believed that a forceful pope would be able to bring peace to Italy, settle the religious issue in Germany and inspire the West to stand firm against the Turk—and when Adrian of Utrecht was elected as successor to Leo x in 1523, men's hopes were renewed. Adrian vi brought to Rome a reputation for statesmanship and scholarship. As tutor to the future Charles v, Adrian had succeeded Cardinal Ximenes as effective ruler of Spain. His election to the papal throne surprised but did not frighten Adrian, who immediately set about planning a series of long overdue reforms which would end the abuses that had made Renaissance Rome synonymous with corruption.

The Italian cardinals did not take to the Dutch professor of divinity, a northerner whom they considered indifferent to artistic beauty and classical antiquity. Their distaste was obviated by Adrian's death only a few months after he was elevated. The loss was an especially unfortunate one, for Adrian's personal qualities were such that, had he lived, his pontificate would surely have been a remarkable one. His successor, Clement vii (1523–34), was a Medici, brought up in the household of the great Lorenzo. Clement had come to dominate the College of Cardinals during the pontificate of his cousin, Leo x, and had proved to be an efficient second-in-command. As Pope, Clement revealed his Medici blood. He seemed more concerned with the salvaging of his temporal possessions than with the salvation of Italy.

A fundamental problem of contemporary politics was the future of French power in Italy. Prospero Colonna brought an imperialist army to Italy in 1522 to drive the French from Milan and restore the Sforza family to power. The French

army's defeat only encouraged Francis I to launch additional campaigns to regain his lost holdings. In subsequent undertakings, the French King's greatest handicap was not a lack of funds to finance those expeditions but the defection of the Duke of Bourbon to Charles v. When an army led by Admiral Bonnivet and the Chevalier Bayard invaded Lombardy in 1524, Bourbon routed them, laid waste to Provence and put Marseille under siege. That winter, the undaunted Francis I crossed the Mont Cenis Pass, easily took Milan and opened the siege of Pavia.

In February, 1525, Bourbon led a well-disciplined army of Spaniards and imperialists to Pavia's aid. The French and their Swiss allies were routed, and casualties exceeded those inflicted in the battle of Marignano some ten years before. Roughly 14,000 men were slain, including Richard de la Pole, pretender to the earldom of Suffolk and the throne of England. Many of the deaths were attributed to the fact that the Spanish infantry used muskets for the first time in the history of warfare. Francis was taken prisoner and transported to Madrid, where months later he had to purchase his release by sur-

Pope Clement VII, more interested in Italian politics than in theology.

rendering the Duchy of Burgundy.

Fearing Charles' domination of Italy, Pope Clement vii soon formed the League of Cognac, an offensive alliance designed to undo the harsh Treaty of Madrid. The League hoped to force Charles to give Francesco Sforza independent sovereignty over Milan and its members planned to press for recognition of the ancient liberties of several other Italian states. All eyes were on Rome in August, 1526, as Cardinal Pompe Colonna plundered the city and forced the Pope to take refuge in the Castle of St. Angelo. In May, 1527, imperial troops under the Duke of Bourbon's command mutinied, looted the city's treasures and killed 4,000 Roman citizens. Bourbon himself was slain and it was nine months before fire, bloodshed and pillage gave place to order. The second sack of Rome marked the end of an epoch: the age of Renaissance Rome as the center of learning and of the arts was over.

The Pope was in as much danger as his city. Besieged in the Castle of St. Angelo for six months, he at last agreed to the Emperor's terms, which included crowning Charles and calling a general council of the Church to deal with the Lutheran problem in the Empire. A day before his scheduled release from St. Angelo, Clement escaped to Orvieto, and in June, 1529, he finally came to terms with Charles v. They agreed that the Medici would be permitted to return to Florence and the Sforzas to Milan—and that Charles would attempt to encourage towns in the Papal States to return to Clement's obedience. Six months later France signed the ignominious Peace of Cambrai, nicknamed "The Ladies' Peace" because it was negotiated by Charles' Aunt Margaret and Louise of Savoy, the Queen-Mother of France. That treaty confirmed Hapsburg rule in Italy, and required Francis I to renounce his claims on the peninsula and his sovereignty over Flanders and Artois in the Low Countries.

Thomas Wolsey

By 1520, Thomas Wolsey was preeminent in England. His power was symbolized by his two residences, Hampton Court and York Place (later Whitehall), both of which were built out of ecclesiastical revenues and the fat fees that he received as Lord Chancellor.

His palaces were the envy of every Englishman, including the King. No Englishman had ever wielded such authority, for Wolsey was both King Henry's chief minister and the Pope's legate—an unprecedented combination of powers. His high-handed rule weakened the Church's resistance to subsequent royal demands—and consequently lay people became antipapal, if not also anti-clerical.

In 1527 Wolsey had become ensnared in negotiations with the

Cardinal Wolsey, who dominated English politics for fifteen years, and fell from power when he proved unable to obtain an annulment of Henry's marriage.

Pope about the validity of Henry's marriage to Catherine of Aragon. Catherine had failed to give Henry a legitimate male heir, and the King was bent on divorce, legally sanctified by Rome. But because Charles v was Catherine's nephew and—unprompted—took her part, the chances of obtaining a favorable ruling from Clement vii, the Emperor's puppet, was remote. For one brief moment, when Clement was seriously ill, Wolsey had hopes of becoming pope himself, but Clement recovered and Wolsey, who knew Henry only too well, realized that he could not remain his chief minister much longer. For all his claims to having influenced events in the courts of Europe, the Cardinal had failed to achieve Henry's wishes. In 1525 he presented the King with Hampton Court and in October, 1529, he gave him York Place as well. Wolsey had fallen from power—and Parliament was as determined as Henry had been to seek revenge. Stripped of all his offices except the Archbishopric of York, Wolsey retired

VIII breaks with Rome

to the north. Within a few months he was arrested as a suspected traitor and he died on the way to London.

Henry VIII was to achieve his divorce by uniting in his own person—as King and Supreme Head of the Church—the same powers that Wolsey had accumulated as Lord Chancellor and Cardinal-legate.

Peasant Revolts

In June, 1524, warfare of a different kind broke out in the West as peasants living on the estates of Count von Lupfen in the Black Forest took up arms to abolish serfdom, feudal services and enclosures, and the payment of tithes. The movement spread rapidly into the Rhineland, Swabia and Franconia and later reached Bavaria, the Tyrol and Alsace. Manifestoes were drawn up which lent an air of respectability to the looting and slaughter that followed. Thomas Munzer, a prist from Saxony who signed orders "The Sword of the Lord and of Gideon," attempted to impose some sort of order on the rebels. But after several initial successes, the peasant army was encircled at Frankenhausen, and in May, 1525, Munzer was executed. Martin Luther, who had disowned the rebels' challenge to secular authority, preached against their political attitudes.

Zwingli of Zurich

Shortly after Luther published his *Theses* in Wittenberg, a very different sort of reformer began to revitalize the life of Zurich. After studying at Vienna University, where he was disciplined for rowdyism, Urich Zwingli (1484–1531) took holy orders and developed his own approach to Humanism. The publication of Erasmus' Greek New Testament added a new dimension to Zwingli's theology, and by the time that he was appointed priest of the Great Minster at Zurich he had grounded his faith on the Bible.

Despite his weak voice, Zwingli was a remarkable preacher. He denounced the sale of indulgences, fasting, the celibacy of the clergy and the use of mercenary armies (in which so many men from the Swiss cantons served). His 1523 dispute with the Bishop of Constance led Zwingli to draw up a set of fundamental articles of religion and to promote disputations on them. Zwingli converted the citizens of Zurich, who demonstrated their faith by removing all images from their churches and refusing to accept episcopal jurisdiction. In 1525, Zwingli completed his liturgical reforms, supplanting the Latin Mass with a service stressing the commemorative nature of the Lord's Supper.

As leader of Zurich, Zwingli envisioned his city as the cornerstone of a wide evangelical confederation—and in 1529 he founded the Christian Civic League as a first step toward achieving that goal. Berne, Basel and Constance joined the league immediately and Strasbourg joined a short time later. In 1529 the League went to war with the Catholic Forest Cantons, which were defeated and forced to abandon their alliance with Austria. That same year Zwingli journeyed to Marburg at the invitation of Philip of Hesse and took part in a disputation with Luther. Philip hoped to effect a reconciliation between the two reformers, but the chasm proved to be too deep.

Zwingli's militancy provoked a second war with the Catholic cantons in 1531, and at the decisive battle of Kappel he was killed. The subsequent peace treaty divided the Swiss Confederation into Protestant cantons—principally Zurich, Berne, Geneva and Basel—and Catholic cantons—notably Lucerne and Freiburg—and that division persisted. As a Catholic soldier noted on the battlefield at Kappel, Zwingli was "a rotten heretic, but a good confederate."

The Reformation reaches Scandinavia

By comparison, the Protestant Reformation made rapid strides in Scandinavia. The kings of Denmark still claimed to rule the three Scandinavian kingdoms under the terms of the Union of Kalmar (1396), but opposition to Danish rule in Sweden had become persistent. The Danish kings imposed a heavy tribute on the Swedish nobility in an effort to force the Swedes to recognize their claims to that country's throne. Christian II, who succeeded to the Danish throne in 1513, was determined to press his claim by force. He defeated a Swedish peasant army on the ice of Lake Asunden in January of 1520. Ston Sture, the leader of Swedish resistance, perished in the battle but his widow, Christina, defended

Catherine of Aragon, who was divorced by Henry VIII.

Stockholm for eight months before surrendering. Christian promised the city amnesty, but after his hurried coronation he summoned an assembly to Stockholm Castle and, with the assistance of Swedish Archbishop Gustavus Trolle, took action against Christina Sture, many nobles, two bishops and the chief burgesses of the city. Trolle was anxious to revenge himself on the nationalist party (which had deposed him in 1517) by extracting a heavy fine—but Christian was out for blood. On November 8, 1520, after a mock trial for heresy, some ninety leading Swedes were executed in the city's market place. The event, known as "The Stockholm Bloodbath," earned its instigator the name "Christian the Tyrant."

Sweden was rescued from Danish tyranny by Gustavus Vasa, a rebel whose father and other relations had been slaughtered at Stockholm. A year before the "Bloodbath," Vasa had launched a campaign to sever Sweden from the Union of Kalmar. He had fallen into Christian II's hands but escaped.

But in January, 1521, Vasa returned to the province of Dalarna —long a center of nationalist resistance—and was promptly elected to lead the peasant army that began the reduction of castles in Danish hands. Increasing numbers of prominent Swedes came over to Gustavus, but Stockholm held out. Fortunately for Gustavus, a rebellion—provoked by Christian's heavy taxation and his quarrel with the Church—broke out in Denmark at this point and the King was deposed in favor of his uncle Frederick. In June, 1523, a fully representative Rikstag unanimously elected Vasa King of Sweden.

Gustavus was the creator of modern Sweden. For years the independence of his state had to be vigorously defended against its Scandinavian and Baltic neighbors —and even from Emperor Charles v. The outstanding event of Gustavus' reign came in 1527, when he severed Sweden's ties with the Church and adopted Lutheranism. The Swedish monarchy had always been elective, but Gustavus feared that his cherished work might be endangered by faction, and in 1544 he established the Vasa dynasty. Gustavus left to his successor an independent nation state, solvent, effectively administered and defended by a superb army. The new Sweden was soon to become an important factor in European politics.

Titian

Titian (1490–1576), the greatest of all Venetian artists, is often considered the founder of modern painting. His contemporary fame was based on the *Bacchanals*, which he painted for the Duke of Ferrara, and on the outsize painting of *The Assumption* in the Frari Church in Venice. Titian eventually aban-

Ulrich Zwingli, who converted Zurich to Protestantism.

doned religious themes for those of classical mythology and for portraiture. The friend of kings and popes, he established what subsequent generations would come to regard as "the official portrait" concept. Titian's later style, with its disregard for contours, was in some respects "Impressionistic," and his technique was equally remarkable. The master constantly revised his canvases and, according to one of his pupils, if he "found something in a painting that displeased him, he went to work like a surgeon."

1520

A Bible for the Masses

The astounding thing about the vernacular version of the New Testament that appeared in Germany in the fall of 1533 was not that it was an able and often forceful translation, but that it existed at all. The translator, the controversial Wittenberg monk Martin Luther, had recently been excommunicated by the Pope—who recognized only the Latin Vulgate Bible—and had been banned by Emperor Charles V. The printer and publishers of "Luther's Bible"—the first complete translation of the New Testament into any vernacular tongue—were therefore taking grave risks in backing the outspoken monk's enterprise. Their gamble paid off handsomely, however; Hans Lufft, Luther's printer, sold nearly 100,000 copies of the monk's Bible. In one bold stroke, Luther had reached the largest lay audience in history—and in so doing, had proved the power of Europe's fledgling popular presses.

During the last days of September, 1522, an extraordinary book was published in Wittenberg, Saxony, a German town of three thousand inhabitants. The volume's short title, printed in highly ornamental Gothic letters, was *Das Newe Testament Deutzsch—Vuittemberg (The German New Testament—Wittenberg)*. No publication date was given, and the name of the translator was not mentioned. The name of the printer, Melchoir Lotter the Younger, and the names of the publishers, the painter Lucas Cranach and his partner Christian Doering, were also omitted. The format, a smallish folio, included twenty-one woodcuts created in the workshop of Lucas Cranach and devoted exclusively to the last section of the book, *Revelation*. The edition appeared in 3,000 copies, each priced at half a gulden, approximately the weekly wage of the best-paid craftsmen of the age.

The printing and publishing of this undated vernacular version of the New Testament had been undertaken in great haste and in full secrecy; the translator, the Wittenberg monk and professor Martin Luther, was under the ban of Emperor Charles V—in addition to his excommunication by the Pope. Names had been omitted for fear that the imperial edict, which threatened anyone who assisted the condemned heretic, might be applied to the printers or to the entire community. Despite those fears, the edition, the first full translation of the New Testament from the original Greek into a vernacular tongue, was soon sold out and a reprint with corrections was issued in December of the same year. At the same time, a pirated edition came out in the Swiss city of Basel, the greatest center of printing and publishing in Europe.

During the next several years, Luther published parts of the Old Testament, which he translated from the original Hebrew with the assistance of collaborators. In 1534, the first complete German-language edition of the Bible was printed in Wittenberg by Hans Lufft, who was to serve as the main printer of the work for decades and who as a result became one of the richest men in the town. Luther himself never received any remuneration for the nearly 100,000 copies of the "Luther Bible" that Hans Lufft printed.

In addition to Lufft's editions, authorized and unauthorized versions of Luther's translation abounded. Pirated editions outnumbered legitimate ones by at least four to one. A form of copyright, granted by special privilege of a local prince, was in existence at the time but in Luther's case this protection was valid only for the dukedom of Saxony—or, to be more precise, for that half of Saxony ruled by the Elector, Luther's patron. In the other half of the country, which was controlled by Luther's enemy Duke George, the monk's books were banned and his Bible was immediately supplanted by another edition. The text of that version, purportedly written by the court-chaplain Emser, was taken without compunction from the Lutheran translation, with some added "corrections." Many other Catholic editions of the time made use of this procedure.

The Holy Roman Empire was without a central authority in the early sixteenth century. The division of the Empire into self-governing principalities—imperial free towns and countless independent possessions held by archbishops, bishops, prince-abbots and mere counts, each eagerly defending his rights or what he called his "liberties"—made it possible to set up printing presses everywhere and to publish almost any book, however dangerous or seditious it might be. Ecclesiastical as well as temporal censorship did indeed exist, but they could be applied only locally; a book suppressed at one place would soon appear at some other place, often in a remote town where the printer was on good terms with his magistrate. This state of affairs, although politically lamentable, accounted for the rapid spread of printing in sixteenth-century Europe. In particular, Bible printing became commonplace, although vernacular versions of the Bible were still

Title of Luther's translation of the New Testament—the first Bible to be translated into German, published in 1522 by Melchior Lotter.

Opposite A woodcut of Luther, 1520, while he was still an Augustinian.

A printing shop in the late-fifteenth century, from a *memento mori*.

Below right The church at Wittenberg where Luther posted his ninety-five theses on October 31, 1517.

regarded as dangerous by ecclesiastical authorities.

Luther himself enjoyed the huge success of his translation and wrote only: "It is easy to plough a field that has been cleared. But no one wants to uproot the forest and tree trunks and put the field in order." He did become irritated, however, when his qualifications as a Biblical scholar were questioned. He retorted: "You are doctors? So am I. You are theologians? So am I. But I can expound the Psalms and the Prophets. You cannot do this. I can translate. You cannot do this." And when incorrectly printed and garbled editions of his work began to appear in rapid succession, he exclaimed: "They do that snip-snap: Money, that's what they are after."

Luther could indeed translate, and in time his work was recognized as the decisive event in the development of the modern German language.

During his own lifetime, Luther's Bible became the cornerstone of the Reformation. It was Luther's belief that Scripture should be the sole guide, the supreme authority in matters of faith. This view was in direct opposition to the tenets of the Roman Catholic Church, which, in Luther's words, "places the Pope above Scripture and says he cannot err."

This principle of "sola scriptura"—Scripture alone—had been Luther's guide and weapon from the beginning of his rebellion against Church stricture. In 1521, one year before the publication of his New Testament, Luther journeyed to the German city of Worms, where, at the invitation of the Emperor, he defended his views before an assembled Church Diet. In his famous final declaration before Charles v and the assembled prelates, Luther declared: "Unless I am convinced by testimony from the Holy Scriptures . . . I am bound by my conscience and the Word of God." The enraged Emperor issued an imperial edict banning Luther as a heretic and rebel against authority. His decree, the most comprehensive edict of general censorship in modern times, also imposed strict supervision of all printed productions, including leaflets, posters, woodcuts and pictures; no one was permitted to "compose, write, print, paint, sell, buy or secretly keep such productions." Luther's answer was the publication of his Bible.

On his return from Worms, Luther was intercepted by the emissaries of his patron, the Elector of Saxony, and brought in secret to Wartburg. There he wrote the first draft of his translation.

A few words must be said about the extraordinary circumstances under which a work of such magnitude and difficulty was undertaken. Luther labored

 Black Letter

 Aldus Roman

 Aldus Italic

Aldus Manutius (Manuci)

Johann Froben

Geofroy Tory

Robert Estienne

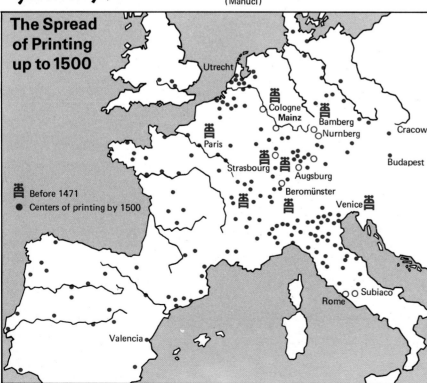

The Spread of Printing up to 1500

Before 1471
Centers of printing by 1500

Utrecht
Cologne
Mainz
Bamberg
Nurnberg
Cracow
Paris
Strasbourg
Augsburg
Beromünster
Budapest
Venice
Rome
Subiaco
Valencia

A tract-writing Junker

without aid from the outside. He had only a handful of books at hand, and he did not have access to any libraries other than his own meager one. During this period, Luther disguised himself as a Junker. He sported a beard and carried a sword at his side. To the great annoyance of his protector and his entourage, who wanted him to keep quiet, Luther wrote numerous letters and tracts from his hiding-place.

Only during the last weeks of his seclusion did the fugitive start on his great translating task. He had nothing to work with except the Greek New Testament published by Erasmus of Rotterdam eight years earlier, the Latin Vulgate, the only officially recognized version of the Bible (which Luther had known more or less by heart since his monastery days), and perhaps two or three books more. It took the monk no more than ten weeks to finish his translation; a mere copyist would have been pressed just to copy the entire text from an existing original in this amount of time, at the standard rate of ten pages a day. Speed was crucial, for Luther was extremely eager to return to Wittenberg, where serious disturbances had arisen among his followers.

Luther therefore broke out of his prison—in defiance of the express order of his protector—and went to Wittenberg, where he corrected the rough draft of his manuscript with the help of his friend, Philip Melanchthon, a twenty-five-year-old professor at the university who was already recognized as one of the most eminent classical scholars of the age. In the midst of the dissension that was shaking the little town to its foundations, the monk's text went into print on three presses at the same time. Luther's concern over such minutiae as the typography of his volume led him to replace his slovenly former printer with Melchoir Lotter, who did his work so well that the list of errata at the end of the first edition of Luther's Bible contained only a handful of minor errors. (There were no major printer's errors like the one contained in the English Bible of 1631. That version, called the "wicked Bible," omitted the word "not" from the Seventh Commandment.)

In the eyes of the Church, Luther's grave and unforgivable error was in undertaking his task in the first place. The Latin text of the Vulgate was the only accepted one, and to translate it into the vernacular was considered an act of willful interpretation, dangerous and possibly heretical. The fight to make the Bible available in the "vulgar tongue" had indeed attached itself to great schismatic movements throughout the centuries of Church history. The Waldensians and Albigensians, heretical sects that sprang up in southern France at the end of the twelfth century, had their own translations of the Bible—and both were equally condemned by the Church.

The first German translations of the Bible were produced in Bohemia during the fourteenth century. These manuscripts were written in secret and distributed clandestinely under threat of death; to be found in possession of a vernacular Bible was often

The burning of John Huss after his condemnation by the Council of Constance in 1415.

Part of a page of Wycliffe's Bible : those who translated the Bible into the vernacular were always suspected of heresy.

The first impact of printing on the masses

sufficient evidence to condemn a man to the stake. The smell of burning hangs on each surviving copy of these Bibles. No Albigensian translations have been preserved, but in spite of severe suppression, more than two hundred manuscript versions of Wycliffe's translation, as well as other medieval versions, are still extant.

The publication of each of these editions was a religious, social and political event of the greatest consequence. The masses—the poor to whom Wycliffe sent out his "poor priests"—wanted to have access to the Word of God in their own language. The fifteenth-century Hussite movement presented the Church, and governments as well, the frightening spectacle of a great rising of the common people, under the banner of Biblical inspiration combined with strong national and social aims. Luther was, therefore, initially accused by his adversaries of being a "Bohemian," a "second Hus."

Persecution of religious dissenters was rampant throughout Europe. William Tyndale, the first to translate the Bible into modern idiomatic English, printed his work at Cologne and Worms in 1524, two years after Luther's New Testament first appeared. Tyndale, whose translation was strongly influenced by Luther's model, perished at the stake. Only a pitiful single fragment of his first edition of the New Testament has been preserved. Later reprints, brought over to England from Antwerp, were publicly burned at Paul's Cross. The list of "Bible-martyrs" is a long one, as is the list of strict prohibitions against the printing or reading of those martyrs' translations. In Spain, all translations in the "vulgar tongue" were placed on the first Index printed by the Inquisition in 1551. Shortly after Luther's death, the Spanish representatives at the Council of Trent described all renderings into the vernacular as "mothers of heresy."

Luther's undertaking had another important meaning, as the crowning achievement of the great Humanist movement. "*Ad fontes*"—back to original sources—had been the watchword of Renaissance scholars. The phrase, applied at first to the Greek and Latin classics, later came to include the greatest

monument of antiquity, the Bible. It was known, of course, that the Bible had originally been written in Hebrew and Greek, but only the Latin Vulgate, derived from a translation made by St. Jerome in the fourth century, was officially recognized by the Church. By 1500, scholars had grown dissatisfied with this state of affairs. Italian Jews printed the Hebrew text of the Old Testament, and in 1516 the Dutch scholar Erasmus published his Greek New Testament. The Dutchman's move was a bold and dangerous one, and only the considerable prestige enjoyed by the man universally recognized as Europe's greatest living scholar saved Erasmus from prosecution. As criticism went further, many differences between the original text and the Latin translation were detected, indicating how corrupted the official version of the Bible had become in the course of more than a thousand years.

From the Church's point of view, however, every single word of the Vulgate remained sacrosanct and unalterable; it was still the basis of Church dogma and of the body of usages, including the smallest details of the worship service. Interpretation of ecclesiastical law, based on the Vulgate, was conducted exclusively by the appointed doctors of the Church, and subject to final sanction by the Pope. Any textual criticism was considered an attack on Church tradition, rather than a philosophical exercise. Indeed, the official revision of the old Latin text of the Vulgate itself, reluctantly recognized as inevitable, was only undertaken at the end of the

St. Luke painting an icon: a picture from Luther's German edition of the Bible, 1540.

sixteenth century. In some instances, arguments regarding the placement of a single comma in the revised Vulgate raged for years.

Luther was not concerned with commas. He translated the Latin text to the best of his ability and with considerable command of Biblical scholarship. The style and sweep of his language has been admired even by his enemies, and his powerful German has been marveled at—particularly since Luther had been educated, from boyhood onwards, exclusively in Latin. During his long years in the monastery and his first academic career, the monk had been obliged to express himself in that language; how he acquired his rich and flexible German vocabulary therefore remains a mystery. It was only in his thirty-fifth year that Luther suddenly broke out of the prison of an alien language—and into the freedom of his native speech. His little tract entitled "On Indulgences and Grace," which followed immediately upon the steps of his *Ninety-five Theses,* was Luther's first German-language publication. It was immediately reprinted, and twenty different pirated editions were soon being sold.

Historically speaking, the publication of Luther's Bible marked the first time that the medium of printing had made a profound impact on the masses of the people. With one bold stroke, Luther had reached a public of incomparably larger dimensions than any former revolutionary or reformer had dreamed of. He continued the fight with his well-

Luther's friend and ally Melanchthon, by Dürer.

Left An engraving of Desiderius Erasmus of Rotterdam, one of the leading humanists of the sixteenth century, by Albrecht Dürer.

The teaching of Christ compared with the teaching of Antichrist; a Lutheran attack on the Roman Church.

Luther with Melanchthon's version of the Bible in Greek and Hebrew: an illustration by Cranach from Luther's translation of the Bible.

known pamphlets and books, and it has been estimated that during the first decade of his public struggle, nearly a quarter of the works published in Germany came from his pen.

Despite the futile edict issued by Emperor Charles v at Worms, printing increased by leaps and bounds in those years. In addition to pamphlets, broadsides, tracts and books, pictorial propaganda became a very powerful weapon as well. It was aimed at the still largely illiterate public, a very large proportion of which was converted to Lutheranism by this means of communication. The papal nuncio, who had been sent to Worms to deal swiftly with the heretical Wittenberg monk, wrote home in near-despair. He counseled the Pope that almost nine-tenths of the Empire had become Lutheran, and that the rest cried out against "Roman tyranny." The publication of Luther's Bible was unquestionably the greatest and most lasting achievement of this period, and therefore that date of September, 1522, may be regarded as no less important than those of such well-known historical events as the publication of Luther's *Theses* in 1517 or his stand at the Diet of Worms in 1521.

Statistical figures about book sales do not tell the whole picture, however. It is not true, as has been repeatedly said, that the Bible was, for all practical purposes, "unknown" before Luther's version appeared. The Latin text of the Bible had been printed on the presses of Gutenberg and his companions at Mainz, in 1450–55, and many editions had followed. There had even been earlier unauthorized German translations, printed during the fifteenth century. More than a dozen of these works, mostly taken from texts printed in the previous century, were in existence. Extracts from Biblical texts, homilies and commentaries abounded.

Nevertheless, the demand for the whole text, the clear and unfettered Word of God, printed in the language of the people, remained and became irresistible. The older editions, written in Latin or in out-dated and halting vernacular, were not read by the people; they were intended for scholars, well-to-do persons or great libraries, and their cost was forbidding (the price of a single volume amounting in earlier times to the value of a good-sized town house). It is significant that a large number of these books have been preserved in excellent condition. By contrast, very few copies of the early printings of Luther's Bible are still extant, and those often badly mutilated from constant re-reading.

In those countries where the book was admitted, Luther's Bible became the great formative influence over the next centuries. The imposing figures regarding distribution of the Scriptures that were published by the great Bible societies in the nineteenth century pale almost into insignificance if compared with the number of old family Bibles in the sixteenth and seventeenth centuries. These volumes were, more often than not, the only book in the house, the only family possession of value, bequeathed from one generation to the next, and consequently bearing the family tree on the fly-leaf. No statistical figures will tell us how often those editions were read aloud to the whole household, servants included. One could, however, design a map of sixteenth-century Europe that divided the Continent into Bible-reading and non-Bible-reading regions. In central France, for instance, the Catholic Church continued to struggle with the stubborn, Bible-reading Jansenists, long after the Huguenots had been thoroughly eliminated.

Bible reading was not an unmitigated blessing. The Roman Church had reservations about individual interpretations of the Scriptures, and Luther himself was forced to struggle, from the time he printed his first draft, with what he called the "heavenly prophets" who interpreted the text in their own light, according to inspiration they claimed to receive from above. Many sects and movements, such as the Spiritualists and the Anabaptists, evolved during this period. Some of these groups developed valuable versions of their own. Bible reading, no longer restricted to matters of faith and religion, became the basis for studies of social and political developments. It was not displaced until the eighteenth century, when secularization arrived in the wake of the Enlightenment.

RICHARD FRIEDENTHAL

Above One of a series of woodcuts on the papacy by Cranach.

Below Luther's meeting with Pope Paul III, by Salviati.

The Reformation creates new divisions in

The Spanish adventurers who explored the western coast of South America in the early 1500s returned to Panama with tales of an empire of untold wealth located in Peru. Those explorers found a ready

Francisco Pizarro, conqueror of Peru.

listener in Francisco Pizarro (1470–1541), a soldier of fortune who had settled in Darien, a port city on the Pacific side of the Isthmus. He and Diego de Almagro patiently explored the coastline of Peru for four years before Pizarro felt that he had sufficient evidence to convince Charles v of the importance of conquering the Incas. He arrived at Charles' court while Cortes was being feted for his victories in Mexico, and the latter's presence insured Pizarro of a fair hearing. The Emperor readily agreed to Pizarro's proposals, and appointed him governor and captain-general of Peru.

Pizarro set sail from Panama in 1530 with one hundred and eighty men, twenty-seven horses and two cannon, and he soon established a settlement on the Peruvian coast. He found the country in the final stages of a war of succession in which Atahualpa, one of the contenders, ultimately defeated his rival, moved the capital from his opponent's stronghold at Cuzco, to Cajamarca in the central plateau, and had himself crowned Inca, or emperor, of Peru. Under the ruse of conferring with Atahualpa, the tiny Spanish force surprised Cajamarca and took the Inca prisoner on November 16, 1532. Incredibly enough, Pizarro's tiny army had conquered the Inca kingdom in the course of a single afternoon.

During the 1530s other Spanish expeditions founded Cartagena in New Granada, conquered Yucatan, colonized La Plata (later Argentina) and settled Buenos Aires.

Spanish attempts to colonize Florida were less successful. Armed with an imperial patent that empowered him to establish settlements on the Gulf Coast, Hernando de Soto (1499–1542) landed in Florida in 1539. He discovered the Mississippi, Arkansas and Oklahoma.

A more persistent attempt to colonize Florida was made by the French in 1564. French fishermen had visited the Newfoundland coasts in the earliest years of the century, but the first planned expedition to the Americas was that of Giovanni da Verrazano, whom Francis I sent out to explore the coast between Cape Fear and Newfoundland in 1524. Ten years later Jacques Cartier made the first of three voyages to the New World.

Calvin at Geneva

By the time that Luther's Bible was published John Calvin (1509–64) had already settled in Paris and experienced what he called a "sudden conversion."

At the age of twenty-six he completed the first draft of his *Institutes of the Christian Religion*, a work expanded over the years from six to eighty chapters. Calvin's work was to have as profound an influence on the direction of the Reformation as Luther's Bible. His style was incisive, and his familiarity with the works of the Early Fathers was complete. Calvin gave a new twist to the doctrine of predestination enunciated by St. Augustine by arguing that a strict moral code was the basis for Christian life. In Calvinistic theology, discipline was fundamental.

In Geneva Calvin was able to put into practice his plans for

John Calvin, father of Presbyterianism.

completely re-organizing religious life. Under a theocratic government, the town became "the most perfect school of Christ." The state was restructured to establish the supremacy of the Christian Church.

Calvin was the most distinguished Biblical scholar of his generation and his teaching was infectious.

The Anabaptists

Lutherans and Catholics alike found a common enemy in the Anabaptists, the extreme left wing of the Reformation movement. Protestantism's radical left was composed of a variety of sects that were collectively dubbed "Anabaptists" by their detractors because they all rejected infant baptism. The Anabaptists believed that baptism was a personal, adult act of repentance. (Indeed, the mass baptisms performed in Amsterdam in the early 1500s astounded Luther and Pope Clement as much as they did the Anabaptists.) Such novel doctrines threatened the very foundations of authoritarian religion, and those who believed in them were mercilessly persecuted.

To escape such treatment, numbers of the Leyden sect settled in Münster in Westphalia. Their leader, John of Leyden, captured control of the city in February, 1534, and established a "communist state," whose excesses—admittedly grossly distorted in contemporary reports—were nonetheless remarkable. Because women outnumbered men four to one in Münster, John of Leyden made polygamy lawful—and he personally took sixteen wives. Attempts to unseat John were repulsed with considerable bloodshed, but in the spring of 1535, a joint expedition of Catholic and Lutheran princes forced Münster to surrender. The sect's leaders were executed and the Bishop of Münster was recalled.

Henry VIII's divorce

Henry VIII's envoys at Rome could make no progress with "the King's great matter." Henry's pleas for special consideration (as one whose attack on Luther's doctrines had earned him the papal title "Defender of the Faith") were ignored, and the opinions favoring his divorce that Cranmer had canvassed from European universities were dismissed by Pope Clement VII. Henry convinced himself that Catherine

of Aragon's inability to provide him with a son was divine punishment for his having married his deceased brother's wife. It was up to Thomas Cromwell to persuade Henry that his divorce did not need papal sanction, but could be effected by the King himself in Parliament. Meanwhile, Anne Boleyn waited in the wings.

In 1531, the English clergy, led by Archbishop Warham, sued for pardon for the offense of praemunire, paid an enormous fine and acknowledged Henry to be their supreme head "as far as the law of Christ allows." A year later—in a move calculated to convince Clement that his determination

Archbishop Thomas Cranmer.

was unfeigned—the King confiscated benefices customarily paid to the Pope. Henry then began undermining the powers of the Church courts, which were already highly unpopular. In 1533, Parliament passed an act that restrained appeals to Rome—and ended the Pope's interference in English affairs. As soon as the act became law, Thomas Cranmer, Warham's successor as Archbishop, opened a court of inquiry into the validity of the King's marriage with Catherine. Their marriage was soon declared void, and Henry was at last free to acknowledge his union with Anne Boleyn (who gave birth to Princess Elizabeth five months later). The final break with Rome came in 1535 when Henry assumed the title Supreme Head of the Church. The clergy, peers, members of Parliament and officials were required to take oaths of loyalty to the King, and Henry VIII became virtual pope in England.

The hopes of England's religious zealots notwithstanding, Church doctrine changed little after 1535. The Six Articles of Religion, a 1539 act that was designed to "abolish diversity of opinions," restated the ancient faith, including the doctrine of transubstantiation—but only after the King had intervened in the debate in the House of Lords to argue with the reforming bishops. The pressures of militant Protestantism soon overcame such reactionary legislation, however, and Archbishop Cranmer found himself swimming with the tide.

Sir Thomas More

The voice of conscience in those times was that of Sir Thomas More (1478–1535), a Humanist and lawyer whom Henry VIII had chosen to succeed Wolsey as Lord Chancellor. More's father had removed Thomas from Oxford when he discovered that his son was learning Greek, a subject that the elder More regarded as one of dangerous modernity. Thomas had been placed at Lincoln's Inn to read law and to prepare himself for the King's service. In his *Utopia* More condemned the abuse of power and preached toleration, and as Speaker of the Commons in 1523 More proved a forceful opponent of Wolsey. His home at Chelsea epitomized the New Learning in England. Erasmus, an occasional houseguest, noted that "in More's household you would realize that Plato's academy was revived, except that in the Academy the discussions concerned geometry and the power of numbers, whereas the house at Chelsea is a veritable school of Christian religion."

More had accepted the position of Lord Chancellor on the understanding that he would not be required to play a part in Henry's divorce, but by 1532 that issue so dominated politics that Sir Thomas felt obliged to resign. He repeatedly refused to take the oath of supremacy to Henry that was required by statue—although he swore to be loyal to the King and the succession—and as a result he was imprisoned in the Tower of London for a year. At his trial, Sir Thomas denied that Parliament could make the King Supreme Head of the Church, and he was executed as a traitor in July, 1536.

English Reformation

While More was still in prison, Henry VIII appointed Thomas Cromwell to be his vicar-general and ordered him to visit England's religious houses and discover the extent of their wealth. As a result of Cromwell's report, 376 houses with property that earned under $480 a year in rents were dissolved and the Crown acquired lands that earned a yearly total of $76,800 in rents. Those lands were soon parceled out by grant to courtiers and by lease to gentry in the shires. The dispossessed monks were granted pensions, and many of them found benefices as secular clergy.

The Pilgrimage of Grace was a conservative protest against Henry's breach with Rome and his confiscation of monastic property, but it was also a reaction against the centralized rule of the Tudor monarchy. Robert Aske, a Doncaster lawyer, recruited thousands of peasants to march under his banner of the Five

Thomas Cromwell.

Wounds of Christ. Their attempt to reverse the course of English domestic policy had no chance of success, however, for the rest of the country, in particular the populous, prosperous south, was solidly behind the King.

In 1539, Henry ordered the dissolution of the greater monasteries, and most surrendered without protest. The abbots of Reading and Colchester had been executed some years before, for denying the king's supremacy and the Abbot of Glastonbury had been martyred for refusing to resign his rule. England's more politic abbots swiftly surrendered their property, and Crown revenues more than doubled. Iconoclasm accompanied the ending of monasticism in England, and St. Thomas Becket's tomb at Canterbury—the focal point of medieval pilgrimages—was pilfered.

The Convocation of Canterbury petitioned Henry VIII for an authoritative version of the Scriptures in English and he was eventually persuaded by Cranmer and Cromwell that Miles Coverdale's translation —the first complete Bible in the English tongue—contained no heresies despite the fact that it had been prepared on the Continent and printed in Zurich. "If there be no heresies," announced the monarch, "in God's name let it go abroad among our people"—and a 1536 injunction required a copy of the Bible to be placed in every church.

Tyndale's New Testament

A few weeks later William Tyndale was burned as a heretic in Antwerp. His tract, *Obedience of a Christian Man*, had prophetically outlined the cardinal principles of the English Reformation: the supremacy of the ruler and the authority of the Scriptures. Tyndale had found it dangerous to continue his work of translating the Bible while living in his native England, and in 1526 he emigrated to Worms, where his English New Testament was printed. Many copies of Tyndale's New Testament were smuggled into England and some of those were seized and burned by the common hangman. Archbishop Warham even sent agents to Europe to buy and destroy copies of Tyndale's work. Ironically, his New Testament, coupled with Coverdale's version of both Testaments, formed the basis of the official "Great Bible" that was prepared under Cranmer's guidance in 1539.

William Tyndale Bible translator.

As a result of the labors of Coverdale and Tyndale, the English became known as "The People of the Book." Later English-language versions of the Bible embodied many of their cadences.

Advances in Science

Scholar-scientists began to examine facts for their own sake, and many of them were prepared to criticize accepted explanations and to pursue new methods without seeking higher justification. The most notable scientific advances were made in surgery and anatomy. Paracelsus (*c.* 1493–1541) published the first manual of surgery in 1528, and Vesalius transformed the study of anatomy by advocating and practicing dissection. Two books marked the progress of technology: Biringuccio's *Pirotechnia* discussed the manufacture of gunpowder and glass, and Agricola's *De re metallica*, described all aspects of mining ores. But in astronomy there were still greater advances.

Sir Thomas More, author of *Utopia*, painted by Holbein.

The Earth Dethroned

By September of 1543, it had become obvious to the citizens of Frauenburg, Poland, that their beloved physician, Nicholas Copernicus, would not live out the year. The good doctor's failing health was a matter of special concern to his brash young disciple, Georg Joachim, who had long urged his mentor—a noted amateur astronomer—to publish his observations on planetary motion. After months of pleading, Joachim had at last been given permission to deliver Copernicus' manuscript to a local printer—and a copy of the published text reached the doctor on his deathbed. That volume postulated the first really new theory of planetary motion in almost two thousand years. Copernicus' insistence that the sun—not the earth—was the center of the universe helped usher in an epoch of broad scientific inquiry that earned the modest astronomer the title "Father of the Scientific Revolution."

A copy by Lorman of Berlin of a contemporary portrait of Nicholas Copernicus.

Opposite A room in the house at Frauenberg that Copernicus inherited from his uncle, and where he carried out most of his astronomical work.

Nicholas Copernicus, the Polish astronomer whose theory of planetary motion helped revolutionize scientific thought in the late sixteenth century, was born on February 19, 1473, at Torun, a Hanseatic community that had fallen under the protection of the King of Poland.

Little is known of Copernicus' childhood. His father died when he was only ten, and Nicholas, his brother Andrew and their two sisters were adopted by their maternal uncle. Lucas Watzelrode (or Waczenrode). A scholar and Roman Catholic priest, Watzelrode was consecrated Bishop of Ermland six years after he adopted the Koppernigk children. At that time, the See of Ermland was virtually an autonomous state, almost encircled by lands controlled by the Teutonic Knights. It owed nominal allegiance to Poland, but the Bishop served as both temporal ruler and spiritual head of the See. His palace was located at Heilsberg (about thirty-nine miles south of present-day Kalingrad, Russia) and his cathedral was located in the coastal city of Frauenberg, some forty miles to the northwest.

In 1491, when Nicholas was eighteen, he and his brother were sent to the university at Cracow, where young Copernicus pursued an interest in astronomy that he had first demonstrated while a schoolchild in Torun. The university of Cracow, one of the first institutions of higher learning in northern Europe to be influenced by the rediscovery of Greek science, was renowned for its high intellectual standards and was consequently attended by numerous foreign students. Copernicus studied mathematics and astronomy at the university.

While still a student, Copernicus began to assemble a collection of astronomical books that he was to keep by him for the rest of his life. The young student's interest in astronomy was looked upon with favor by the Church, which was at that time much concerned with the possible reform of the calendar. When Copernicus left Cracow, his uncle wanted to have him installed in a canonry in Frauenberg, but until a suitable vacancy occurred, the Bishop felt that his nephew might profitably seek a degree in ecclesiastical law. Accordingly, Nicholas departed for the famous law school at Bologna in 1496.

While in Bologna, Nicholas lodged at the home of Domenico Maria de Novara, a professor of astronomy. The two men observed the heavens together, and spent many hours discussing possible improvements that they felt could be made in the prevailing theory of planetary motion. Nicholas remained in Bologna for three and a half years and then journeyed to Rome for the celebrations attending the 1,500th anniversary of Christianity. He lingered in the city for a year, and during that time made some celestial observations, particularly of an eclipse of the moon, and gave informal lectures on astronomy and mathematics.

During the years that he was in law school, a canonry became vacant at Frauenberg and Nicholas was elected to fill it. On July 27, 1501, he was duly installed—and promptly was granted further leave of absence so that he might go to Padua to study medicine and complete his law studies. Nicholas chose, however, to graduate in ecclesiastical law at Ferrara, and in 1503 was made a Doctor of Canon Law there. He then returned to medical school at Padua.

In Italy, as elsewhere in sixteenth-century Europe, medical training was largely theoretical. The teaching of medicine was based on certain rules attributed to Hippocrates, a Greek physician who lived in the fifth century B.C. Those rules, coupled with the writings of the Roman surgeon Galen (circa A.D. 200) and those of the eleventh-century Arabian chemist and physician Avicenna, composed the bulk of contemporary medical lore. Practical treatment involved the study of astronomy, because the current belief was that the celestial bodies exerted an influence on the human body and on the herbal drugs that were prescribed as cures.

When Copernicus, by then in his early thirties,

A picture from *The Travels of Sir John Mandeville*; astrologers as well as travelers found that the stars had their uses.

returned to Heilsberg in 1506, he was appointed medical attendant to his uncle (with whom Nicholas shared certain governmental duties). In March, 1512, Watzelrode died, and by June of that year Copernicus was installed at Frauenberg cathedral. Nicholas' gratitude for all that the old man had done on his behalf was expressed in a book that he published in 1509, three years before the Bishop's death. The work, a Latin translation of some Greek verses by Theophylactus, was dedicated to Lucas Watzelrode.

At Frauenberg, Copernicus carried out a number of ecclesiastical and temporal duties. He lived in the modest style expected of canons, possessing but two servants and three horses. He set up his own astronomical observatory. In 1514 he was invited to Rome to assist in the reform of the calendar but felt it necessary to refuse, believing that the proposals were premature and that more research was needed into the motion of the sun and moon. Two years later he moved about fifty miles from the cathedral in order better to administer several of its large estates. Copernicus was now forced to spend long periods away from his observatory, and his absences grew more frequent when war broke out between Poland and the Teutonic Knights in 1519.

When, at the end of the war, a new Bishop was appointed, Copernicus returned to Frauenberg. The astronomer's final years were spent tending not only the Bishop and his successors, but also the town's poor, who grew to love him. Indeed, in Copernicus' own lifetime, it was for his medical skill and not his astronomical theory that he was noted.

Copernicus carried out his astronomical work whenever he was freed of his other duties. Initially, he had become dissatisfied, as many astronomers of his day were, with the generally accepted theory of the universe. That concept, based on the teachings of Greek philosophers, placed the Earth, fixed and immovable, at the center of the universe. Around it, in order, orbited the moon, Mercury, Venus, the sun, Mars, Jupiter and Saturn. Beyond Saturn lay the sphere of the fixed stars, which supposedly rotated once every twenty-four hours. Heaven lay beyond this starry sphere.

The problem with this theory—one that still troubled astronomers in the sixteenth century—was how to account accurately for the movements of the sun, moon and planets. To resolve this dilemma, ancient astronomers had evolved three basic provisos: first, that motion took place about the Earth; second, that such motion was uniform in speed; and third, that movement must be in a circle. The great difficulty was that the sun, moon and planets did not move across the sky evenly; they moved faster at some times than at others, and, worst of all, the planets appeared to perform loops in the sky as they wandered across the background of the stars.

Throughout antiquity solutions designed to explain some or all of these observed effects had been proposed, and in the second century A.D. the Alexandrian astronomer Ptolemy had worked out a comprehensive scheme of planetary motion that was still in use in Copernicus' day. Ptolemy explained planetary motion by using a collection of circular motions devised in the fourth century B.C. by Apollonios of Perga. Basically, each planet was conceived of as orbiting in a small circle, known as an "epicycle." The epicycle, in turn, moved at a regular rate around the circumference of a larger circle, known as a "deferent," at whose center lay the Earth. Ptolemy ingeniously modified this system not only to account for the planet's orbital loops, but also to account for changes in the apparent distances of given planets from the Earth, and for unevenness in their motion. He did this by offsetting the deferents from the center of the Earth, by allowing the deferents and epicycles to rock, and by using more than one epicycle for each planet. It was a brilliant system, and it remained in use (in modified form) for nearly 1,400 years.

By Copernicus' time, Ptolemy's system had been interwoven with the ideas of Aristotle, who had conceived of the universe as composed of a series of concentric spheres, with the Earth at the center. Many sixteenth-century astronomers thought of Aristotle's spheres as real, although transparent, and made of the purest crystal. According to Aristotle's generally accepted laws of physics, celestial bodies

Dissatisfaction with Ptolemy's ideas

were eternal and composed of a heavenly material—quite different from anything on Earth—whose natural place was the sky. Heavy bodies fell to the ground, Aristotle taught, because their natural place was the center of the universe (which was, of course, the center of the Earth). These laws were to have an important bearing on the acceptance of Copernicus' proposals.

While still a university student, Copernicus had had grown dissatisfied with the views of Ptolemy. He decided to read the Greek authors for himself to see whether he could find a clue to any other explanation of planetary motion. To seek new ideas from ancient writings was not unusual: for one thing, it was commonly held that the Greek philosophers had special knowledge of scientific matters; and for another, appeals to ancient authority—to the Scriptures, the teachings of the Church or some other early source—were customary. In his reading of Greek authors, Copernicus discovered that several did not accept the geocentric view of the universe. At least one bold thinker had even gone so far as to suggest that the Earth and planets orbit the sun—and it was this view that Copernicus eventually revived.

The resurrection of some unusual and unfamiliar Greek speculations would not have been enough—by itself—to make Copernicus famous, had he not spent years perfecting the mathematics of his new view, computing future planetary positions and making observations to provide additional evidence. He prepared a carefully reasoned argument in support of his theory, using arguments somewhat similar to those adopted 1,800 years before by Aristotle, but reaching a different conclusion. In 1530, while Copernicus was at work on his theory but before he was ready to set down his views in detail, the astronomer issued a manuscript that contained the essential facts. The manuscript was called *Commentariolus (The Litttle Commentary)*, and although it boasted no diagrams or detailed descriptions, it aroused considerable interest. Indeed, in 1533 John Widmanstad, the Papal Secretary, lectured to the Pope and some of his cardinals on the views it contained. At this time, such religious opposition as there was to Copernicus' theory of a moving Earth came from the Protestants, who believed it to be contrary to a literal interpretation of the Scriptures.

Copernicus was urged to publish his theory in full, but claimed that he was not ready. Indeed, he might never have agreed that his facts and figures were sufficiently complete had it not been for the efforts of George Joachim, a young Protestant scholar who came to see him in the spring of 1539. Better known by his Latinized name Rheticus, Joachim remained with Copernicus for almost three years, and it says much for the characters of both men—and for the stimulation that their scientific study provided—that in an age torn by religious dissension, the two men worked harmoniously together.

In 1540 Rheticus persuaded his host to publish a summary of his views, which was subsequently printed in Nürnberg under the title *Narratio Prima (A First Narrative)*. Not content with this, Rheticus continued to urge Copernicus to draw up his theory in detail. In the end he prevailed, and in 1543 a complete manuscript was delivered to Johann Petrejus, the Nürnberg publisher who had printed the *Narratio Prima*. Unfortunately, Rheticus moved to the University of Leipzig soon after delivering the manuscript, and he was forced to leave the technical details to his old tutor, Johannes Schoner, and a Lutheran divine, Andreas Osiander.

Osiander, worried about religious opposition to Copernicus' work, gave the publication a title without consulting Copernicus. (Copernicus had left his manuscript untitled, and was therefore partly to blame.) The book appeared as *De Revolutionibus Orbium Coelestium (On the Revolutions of the Celestial Spheres)*, although it is clear that Copernicus himself did not believe in the reality of Aristotle's spheres. More significant, however, was the fact that Osiander inserted an unsigned preface, disclaiming any physical reality to the movement of the Earth and explaining that Copernicus' theory was no more than an ingenious way of computing future planetary positions. The book appeared in 1543, and tradition has it that a copy reached Copernicus on his deathbed in October of that year.

Copernicus' theory as set out in *De Revolutionibus* places the sun firmly at the center of the universe, with the planets orbiting around it. The Earth is dethroned from its privileged position in the midst of all creation and is relegated to the role of mere satellite, orbiting the sun and rotating once on its axis every twenty-four hours. (It still acts as the body

The Lutheran divine, Andreas Osiander, who gave Copernicus' book its misleading title, and explained away many of his ideas in order to reduce opposition to Copernicus' theories.

The Copernican solar system as depicted by Thomas Digges in the 1576 edition of his father's *Prognostication Everlasting*.

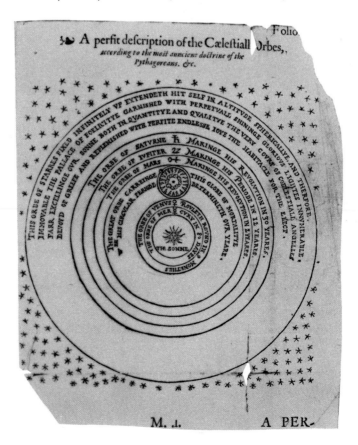

Opposition to Copernicus—scientific and religious

Sixteenth-century astrolabe used to tell the altitude of stars and planets.

about which the moon performs its monthly orbit, however.) The epicycles and deferents of Ptolemic astronomy are retained, and no changes are made in Aristotelian physics. Copernicus could not free himself from the ancient Greek beliefs that the heavens were incorruptible and that celestial movements must be circular and regular. Yet his system did possess regular motion centered on the sun, instead of off-centered motion about the Earth, which Ptolemy had advocated.

To Copernicus, this new scheme seemed virtually a moral victory, for it kept the true spirit of the Greek belief in circular motion. Moreover, his system was more elegant mathematically—as contemporary mathematicians were quick to realize—and it appeared to give more accurate results when used for computing the future positions of the planets. The tables in *De Revolutionibus* were used by the mathematician Erasmus Reinhold to prepare, under the patronage of Duke Albert of Prussia, a new set of tables of future planetary positions. These *Prussian Tables*, as they were called, were more precise than any previously published.

In England, the new theory received considerable support, particularly from Thomas Digges, a distinguished Elizabethan mathematician. Digges followed up a new consequence of the Copernican theory, which he realized affected all commonly held assumptions about the extent of the universe. Aristotle and other Greek philosophers had argued that since the sphere of the stars rotated once every twenty-four hours, that sphere must be finite in size —for if it was infinite, it would have to rotate at an infinite speed to complete a revolution in the same period. Digges appreciated that in a heliocentric

universe, where the Earth turned on its axis while orbiting round the sun, this argument was no longer valid. In an astronomical handbook published in 1576 and titled *Prognostication Everlasting*, Digges proposed an infinite universe of stars, each similar to our sun; his proposition completely refuted the idea of a spherical universe.

But if the Copernican theory met with support in England and much of Germany, it also faced some opposition. That opposition was of two types— scientific and religious. The former was based on arguments founded on Aristotle's physics: how could so heavy a body as the Earth be thought to move? Why, if it moved, should bodies still fall to the ground and the moon remain with it in space? How could it rotate once a day without setting up tidal waves and hurricanes as it rushed around in the surrounding air? Another significant scientific argument was based on observation: If the Earth orbited the sun, then at one time of year it would necessarily be nearer to some stars than to others, and as it moved, the nearer stars would be replaced by others. Some change in star positions ought, then, to be observable, but the most careful examinations of the sky showed no change at all. Copernicus, who had foreseen this argument, countered it by saying that the stars were too far away for any change to be observed. This deduction was perfectly correct, as we now know, but in the sixteenth century, it seemed insane to assert that God had made a universe with an immense gap between the planetary orbits and the stars. Only telescopic observations made from 1600 onwards, coupled with the gradual rejection of Aristotle's physics, removed these objections.

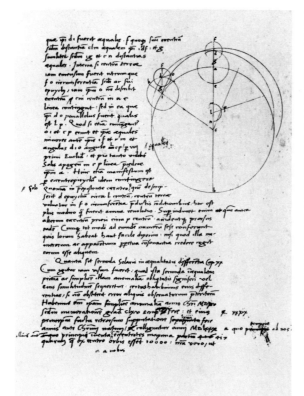

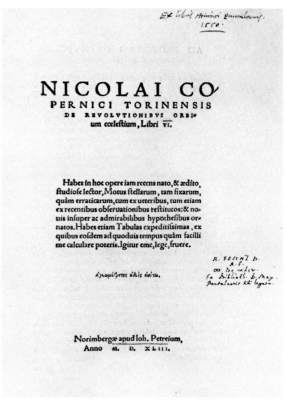

A page from the original manuscript of Copernicus' *De Revolutionibus,* and the title page of the first edition.

A celestial globe of the
mid-sixteenth century.

Some Protestants rejected the theory from a religious point of view, citing Biblical passages which asserted that the Earth stood still. There were others who were less committed to so literal an interpretation, however; Copernicus had dedicated *De Revolutionibus* to Pope Paul III, and the Roman Catholic Church had raised no objections to the theory. Copernican astronomy was strongly advocated by Giordano Bruno, who learned of it while on a visit to England in 1583. Bruno, a former Dominican, had found much to criticize in his Church and had published many contumacious books attacking it. In these books, which supported a magical form of anti-authoritarian government, Bruno extolled the Copernican view of a heliocentric universe (although not for scientific reasons) and it was this, more than anything else, that led to *De Revolutionibus Orbium Coelestium* being placed on the Index of Prohibited Books in 1616.

Although his detailed descriptions of planetary motion were to be superseded within the next 150 years, Copernicus' theory was nonetheless a profound break with scientific tradition—the first dramatically new view of the universe in almost two thousand years. Copernicus' work acted as a powerful stimulus to future scholars, encouraging them to re-think the principles underlying the behavior of the universe. The new laws of planetary motion described by Johannes Kepler between 1609 and 1621, and something of Galileo Galilei's mathematical physics published in 1638 and his earlier observations with a telescope, owe a debt to the spirit of *De Revolutionibus*. The publication of Newton's *Principia* in 1687 culminated an era of intense scientific enquiry of which Nicholas Copernicus had been one of the pioneers.

COLIN RONAN

Elizabeth fears for her throne so Mary

A great spiritual revival lay at the heart of Rome's reply to Wittenberg and Geneva, for in truth the Counter-Reformation was already under way when Luther posted his *Theses*. The calling of the Lateran Council in 1512 and the program of reforms drawn up by Adrian VI some eleven years later were more than straws in the wind. Early in his pontificate Paul III (1534–49) appointed a Reform Commission and, despite his own conservatism, he was persuaded by his cardinals to call a general council. The council, which met at Trent in 1545 to determine policy and restate doctrine, concluded its work under Pius IV in 1562–63. But it was new religious orders, rather than general councils, that gave impetus to the Counter Reformation.

A number of new orders were established at this time, principally in Italy. Paoli Giustiniani, a Venetian of noble birth, embraced poverty in 1528 and founded the Capuchins, an order dedicated to working among the sick and needy. In 1535, Angela Merici formed the Ursuline Order, as an association of lay women pledged to a life of good works. And in 1540, Philip Neri (the future apostle of Rome) founded the Congregation of the Oratory.

The most significant of the new orders was the Society of Jesus, founded by Ignatius Loyola. Loyola (1491–1556) was a Spanish soldier and courtier who underwent conversion and wrote his *Spiritual Exercises*. While studying at Paris in 1534, the young Spaniard and his friends renounced wordly possessions and pledged to dedicate their lives to God's Word. They ultimately intended to undertake a barefoot pilgrimage to Jerusalem, but in the interim Loyola's followers worked in Italy. The Jesuit Order

S. IN CHRISTO PATRIS ET Dñi
N.D.Pii diuina prouidentia Papæ. iiii.

Bulla

Indictionis SACRI Oecumenici Concilii
Tridentini Celebrandi.

Pius IV's Bull recalling the Council of Trent, 1560.

Ignatius Loyola, founder of the Jesuits.

was formally recognized by Paul III in 1540. Their Rule involved unquestioning obedience to the Pope —and almost from the beginning they served as the Church's shock troops, propagating the faith wherever they were sent. Their task was to reconvert the lands lost to Protestantism and to convert the heathen.

As Spaniards, both Loyola and his compatriot, Francis Xavier, were more at home among the heathen in the Moslem world than among Lutherans in North Germany. Their plans for missions to India, Brazil and the Congo received enthusiastic support from John III of Portugal and in 1542 Xavier set out for Goa. Meanwhile, in Europe the Society of Jesus quickly won a reputation as a teaching order with high standards in both classical studies and theology. The Jesuits established their first college at Padua, but their most famous was the College at Rome, which was founded in 1551.

To combat heresy, Paul III established the Inquisition in Rome in 1542 and issued the first papal Index of Prohibited Books some fifteen years later. The decrees of the Third Session of the Council of Trent further revitalized Catholicism and a new breviary was issued. Work on the dome of St. Peter's proceeded according to Michelangelo's plan and masses composed by Palestrina, director of music at St. Peter's, were sung in the Great Nave of the Cathedral.

Henry VIII

After executing Anne Boleyn in 1536 for adultery and incest, Henry VIII married Jane Seymour, who gave the King his longed-for son before dying in childbed. Henry's 1540 marriage to Anne of Cleves was arranged by Thomas Cromwell as part of a grand alliance with the German Protestant princes. The

union lasted only six months, and as soon as Henry had shed Anne, the Duke of Norfolk, who had ousted Cromwell on a charge of treason, cemented his position by marrying his niece Katherine Howard to the King. Katherine eventually trod the same path to Traitor's Gate that her cousin Anne Boleyn had walked, and Henry ended his matrimonial adventures in 1543 by marrying Katherine Parr, a widow of scholarly tastes— who managed to survive him.

Henry's unslakable thirst for military glory squandered his resources. The King's victory over the Scots at Solway Moss in November, 1542, was overshadowed by his disastrous campaigns in France. Charles V came to terms with

Henry VIII; Tudor despot.

Francis I without consulting his English ally, and all Henry could salvage from his conquests was Boulogne. Yet for all his excesses, Henry VIII laid the foundations of a strong national state. To Europe's considerable astonishment, he had defied the pope and had brought both Church and State under his forceful rule in England and Wales.

Defying the arrangements that had been made for Edward's minority, the prince's uncle, Edward Seymour, seized power as Lord Protector, took the title of Duke of Somerset, and unleashed a doctrinal Reformation. A prayer book compiled by Cranmer was forced upon the Church in 1549 by the Act of Uniformity, and the West Country rose to demand the restoration of the Catholic liturgy. Before the rising was put down, Robert Kett led a revolt in Norfolk in protest at the enclosure movement. John Dudley (who was soon to become Earl of Northumberland) defeated Kett and conspired to replace Seymour. In October, 1549, Seymour was ousted and Northumberland assumed effective control of the government; he was to rule England for the remainder of Edward's reign. In 1552 a second, more radically Protestant prayer book was approved.

To remain in control of the

government and to insure the survival of a Protestant England after the sixteen-year-old King's death, Northumberland married his son Guildford Dudley to Lady Jane Grey, eldest claimant to the throne in the Suffolk line of the succession. He prevailed upon the dying King to bestow the crown on Lady Jane rather than on Princess Mary, the rightful heir. Against her will, Jane was proclaimed Queen in July of 1553, and she reigned for thirteen days. Meanwhile, Mary's supporters rallied in East Anglia, and when an army sent to engage them deserted or disbanded, Northumberland surrendered.

Mary I's Spanish marriage

Queen Mary (1553–58) reintroduced the Roman Mass and, as the child of Catherine of Aragon, reconciled England with the papacy. Protestant bishops—among them Cranmer, Latimer and Ridley— who refused to recant were burned and others took refuge in Zurich and Geneva. In 1554, Mary married Philip of Spain, son of Charles V, but when Parliament opposed his plans to secure an English crown, Philip left the country. He returned only once, to insure that England would join Spain in her war against France—a war in which the English lost Calais, the last English foothold on the Continent. The seizure

Mary Stuart, Queen of Scots.

of Calais in 1558 ended Philip's hope of succeeding to the throne.

Mary, acknowledging at last her inability to produce an heir, became reconciled with her sister, Elizabeth, who succeeded the barren Queen on November 17, 1558. Protestants regarded Elizabeth's accession as the dawn of a new age, but Elizabeth I was determined to find in religion, as in politics, a

Queen of Scots is imprisoned

moderate course—to heal the wounds inflicted by extremists.

James V and Mary Queen of Scots

Buttressed by interlineal marriages, Scotland maintained the "Auld Alliance" with France until 1560. Within a year of the death of his first wife, Madeleine of France, James V married Mary of Guise. Continuing border strife with Henry VIII's troops culminated in the Scots' defeat at Solway Moss in 1542. James V, who was mortally wounded in the battle, left as his successor a six-day-old daughter, Mary Queen of Scots. She was betrothed to Edward Tudor under the peace treaty of Greenwich in July, 1543, but after Cardinal Beaton's bid for the regency, the treaty was repudiated by the Scottish Parliament. Protector Somerset invaded Scotland again in 1547 and captured Edinburgh in a vain effort to reimpose a marriage treaty that would unite the two kingdoms. The young Queen of Scots, who was already betrothed to the Dauphin, was whisked away to France, leaving the rule of Scotland to her mother. The "Auld Alliance" had never appeared as menacing to England as it did in the years that Mary of Guise ruled a Scotland garrisoned with French troops while her brothers, Francis, Duke of Guise and the Cardinal of Lorraine, dictated French policy.

The growth of Protestantism north of the border altered the entire situation. Enflamed by Cardinal Beaton's persecution of heretics, the Protestant party assassinated him in 1546, and in 1555 John Knox returned from Geneva to preach reform of the Scottish Church. The first Covenant was signed in 1557, and Knox urged the Protestant Lords of the Congregation to rebel. In 1559 they sacked religious houses, seized Edinburgh and deposed Mary of Guise. Elizabeth answered the Scottish lords' appeal for help by sending troops and ships north to drive the French from Scotland. The following summer she signed the Treaty of Edinburgh with the Protestant Council of Regents, thus ending the endemic strife between the two kingdoms that had persisted for centuries. The Parliament in Edinburgh abolished papal jurisdiction and approved a Calvinistic Confession of Faith, drawn up by Knox, that established the Presbyterian Church of Scotland.

The Dauphin, whom Mary Queen of Scots had married, succeeded his father as Francis II in 1559, but reigned for only eighteen months. Mary, who claimed the throne of England as the granddaughter of Henry VIII's elder sister Margaret, regarded Elizabeth as a usurper and never ratified the Treaty of Greenwich. After Francis' death she returned to Scotland. She longed for a meeting with Elizabeth and an assurance that she would inherit the throne of England, but her claims and her search for another husband exasperated Elizabeth, The beautiful, imperious and impulsive widow outraged her own subjects by her devotion to Catholicism, and the gaiety of her court at Holyrood House angered Church elders, who soon questioned her fitness to rule.

Mary married the worthless Lord Darnley in 1565. Darnley was soon discredited for his complicity in the murder of David Rizzio, the Queen's Italian favorite. He was assassinated in Edinburgh in 1567 on the orders of James, Earl of Bothwell, who then seized Mary and married her. In a matter of weeks

Francis II of France.

the Lords of the Covenant had routed Bothwell's supporters at Carberry Hill, placed Mary in Lochleven Castle and forced her to abdicate in favor of her infant son James VI. Mary's step-brother, the Earl of Moray, was named regent. In May, 1568, Mary escaped to England, where she expected to find support for her efforts to regain the Scottish throne. Elizabeth, who feared Mary's influence among English Catholics and was wary of her designs upon the kingdom, decided to keep her in captivity.

Europe after 1540

The European scene changed rapidly after the mid-1540s. Luther,

Henry VIII and Francis I died in rapid succession. Emperor Charles V, the lone survivor, seemed to be at the height of his power when, in April, 1547, he won the decisive Battle of Muhlberg and ended his struggle with the Schmalkaldic League. Within a few years, however, his vast Empire began to collapse.

Fearing Hapsburg domination, the Empire's Protestant princes formed a defensive league. Henry II of France joined the League on the condition that he receive the bishoprics of Metz, Toul and Verdun in exchange for subsidizing a campaign against Charles. Henry occupied the bishoprics in 1552, and Maurice of Saxony invaded southern Germany at the head of a French army. The Emperor was forced to flee from Innsbruck, barely escaped capture and rode across the Brenner Pass to Villach. He made a last attempt to regain his Empire in 1554 with the aid of the Duke of Alva and the unpredictable Albrecht Alcibiades. The latter's defeat at Schwarzach in June ended the fighting and Charles, empowering his brother the Archduke Ferdinand to settle the religious question at the Diet as best he could, left Germany to her fate.

Thirty-eight years after the publication of the Wittenberg *Theses*, Germany finally acknowledged Lutheranism at the Peace of Augsburg in 1555. Charles was forced to abandon his hopes that his son Philip would be permitted to succeed him in the Empire, for both the princes and Archduke Ferdinand were opposed. Philip formally renounced his claims at the Diet of Augsburg and in September, 1556, Charles abdicated in favor of Ferdinand I. Charles had previously resigned the government of the Netherlands, Milan and Naples to Philip at a grand ceremony in Brussels, and in 1598 he surrendered the Empire and returned to Spain.

A general peace treaty was signed at Cateau-Cambresis in April, 1559. By the terms of that treaty France retained Calais and the bishoprics of Metz, Toul and Verdun. Piedmont was returned to Savoy—although both France and Spain kept garrisons at various key points —and Spanish possession of Franche-Comte was confirmed. During a tournament celebrating the end of Hapsburg-Valois strife, Henry II of France was accidentally killed, bringing Francis II, husband of Mary Queen of Scots, to the throne.

Upon returning to Spain in 1558, Philip II established Madrid as his capital and began building his great palace of the Escorial in the solitary foothills of the Sierra de Guadarrama. For forty years Philip ruled from the Escorial—directing policy, weighing reports, annotating despatches and making calculations.

Mary Tudor, Queen of England, and Philip II, King of Spain.

By 1558 both France and Spain were on the verge of bankruptcy, despite the seemingly inexhaustible resources of the New World. The riches of Mexico were being systematically exploited, and the silver mines that had been opened at Potosi, Peru, in 1545, were operating under the able administration of Francis de Toledo, the greatest colonial administrator of Spain's golden century. Yet each sailing of a treasure fleet to Europe added a new spiral to the price revolution.

Philip II, as his nickname "the Prudent King" implies, was sufficiently realistic to place politics before religion when the two interests clashed. Though a devout Catholic, much of his policy was distinctly anti-papal. He was never so happy as when national interests coincided with crusades against heretics and infidels—and his long struggle against the Dutch Calvinists, his eventual war with England, his cruel suppression of the Moriscos in Spain and his ending of Turkish supremacy in the Mediterranean were all undertaken for political as well as religious reasons.

In the last months of his reign, Suleiman the Magnificent embarked on another campaign in Hungary, took Belgrade and opened the siege of Szigeth. The fortress fell three days after the Sultan's death, and Emperor Maximilian II, whose army had melted away, came to terms with the new Sultan, Selim II (1566–74). Selim then turned his attentions to a naval war against Venice.

Cutting the Sultan's Beard

On September 16, 1571, a mammoth fleet composed of some three hundred ships weighed anchor in the Sicilian port of Messina and sailed for the Levant. Pope Pius V, who had summoned that navy and blessed its undertaking, hoped that the combined might of his Holy League fleet could strike a crippling blow against the Ottoman Empire. The Turks' increasing boldness on both land and sea threatened not only Venetian trading rights in the eastern Mediterranean but the Pope's none-too-secure empire as well. Pius himself chose Don Juan, natural brother of Philip II of Spain, to lead the Holy League against the Infidel—and he chose well. In an epic sea battle that pitted the Christian fleet against the combined navies of Ottoman Emperor Selim II and his Near Eastern allies, Don Juan captured or sunk more than two hundred Turkish vessels and inflicted some 25,000 casualties. His stunning victory ended Turkish incursions into Europe for decades.

The victor of Lepanto, Don Juan of Austria, bastard son of Charles V, from a portrait by Alonso Sánchez Coello.

Opposite Bruno del Priore's picture celebrating the victory at Lepanto. The figures in the lower left-hand corner represent the Republic of Venice, Philip II of Spain and Pope Pius V, while on the right, Death, with his scythe, mows down the Turks.

The first of July, 1571, was a day of rejoicing in Barcelona, Spain's principal seaport. On that scorchingly hot morning, a fleet of forty-seven war galleys lay at anchor in the harbor, and the city rippled with gaiety and excitement. Don Juan of Austria, half-brother of Philip II, the King of Spain, had just gone aboard the *Reale*, the flagship of the fleet, to introduce himself to its crew. The *Reale*, built in the shipyards of Barcelona, was painted red and gold—Don Juan's colors—and was bedecked with elaborate carved emblems. Multicolored pennants hung from the ship's rigging, and rose-colored velvet was draped over the planking.

Curiously, this day of triumph was to end with a humiliating rebuff for Don Juan. Upon returning to his quarters in the viceroy's palace, the young prince found a letter waiting for him from his half-brother, Philip II. The letter curtly ordered him to refrain from calling himself by the title of Highness and to confine himself to the title of Excellence, as befitted his station. Philip's note was a blunt reminder that Don Juan was illegitimate; he was the natural son of Charles V and a Flemish washerwoman, Barbara de Blomberg—and he was, therefore, a bastard. Don Juan began his proud reply to the King with the words: "God has made me the brother of Your Majesty. . . ."

In the eyes of history, Don Juan of Austria was the triumphant victor at Lepanto, but he was not the only actor in the drama by any means. Other personalities were to play equally important parts before, during and after the battle.

At the time of the Battle of Lepanto, Philip II was at his most powerful, and Spain was at the height of her glory. The Spanish regent had not inherited the great European hegemony that his father, Charles V, had conquered and subsequently relinquished. Nevertheless, Philip reigned over a completely independent Spain, which was no longer just another province of the Holy Roman Empire. In addition, he controlled the Netherlands and Spain's profitable New World possessions, Mexico and Peru. As the ruler of Milan, Naples and Sicily, Philip also controlled nearly the whole of Italy—with the notable exception of Venice, which had maintained its independence ever since the ninth century, experiencing both prosperous and difficult times during that period.

The history of Venice has the rich, colorful texture of silk about it, and the flavor of Oriental spices. The Venetian merchants, creators of the sturdy *galeazza de mercanzia*, the huge trading vessels that were to prove their worth at Lepanto, were expert in the art of importing and exporting. For centuries they had been the custodians of the great international markets, and the principal suppliers of merchandise from the Orient to the Western countries. And from time to time the Venetians had found it necessary to defend their flourishing trade by force of arms. In the fifteenth century, Venice—which already ruled a Mediterranean empire that stretched from Istria and the Dalmatian coast to the Ionian islands and Crete—adopted a policy of territorial as well as maritime expansion. The Sultan of Turkey granted the Venetians exclusive trading rights within the Ottoman Empire, and in 1489, Venice annexed the island of Cyprus.

In Turkey, Selim II had succeeded his father, Suleiman the Magnificent, to the Ottoman throne. The new Sultan was very concerned about the annexation of Cyprus by Venice, for it hindered the free passage of Turkish ships across the waters lying within the vast Ottoman Empire. He determined that the Venetians had to be driven off Cyprus; if they refused to cede the island of their own free will, the Turkish fleet would have to intervene. Needless to say, the Venetians found the demands of the Sultan totally unacceptable, and when the Doge of Venice presented Selim's proposals to the Senate, they were angrily rejected as being contrary to the

Don Juan: an admiral chosen by the Pope

Philip II of Spain regarded Lepanto as a minor victory; he was more interested in stamping out heresy and crushing the Berbers. He was also jealous of the reputation of his half-brother, Don Juan.

The palace of the Escorial, the center of Philip II's vast empire.

peace treaty signed some years earlier with the Sublime Porte (the Ottoman government in Constantinople).

While the Venetians were trying to preserve their territorial possessions in the Mediterranean, Philip II of Spain was organizing an expedition to conquer the coastal strip of North Africa. Consequently, although there was little love lost between Spain and Venice, events combined to make a military alliance between the two states mutually beneficial. This community of interests needed only a moral justification, pronounced by some supreme and undisputed authority, to transform it into a true pact. The logical person to serve as this authority was Pope Pius V, and it was he who fashioned the Venetians' war of reprisal against the Turks into a religious crusade against the Infidel. Pius' creation, the Holy League, was ably supported by the fanatical Catholicism of Philip II.

The Holy League was confirmed by a treaty drawn up between Venice and Spain and approved and promulgated by the Pope, who was also one of the signatories. It consisted of a common declaration of war against the Turks and the Moors in Algeria, Tunis and Tripoli. It laid down the terms and conditions of intervention by the respective parties, and detailed the military contributions and the division of expenses between the two states and the Papacy. It was agreed that the conduct of the war should be under the leadership of three commanders: a Venetian, a Spaniard and a representative of the Papacy. However, in accordance with the wishes of the Holy Father, one paragraph of the treaty stipulated that Don Juan of Austria should become commander-in-chief of the joint forces.

The Holy League treaty was drawn up and signed in Rome on May 20, 1571. Two months later, on July 11, a convoy of eleven galleys, a protective vanguard for the main Spanish fleet, raised anchor and set sail from Barcelona. Nine days later, a second convoy, consisting of thirty-seven ships and led by the *Reale*, weighed anchor. It too was bound for Genoa. Don Juan stopped only briefly at this Italian port before pressing on to the Sicilian port of Messina, the assembly point for the allied squadrons.

The *Reale* reached her destination on the evening of August 23. By that time more than three hundred ships, thirty thousand soldiers, and fifty thousand rowers and sailors were gathered in Messina. Galleys and troops from Venice, Genoa, Naples, Sicily and the Papacy had joined Don Juan's fleet. Savoy and the Knights of Malta sent their contributions.

Don Juan carried out a lengthy, careful inspection of the force under his command. On board the *Reale*, he held meetings with his chief officers: the Genoese Andrea Doria, the Venetians Sebastiano Venier and Agostino Barbarigo, the Pope's delegate Marco Antonio Colonna, the Spaniards Santa Cruz and Requesens, and Alexander Farnese, Don Juan's childhood companion. The ships' captains received precise and secret instructions as to the order of battle and their own special duties.

The Turks, meanwhile, had left a trail of blood and fire behind them in Cyprus, where they occupied the main town of Famagusta, and in Corfu, which they destroyed. The city was in ruins when Don Juan stopped there on September 28. Two days later, he gave orders for his fleet to set sail for the Bay of Gomenitza, on the Albanian coast, for Don Juan had discovered that the enemy fleet was lying not far from the Turkish base of Lepanto, at the mouth of the Gulf of Patras in western Greece. The enemy fleet was composed of two hundred and eight fighting galleys, sixty-six galliots, or small galleys, and eighty-eight thousand men, twenty-five thousand of whom were soldiers.

On October 3, the Christian fleet left Gomenitza, and sailed south past the island of Corfu. Three days later, it passed the fortress of Preveza on the eastern shores of the Ionian Sea. During the night of October 6, the fleet moved south toward the island of Cephalonia, and anchored off Lepanto, north of the Gulf of Patras and close to the Cape of Actium (where Octavius and Marc Antony had fought their famous battle for control of the Roman Empire). At dawn on Sunday, October 7, Don Juan of Austria carried out a final inspection of his fleet. Everything seemed to be in order, and the prince felt confident, particularly when a light westerly breeze sprang up, giving the Christian fleet the advantage. At 11:45 A.M., Don Juan gave the order for the white banner of the Holy League to be hoisted on the mast of the *Reale*. The guns were fired, and the battle was on.

The Christian fleet, which consisted of two hundred and eight fighting galleons, six large galleys, and one hundred and two smaller craft carrying twelve to seventeen oars, formed a rectilinear front. Barbarigo was in command of the left flank of the fleet, and Doria of the right flank; the *Reale* lay in the center, surrounded by the galleys of Colonna and Venier. A relief galley, belonging to Requesens, lay next to the flagship, so close that the two were almost touching. Behind them, a fourth division, under the command of Santa Cruz, was waiting in reserve. The six huge Venetian *galeasses*, each weighing six hundred tons and each armed with 180 guns, were lined up in front of the main fleet. These enormous ships which were so ponderous that they had to be towed into position by galleys, were manned by a crew of one thousand men and four hundred and fifty rowers, eight men to each oar.

The Ottoman ships were spread out in a crescent-shaped formation facing the battle fleet of the Holy League. Scirocco, Pasha of Alexandria, and Ulüch Ali, Dey of Algiers, were in command of the right and left extremities of this curve, while the center of the formation was occupied by Pertev and Ali Pasha, whose flagship, the *Sultana*, lay opposite the *Reale*.

The two fleets joined battle, attacking each other with great violence. The Christian and Ottoman commanders-in-chief eyed each other warily from the two opposing flagships, separated by a distance of not more than five yards. Ali Pasha was wearing a caftan made of white brocade embroidered with precious stones, and on his head was a turban, wound around a steel helmet. He was surrounded by three hundred janissaries and a hundred archers. The two flagships collided with a tremendous crash. Drums were beating; bugles were blowing. The bright sun lit up the vivid yellows, greens and reds of the Moslem flags and glittered on the helmets of the Christian soldiers. Don Juan, standing on the forecastle of his galley, raised his sword high into the air, made the sign of the cross and plunged into the attack. Four hundred leather-booted Spaniards followed close behind, brandishing their halberds.

The battle lasted for five hours, and until the very end the outcome remained uncertain. Both the *Reale* and the *Sultana*, symbolic prizes in the contest, were invaded by the opposing side and then almost immediately abandoned. Turks and Christians alike displayed extraordinary valor: Alexander Farnese single-handedly captured the galley in which the treasure of the Turkish fleet was stored. A party led by Ulüch Ali, taking advantage of a breach in Doria's division, plunged forward to attack the galleys of the Knights of Malta, strangled the thirty knights, and captured the black flag of their Order. It looked as though the battle would go in favor of the Turks until the Holy League's reserve division, under the command of Santa Cruz, intervened.

Late in the afternoon, Don Juan himself managed

Andrea Doria of Genoa, who, acting on secret orders from Philip II, refused to fight. This unsuccessful attempt to reduce the effect of Don Juan's victory was part of Philip's campaign to subjugate the Republic of Venice.

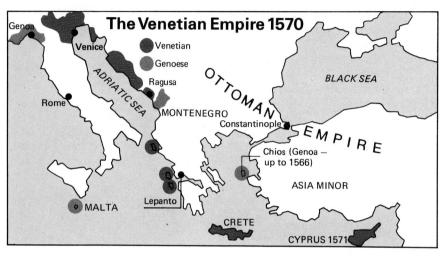

The Venetian Empire 1570

- Venetian
- Genoese
- Ragusa

Genoa
Venice
ADRIATIC SEA
Rome
OTTOMAN EMPIRE
BLACK SEA
MONTENEGRO
Constantinople
Chios (Genoa — up to 1566)
ASIA MINOR
Lepanto
MALTA
CRETE
CYPRUS 1571

to set foot on the deck of the *Sultana*. Just as he was about to capture Ali Pasha, the Turkish commander was struck in the head by a shot from an harquebus and fell dead. A Spaniard cut off the fallen leader's head and offered it to Don Juan. It was then stuck on the end of a pike and displayed to all the combatants. The air was filled with cries of joy from the Christians and cries of despair from the Turks at the sight. From that moment, the Holy League was assured of victory. Colonna succeeded in disengaging the *Reale* from the Turkish galleys that were hemming it in, and the battle deteriorated into a massacre. The Turkish galleys, inexorably blasted by the guns of the Christian ships, were set on fire, sunk or captured. The strength of the Christians, combined with the superiority of their armaments, was too much for the Moslems, despite the fact that the latter were more skilled at maneuvering their ships. By five o'clock in the afternoon it was all over; at the masthead of the Turkish flagship, the *Sultana*, the crucifix had replaced the flag of the Prophet.

A total of twenty-five thousand Turks were killed and five thousand taken prisoner—a total loss of thirty thousand men. Twelve thousand Christian slaves were freed from the captured galleys.

Not surprisingly, the whole of Christendom was filled with joy at the news of the victory at Lepanto. The Turks had suffered a spectacular and decisive defeat, at least when judged solely from the number of casualties sustained and ships lost. The Turkish fleet had not been wholly destroyed, however; the Algerian Ulüch Ali had managed to escape with forty ships. According to Pertev, the comrade-in-arms of Ali Pasha, the Christians' victory "had only

Alexander Farnese, a childhood companion of Don Juan, who was one of the leaders of the expedition.

A breathing-space for Christendom

A coin struck by Pope Pius V to celebrate Lepanto. The motto reads "O Lord, Thy right hand destroyed the enemy."

The Battle of Lepanto, by an unknown artist.

cut off the beard of the Sultan." His taunt implied that the beard would grow back again.

Nevertheless, the Republic of Venice had been saved for the time being from the danger of further attacks by the Ottomans, who had been menacing its frontiers, laying waste to its possessions and massacring its subjects. But for this setback, the Sultan might well have conquered Venice itself. All the same, Venice had lost the flower of its young nobility and a substantial portion of its fleet. Moreover, it had managed to maintain its political independence, but it was gradually losing its commercial supremacy. During the years that followed the Battle of Lepanto, Venetian galleys, driven out of the Levant, found that they no longer had any call to sail to northern ports. The British, unable to obtain the merchandise from the Mediterranean that they had grown to expect, decided to get it for themselves. They sailed through the Straits of Gibraltar, and soon established commercial relations with the Christian trading stations located in the eastern Mediterranean. They then went a step further, and opened trade negotiations with the Sultan, who badly needed tin for his guns. Thus, only ten years after Lepanto an English fleet of merchant ships flying the flag of the Levant Company was plying the Mediterranean. They sold English metals and manufactured articles to the Ottoman Empire and, in exchange, bought silks and spices from the Turks. These English traders were soon joined by Dutch merchants, who established commercial relations with the Sultan.

In this way, Venice was deprived of both its suppliers and its clients at the same time—to the benefit of the Turks. For the first time in history, northerners were trading in the Mediterranean, a sea that until then had been reserved for Mediterranean peoples. Venice, which suffered a great loss of economic prestige, grew apprehensive, for it still feared the possibility of a Turkish attack. To rectify this situation, Venice concluded a separate peace treaty with the Ottoman Empire several months after the Battle of Lepanto. The terms of the treaty were relatively honorable, but Cyprus became a Turkish possession once again.

The breaking of the pact of the Holy League by the Venetians, through their separate treaty with the Turks, did not anger Spain, as might have been expected. It had quite the contrary effect, for this move served Spain's interest admirably. And those interest were synonymous with the interests of Philip II, who had complete political control over the country. The personal policy he adopted in regard to the Lepanto expedition was so riddled with secret, subtle intentions that it often seemed to run counter to the national interests. For instance, when the Genoese Andrea Doria, who was in command of the right flank of the Christian fleet, abandoned his position and withdrew his forces—thus allowing the Algerian Ulüch Ali to penetrate the League's formation—this move was not in fact a miscalculation, but a positive decision not to fight. Nor was this refusal to fight a voluntary action on the part of

Doria—it was carried out on the secret orders of the King of Spain himself, without the knowledge of Don Juan of Austria. Philip II wanted a victory over the Turks, but he did not want this victory to be too spectacular. He wanted to save Venice only so that he could later annex it.

Although Philip II had seen to it that he did not become too deeply involved in the Lepanto expedition, he was prepared to pay the larger part of the expenses. The Spanish treasury had not merely run dry, but was also heavily mortgaged by costly loans contracted with the bankers of Genoa. However, the King of Spain refused to permit financial worries to divert him from his main objectives: crushing the Berbers and stamping out heresy. He expelled the Moriscos and Marranos from Spain—the Moslem and Jewish inhabitants who had been converted to Christianity—because he doubted the sincerity of their conversion and feared especially that the Moriscos might be the vanguard of an eventual Islamic invasion of Spain. Philip had good reason to fear the Moslems; less than a century had elapsed since Ferdinand and Isabella, Philip's great-grand-parents, had succeeded in driving the Moors from Iberia. The King's religious zeal concealed a more practical motive, however. By confiscating the possessions of the Moriscos and Marranos, he was able to replenish the empty coffers of Spain.

Taking advantage of the psychological effect of Don Juan's victory over the Turks, Philip II sent him off forthwith to conquer Tunis, in an effort to regain

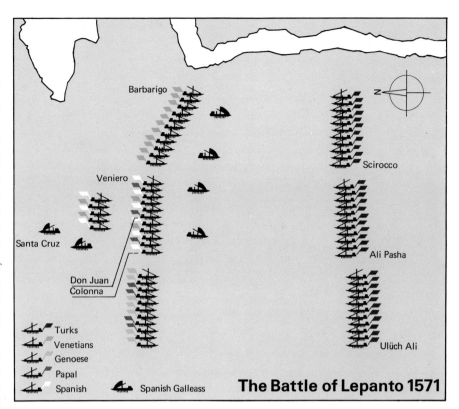

The Battle of Lepanto 1571

the Protectorate, which had been under Arab rule for many years. Within a month, Don Juan had captured Tunis; he begged leave of Philip II to be proclaimed king of it, but his request was refused. In any case, Don Juan's victory was only temporary: a year later, Ulüch Ali retook Tunis and the fort of La Goletta and exterminated the eight thousand Spaniards living there. Thus, Spain's military gains as a result of the Battle of Lepanto were negligible. Nevertheless, since he was at last safe from the menace of a Turkish attack, Philip II was able to turn his attention and energies to Great Britain and the Netherlands.

In short, the real victory of the Battle of Lepanto was gained by Christendom. The powerful Ottoman Empire suffered a decisive defeat in the waters of the Ionian Sea, a defeat that was to put an end to its territorial expansion. If there had been no Battle of Lepanto, the whole of Europe might have fallen into the hands of the Turks. Italy might have suffered the same fate as that of Greece, and Western Europe might have disintegrated in much the same way as the Roman Empire did during the fifth century. Moreover, the psychological and moral effects of Lepanto were profound, for this victory destroyed once and for all the myth of the invincible Turk.

JEAN DESCOLA

A mid-sixteenth-century Turkish quiver and arrows.

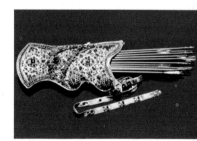

Three thousand Protestants are murdered

By the middle of the sixteenth century, many prominent French nobles and a substantial portion of the middle class had adopted Protestantism — despite continued threats of persecution. As regent for her son Charles IX, Catherine de' Medici attempted to achieve a balance of power between the Catholic supporters of the House of Guise and the chief Huguenot nobles. In January, 1562 — the month that the final session of the Council of Trent opened — Michel L'Hopital, the moderate constable of France, promulgated the Edict of St. Germain. For the first time, the Huguenots received official recognition. In the face of this threat to French Catholicism and to stable

Claude de Lorraine, Duc de Guise.

government, the Duke of Guise, the Cardinal of Lorraine and the Duke of Montmorency created a militant league to renew persecution of the Protestants. The Guises ordered the massacre of 1,200 Huguenots at Vassy in 1562, an action that provoked the first of seven Wars of Religion. Those clashes, which continued intermittently until 1580, led in turn to a war of succession. In 1598, after thirteen years of dynastic war, Henry of Navarre was able to achieve a lasting peace. His Edict of Nantes, promulgated in 1598, granted Huguenots equal political rights with Catholics and insisted upon limited toleration of their worship.

By the turn of the century, France had been a battlefield for thirty-six years. Incessant civil war, broken by periodic, uneasy truces, had claimed the flower of her nobility. In the beginning Conde, the Huguenot commander, had pinned his hopes for military victory on English support, but the army that Elizabeth I sent to garrison Le Havre was decimated by the plague in 1563, and thereafter English aid took the form of

subsidies. John Casimir of the Palatinate was one of a group of German soldiers of fortune who had answered the Huguenot summons and marched his mercenary armies into France. The modest concessions that the Huguenots and their allies secured through the Peace of Amboise in 1563 and by the Treaty of Longjumeau, some five years later, satisfied neither side. The terms of the Peace of 1570, which ended the third war, were more encouraging for the Huguenots, who were granted amnesty, liberty of conscience and permission to retain their strongholds in La Rochelle, Montauban, Cognac and La Charité.

Massacre of St. Bartholomew

Two years later, in August, 1572, Paris prepared for a royal wedding. Margaret of Valois, Charles IX's Catholic sister, was to wed Henry, Duke of Bourbon and King of Navarre, who had become the leading Huguenot in France. In a more mature age, the marriage of a Catholic princess and a Protestant king might have healed the divisions of the realm, but the atmosphere of Paris in 1572 was too explosive. Four days after the wedding Admiral Coligny, the Huguenot commander-in-chief, was wounded by an assailant who

Gaspard de Coligny, Protestant leader.

was working for the Duke of Guise. Catherine de' Medici, the Queen Mother, fearing Huguenot reprisals on the royal family, proposed an immediate massacre of all Huguenots in the capital. Catherine's weakling son Charles IX agreed — and lists were swiftly compiled.

The massacre of St. Bartholomew's Day.

Henry of Navarre was spared in the Massacre of St. Bartholomew, but the Duke of Guise personally executed Coligny and some 3,000 other Protestant Parisians were slaughtered. The massacre touched off similar attacks in the provinces — notably in Bordeaux, Orleans, Lyons, Rouen and Toulouse — in which an additional 10,000 Huguenots died. Deprived of their generals, the Huguenot army withdrew to La Rochelle and other strongholds. Many civilians emigrated from France at this time, and refugees by the thousands poured into England and Germany. In general the Huguenots, many of whom were skilled craftsmen, were welcomed in the lands to which they fled.

The events of 1572 drove the Center Party, which was composed of moderates such as L'Hopital, to support the Huguenots. Navarre, the future King Henry IV, feigned conversion to Catholicism to save himself during the massacres, but four years later he abjured Catholicism and was recognized as head of the Huguenot Party. Protestant Europe was shocked by the massacres, which left it more vulnerable than ever to militant Catholicism. Coupled with Don Juan's victory at Lepanto and the success of Alva against the Dutch rebels, events in France made the future of Protestantism look very bleak.

Philip II and "The Beggars"

Charles V had begun his life as Charles of Ghent — and despite his Spanish crown and imperial office, he had been regarded with affection by his subjects in the Low Countries. Those same subjects looked upon Philip II, Charles V's son, as an interfering Spaniard — and not without reason. One of Philip's first acts as ruler of the Netherlands

was to introduce the Jesuits, and when he returned to Spain he left his natural sister Margaret, Duchess of Parma, as regent. During Margaret's rule, Dutch policy was directed by Cardinal Granvelle, Bishop of Arras, who provoked disturbances in Holland and Zeeland by establishing new Catholic bishoprics. The northern provinces — those that eventually formed the Dutch Republic — were already strongholds of Calvinism, and they protested Granvelle's actions through a series of risings. Margaret was forced to call in the Spanish army to suppress the rebels. The Nationalist Party, headed by Count Egmont, persistently demanded that the Spanish soldiers leave, Granvelle be replaced and the provinces be left to enjoy their ancient liberties — and in 1564 the Cardinal was dismissed.

In 1566, Prince Louis of Nassau, brother of William of Orange, and Philip of Marnix organized the lesser Dutch nobility into a confederacy — soon nicknamed *Les Gueux* (the Beggars) — which demanded that the Inquisition be withdrawn and freedom of worship reinstated. Margaret of Parma promised concessions, but these failed to satisfy the Dutch extremists. In August there were violent waves of iconoclasm in Hondschoote, Valenciennes, Antwerp and Groningen: some four hundred churches were sacked, statues and images were broken and abbeys were burned. Those spontaneous outbreaks, as much social as religious in nature, forced Margaret to withdraw the Inquisition; yet she retaliated by raising an army of German mercenaries that annihilated 2,000 reformists near Antwerp.

Philip chose his ablest general, the Duke of Alva, to bring the Netherlands to heel, and Alva arrived at Brussels in August, 1567, with an army composed of 20,000 seasoned

Spanish and Italian soldiers. As military governor, Alva established the Council of Blood, a tribunal that instigated a reign of terror, and Margaret handed the office of regent over to him. Calvinist refugees began to leave for England and Germany, and their numbers increased after counts Egmont and Hoorn—who personified resistance to Spanish rule—were executed for high treason.

In 1568 the outlawed William of Orange, who was destined to be the savior of the Dutch, defeated the Spanish with a mercenary force raised in Germany. That action at Heiligerlec marked the outbreak of the Revolt of the Netherlands, a conflict that was to dominate European politics until the close of the century. Out of the long struggle with Spain emerged an independent Dutch Republic composed of the Protestant northern provinces. The Catholic southern provinces—the future Belgium—remained under Spanish rule.

The Spanish dominated mid-sixteenth-century Italy with the exception of Savoy, which was restored to Emmanuel Philibert by the Treaty of Cateau-Cambresis. Emmanuel, who succeeded his father to an apparently empty title and sought fame as a general of Philip II, proved to be the lone Italian ruler capable of building an independent, centralized state. His victory over the French at St. Quentin in August, 1557, earned him the lost provinces of Savoy and Piedmont at a subsequent peace conference. (France was permitted to retain her garrisons in Turin and Pignerolo, however, and Spain continued to hold Asti.) The wars had devastated the duchy to such an extent that there were "no citizens in the cities, neither man nor beasts in the fields." Emmanuel Philibert inaugurated a series of reforms, stabilized the currency and formed a standing army that was the envy of his neighbors. After initially repressing the Protestant Waldenses in the valleys of Piedmont, he was persuaded to grant them religious toleration.

Brahe's "new" star

The Danish astronomer Tycho Brahe (1546-1601) was a curious contradiction. The modernity of his instruments and calculations was balanced by the reactionary nature of his intellectual outlook— Brahe regarded astronomy as a

Tycho Brahe in his observatory.

"divine" science and rejected the Copernican theory of a heliocentric universe. While studying chemistry at Augsburg, he made a nineteen-foot quadrant and a celestial globe five feet in diameter, and when he returned to Denmark his noble uncle encouraged him to build a laboratory in his castle. From that vantage, Brahe observed the "new" star Cassiopeia on November 11, 1572. Brahe's discovery brought him unprecedented royal patronage: Frederick II granted the astronomer the island of Hveen, on which Brahe built his Uraniborg Observatory in 1576. Brahe designed his own instruments and with them achieved new standards of accuracy, but his fame rests primarily on the voluminous observations that he recorded in great detail. Those records form the basis of modern astronomy.

Ivan IV of Russia

The excesses of the Glinski and Shuiski factions in Russia during Ivan IV's minority were a disastrous preparation for his eventual rule (1547-84). Until her early death, his consort Anastasia had a restraining influence on the Tsar, but for most of his reign he acted like a possessed monster, plunging the country into unprecedented carnage that earned him the name "Ivan the Terrible." His early campaigns against the Tartars enabled him to annex Kazan in 1552 and Astrakhan in 1556, and gave the Tsar complete control of the Volga River. Ivan fought a long and costly war with Livonia between 1557 and 1582, but he failed to acquire his objective—an outlet on the Baltic. English adventurers under Chancellor arrived at Archangel in

1553 and established trading privileges in Moscow, but for the most part Ivan's contacts with the West were less numerous and less significant than his predecessor's had been.

Ivan's cruelty was legendary. He left Moscow in 1564—to escape from a boyar rising led by Prince Kurbski, and upon his return he inaugurated a reign of terror that lasted for the rest of his life. The Tsar murdered his eldest son in a fit of rage in 1580; and when he was overcome by the beauty of the new Cathedral of St. Basil in Moscow, he put out the architect's eyes—to prevent him from being able to design another so great. Ivan personally directed the Massacre of Novgorod, in which some 60,000 men and women were slaughtered in the streets for contemplating an alliance with Ivan's enemy, Livonia.

Ivan the Terrible.

"I am your god and God is mine," Ivan thundered, and his people came to accept their Tsar's violent nature as readily as they accepted his near divinity.

Japan

The early history of Japan is a chronicle of prolonged anarchy. The country was devastated by wars of succession and lives were sacrificed on a Muscovite scale. The arrival of Portuguese ships in 1542 brought Japan into contact with the West for the first time, and in 1549 St. Francis Xavier and two companions landed at Satsuma and set about converting the inhabitants. The princes of Japan were more interested in muskets than in missals, however—and it seemed likely for a time that the importation of more sophisticated methods

of warfare would lead to unprecedented carnage. The country's eventual recovery from endemic civil war and its emergence as a unified state in the late sixteenth century resulted from the efforts of three remarkable leaders, Ota Nobunaga, Hideyoshi and Ieyasu.

Nobunaga, who seized power in Kyoto in 1568, soon managed to impose his rule upon the central provinces and gradually weakened the power of the Buddhist monasteries (notably the military community on Mount Hiei). Profiting by Western methods learned from the foreign traders who came to the free port of Nagasaki, Nobunaga built Japan's first castle on the shores of Lake Biwa.

In 1582, Nobunaga was assassinated by one of his generals, who also destroyed the castle on Lake Biwa. Upon his return from campaigning in western Japan, Hideyoshi avenged Nobunaga's death—and in the next few years he overcame all opposition and became the virtual dictator of a unified Japan. When, in 1592, the Koreans refused to permit Hideyoshi's troops to pass through the peninsula on their way to China, he invaded Korea. Confronted by a huge Chinese army, Hideyoshi was forced to retreat. The dictator's last years were clouded by the persecution of Christian missionaries, whom Hideyoshi accused of seeking to divide his people in preparation for a conquest by European powers.

Persia

While Akbar was consolidating the Mogul Empire, Shah Abbas I (1587-1629) was establishing a strong personal rule in Persia. In order to expel the Uzbeks from Khorasan, he came to terms with the Turks and surrendered Tabriz and Georgia to them. His army then won a decisive victory near Herat, ending the long series of Uzbek depredations. Abbas the Great resumed the war with Turkey in 1602 and regained Tabriz, Shrivan and subsequently Baghdad. His successes continued and, by the time of his death, his kingdom stretched from the Tigris to the Euphrates. Although cruel to his own family and subjects, Abbas was remarkably tolerant of foreigners. He profited greatly from the advice of two Englishmen, Anthony and Robert Shirley, who came to his court on a diplomatic mission and remained in his service.

A New Empire for India

In February, 1573, following a protracted siege, the Afghan stronghold of Surat capitulated to the Mogul Emperor Akbar. The Indian monarch's victory added the textile-rich province of Gujarat and its busy ports on the Arabian Sea to Akbar's burgeoning Empire—and it effectively ended decades of internecine strife in northern India. A generation earlier, Akbar's father, Humayun, had captured and briefly held Gujarat before launching an impetuous and disastrous campaign in the east. Akbar's reconquest of the province consolidated his holdings and radically diminished both internal and external threats to the Mogul throne. From this secure power base, Akbar was able to quell further outbreaks, promote amicable Moslem-Hindu relations, promulgate a new religion and lay the groundwork for a truly pan-Indian nation.

In the traditional view of Indian historians, the Mogul Empire in India was established in 1526 when Baber, a descendant of Genghis Khan, defeated the Afghan prince Ibrahim Lodi in the First Battle of Panipat. After the great Sikandar Lodi's death in 1517, the old Delhi sultanate—which dated from the first Moslem conquest at the end of the twelfth century—had been split up among contending members of the Lodi family, each of whom was supported by a different Afghan tribe. Disputes over the succession had raged for nearly a decade when Baber intervened in 1526. His action was clearly prompted by hopes of personal gain and not out of any sympathy for the squabbling Afghans, for Baber had already extended the boundaries of his central Asian empire of Farghana into parts of Afghanistan, and he was eager to acquire the Punjab and Delhi itself. The deeper Baber advanced into India, the less secure his own northern possessions became and he was obliged to wage a continual struggle to convert his implicit sovereignty over the Lodi into actual domination.

By the time of his death in 1530, Baber had become master of Delhi and Agra, moved down the Ganges to establish himself in Jaunpur, secured his western frontiers against the martial princes of Rajasthan and extended his sway in the east down to the border of Bengal. The conqueror established little more than his sovereignty in those regions, however; Baber introduced no new cultural or administrative ideas, developed no Indian "policy" and built no distinguished public structures. From the natives' point of view, one foreign ruler had been replaced by another; the difference was only one of tenancy of the Delhi sultanate.

Baber's son, Humayun, was even less effectual as an emperor. He assigned the government of the Punjab, Kandahar and Kabul to a brother in order to be free to direct the continuing Indian campaigns. Those campaigns were numerous and sizable, for both the Hindu kings and the Moslem rulers of India opposed Humayun. The beleaguered monarch was also at odds with his kinsmen the Mirzas—descendants of the great conqueror Timur (Tamerlane)—a turbulent lot who were only too anxious to grab for themselves any convenient slices of the cake that Baber had carved out of India. The Mirzas' hostility was ironic, for Baber had deliberately brought them to India to strengthen his hold over northern India.

In the course of his campaigning, Humayun defeated Bahadur, the Sultan of Gujarat, drove him out of the province, and then abandoned the chase to launch a vigorous assault against an Afghan force in the east. That Afghan army was led by Sher Shah of the Sur tribe—a man who was one of India's ablest sovereigns. While Humayun was preoccupied with Bahadur, with the Mirza rebellion and with safeguarding his western lands against his ambitious brother, Sher had established a trained army in southern Bihar and had extended his personal control into Bengal by defeating its sultan in 1538. Alarmed by Sher's welling strength, Humayun marched into the Bengal capital—only to find the city empty. Sher had withdrawn—and his army was sitting astride Humayun's sole line of communication with Delhi. The outgeneraled Mogul ruler was hounded back to his capital, and in 1540 he was driven out of India. The Delhi sultanate had a new ruler.

Sher Shah's accession marks the first great turning point in sixteenth-century Indian history, for Sher did much more than simply assume sovereignty over Humayun's former possessions. He retook Malwa, which Humayun had given up, established his authority in Rajasthan, and—more than any other contemporary Indian ruler—inspired a nationalistic following.

The keystone of Sher's reforms was a new revenue system: he abolished the old hit-and-miss system of crop-sharing in favor of a system based on the crop-bearing potential of measured areas, and employed

A portrait of Akbar, Mogul Emperor.

Opposite Building the city of Fathpur Sikri as part of the celebrations for the birth of Akbar's son.

into the system, but the fundamental structure of the Mogul revenue system—devised by Sher Shah—remained unchanged throughout the whole Mogul period. Indeed, Sher's reforms put India on a stable economic footing that lasted long beyond his own short reign.

After Sher Shah's death in 1545, political turmoil broke out afresh in northern India. Sher had left no one to succeed him, and Afghan tribal groups rallied to the support of a number of nobles of the Sur tribe. By 1554 the empire had been divided among three such nobles, each of whom was calling himself sultan. In the midst of the confusion Humayun—who had managed to recapture the Afghan capital of Kabul after fifteen years of wandering—marched on India to regain his lost kingdom. He defeated a Sur army at Sirhind in the Punjab in 1555 and went on to occupy Delhi without opposition. Within six months he died and his son Akbar—born during Humayun's exile and not yet fourteen years of age—succeeded to the somewhat precarious Mogul throne.

The affairs of Mogul government were initially well served by a council of regency, and the council in turn was blessed with competent generals. The three Sur pretenders to the throne were defeated, as was a former minister of one of the Sur "sultans." Hemur, a low-born man with a natural head for soldiering, was perhaps the most dangerous enemy of the Mogul state. He actually managed to occupy Delhi in 1556, but was killed in a clash between his followers and the Mogul forces at the Second Battle of Panipat. With these dangers removed, the Mogul generals soon recaptured Gwalior and Jaunpur.

In 1562, Akbar married the daughter of a Hindu rajah. Such interfaith marriages were by no means unknown, but in Akbar's case there was one outstanding difference: by the Moslem ruler's decree, his wife's Hindu relatives were regarded as members of the royal family, were frequently appointed to high office and were permitted to practice their own religious rites. This policy, which earned Akbar the support of the Rajput princes, was continued by his successors during the heyday of the Mogul dynasty. It is noteworthy, however, that the rigid orthodoxy of Aurangzeb, Akbar's great-grandson, lost the Mogul Empire the support of its Hindu population and contributed to the Empire's decline. Akbar's decree was the first of many steps taken by the Mogul Emperor to make himself the ruler of all his people, Hindu as well as Moslem.

During the 1560s, the young ruler gradually rose to a position of strong personal power. Akbar's armies invaded Malwa and held the region despite some reverses; the Gond kingdom in east central India was annexed; Mogul armies captured Bihar, where there had been another attempt at Afghan resurgence; and military supremacy over the Rajputs was won. The Rana of Chitor, acknowledged head of the Rajput clans, had remained haughty and aloof during the early 1560s. He had spurned all contact with the Moguls, and had indicated his readiness to take up arms against them at any time.

Baber, Humayan and Akbar, the first three Mogul emperors of India.

a well-drilled civil service to conduct the necessary surveys, collect the revenues and maintain the accounts. Chief administrative officers were appointed in each district to insure that the revenues were collected, to settle cases of injustice in the system and to make sure that the cultivators were not being subjected to any form of oppression. The civilian population was further relieved from anxiety by a rigorous campaign against organized brigandage and other crime. "An old woman with a basketful of gold," says a contemporary historian, "could sleep safe out doors at night without a guard."

Sher Shah's achievements were a source of embarrassment to later Mogul historians, who sought to credit their own rulers with the achievements of his reign. The administrative measures that he introduced were later attributed to Baber's grandson Akbar by his sycophant-biographer, Abu'l Fazl. It is true that in 1571 Akbar's revenue minister, Todar Mall, eliminated some abuses that had crept

Suppressing rebellion in Gujarat

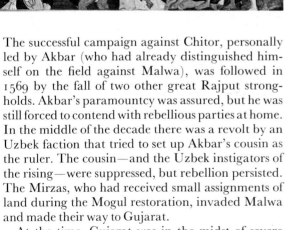

sultans who were installed as puppet rulers. Suspicious nobles plotted against one another and against the best interests of the state, faction was rife and the ambitious Portuguese were a constant menace on the coasts.

The Portuguese, who had been established at Goa since 1510, were masters of the western seas. (Gujarati sailors were competent enough as coastal pirates, but naval warfare was scarcely known in India.) The foreigners sacked and burned more than one town on the Gujarat coast and—most disturbing of all to the Moslem powers of India—they were able

Rejoicing at the birth of Akbar's child.

While watching an elephant fight, Akbar is told that his wife has had a baby.

The successful campaign against Chitor, personally led by Akbar (who had already distinguished himself on the field against Malwa), was followed in 1569 by the fall of two other great Rajput strongholds. Akbar's paramountcy was assured, but he was still forced to contend with rebellious parties at home. In the middle of the decade there was a revolt by an Uzbek faction that tried to set up Akbar's cousin as the ruler. The cousin—and the Uzbek instigators of the rising—were suppressed, but rebellion persisted. The Mirzas, who had received small assignments of land during the Mogul restoration, invaded Malwa and made their way to Gujarat.

At the time, Gujarat was in the midst of severe troubles. Sultan Bahadur had been assassinated through Portuguese treachery in 1537. His nephew, the ruler of the neighboring state of Khandesh, had died within weeks of receiving his summons to the Gujarat throne, and from that time the Gujarat sultanate had been held by a succession of minor

The central pillar of the Diwan-i Khassat at Fathpur Sikri, the city built by Akbar to celebrate the birth of his son.

to menace the peaceful pilgrim traffic to Mecca and the Hejaz.

The Gujarat state, which by the 1560s was little more than a polite fiction, was not strong enough to contain its own nobles, much less foreign aggressors. Gujarati nobles parceled out the land among themselves, and they were joined in their depredations by the Mirzas and by the local Habshis—a nominally Abyssinian group, which had been brought to India as slaves, soldiers and palace guards, but had risen to considerable local prominence. The nominal regent of Gujarat during this time of civil strife was I'timad Khan, a converted Hindu. Powerless and desperate, he invited Akbar's intervention.

Akbar had, in the meantime, grown disturbed by his failure to produce an heir. A visit to a Moslem mystic and recluse in the village of Sikri, twenty-three miles southwest of Agra, had given him hope, however, for the mystic, Shaykh Salim Chishti, had prophesied the birth of three sons. In 1569, Akbar's Hindu wife, sent to Sikri to live under the Shaykh's protection, gave birth to a son (who was later to succeed his father as the emperor Jahangir). In his delight, Akbar decided to build a vast mosque at Sikri in the Shaykh's honor, and to transfer his court to the city that he planned to build there. Construction began in 1571, and the spacious and varied structures bear witness to Akbar's taste. In general the styles owe more to Hindu tradition than to Moslem; only the mosque and the tombs show the influence of the builders and masons of Gujarat and Malwa. It was from Sikri in 1572 that Akbar set off in response to I'timad Khan's invitation.

A Mogul officer on horseback.

Akbar expands his Empire

Akbar's Empire

Kandahar 1595
BALUCHISTAN
KASHMIR

Fathpur Sikri
Agra

SIND 1591
BIHAR
1576
Calcutta

GUJARAT

Daman 1559
Bombay 1530
Chaul 1509
Surat

ORISSA

KHANDESH

Goa 1510
Masulipatam 1570

Kotschim 1502
Negapatam 1519

◄ Mogul Possessions 1526
▲ Portuguese Colonies

The monarch's reception at Patan and Ahmada-bad—where he received the submission of the Gujarati nobles—was more of a triumphal procession than a campaign. There was little resistance in the disheartened north, and what opposition there was came from the southern section of Gujarat, where the Mirzas and the rebellious Habshis formed a resistance party. They were defeated in battle by the Mogul forces at the end of 1572, and a protracted siege of the rebel stronghold at Surat ended in a Mogul victory in February, 1573. Akbar returned in triumph to Sikri, and Gujarat became a province of the Mogul power. In commemoration of the victory, the city of Sikri received the new name of Fathpur, "town of victory," and Akbar built a vast portal on the south wall of the mosque as a triumphal arch.

Moslem historians have probably attached too much importance to the "conquest" of Gujarat, for the victory over the province was by no means hard-fought. But although we can scarcely consider the conquest of Gujarat one of the decisive battles of history, the acquisition of the province did mark a new phase in Mogul affairs. Gujarat was a rich country, famous for its textiles and other valuable commodities such as indigo, saltpeter and salt.

Another province was soon added to Akbar's Empire: Bengal fell to the Moguls in 1576. By this time the Mogul ruler's attitude had outgrown the old concept of the Delhi sultanate, and had attained many of the qualities of an *imperium*. Akbar, who ruled a wider range of subjects than any of his for-bears, soon set about organizing and unifying his Empire. He introduced a series of administrative reforms.

After his return from Gujarat, something happened that provoked Akbar's curious mind: a Moslem divine expressed the hope that Akbar might become his people's spiritual as well as their temporal ruler. Within seven years Akbar acted upon that suggestion. A document was issued that gave the ruler authority to pronounce on any question pertaining to the religion of Islam. In addition, Akbar initiated discussions on theological questions —and through those discussions it became increasingly obvious that the Emperor was entertaining doubts about the sufficiency of Islam. From 1579, representatives of faiths other than Islam were summoned to the debates, and a dispatch was sent to Goa asking that priests be sent to the court to satisfy Akbar's curiosity about the Christian faith. By the time that the two Jesuit missionaries arrived in Fathpur Sikri, Akbar's revisionist ideas had led him to forbid mention of the prophet Mohammed's name in public prayers. His partiality for the Jesuits, and for the Jains and Parsis that he invited to the court, alarmed his orthodox subjects and brought about the most serious crisis in his reign.

"Islam in danger" had more than once been a rallying cry in Moslem India, and it was invoked again in 1580. Aided by Akbar's half brother, Mohammed Hakim, who advanced on the Punjab, discontented Afghan settlers in Bihar launched an open rebellion against Akbar's Christianized

The Great Gate at Fathpur Sikri.

Akbar's siege of a fort in Rajputam, 1568.

Flourishing arts of an oriental realm

Above A late-sixteenth-century carpet from Lahore.

Left Akbar receives a Western embassy.

administration. A false step would have meant Akbar's ignominious disappearance from the Indian scene. He sent his most competent generals to deal with the rising and prepared an overwhelming force to counter his half brother's advance. The embattled Emperor's display of power terrified Mohammed Hakim, and Akbar soon subdued the traitor. The Emperor's generals dealt severely with the rebels in the east, and when Akbar returned to his capital at the end of 1581, he had overcome all obstacles.

In 1582 he renounced Islam and promulgated a rather naive syncretistic eclecticism, known as the *Din-i Ilahi*, or "Divine Faith," as the official religion of the Empire. Akbar became the supreme spiritual power in his realm, and the Jesuit mission withdrew. The Portuguese remained a threat in the west, but elsewhere his Empire continued to grow: Khandesh fell to the Moguls in 1577, Kashmir capitulated in 1586, and Sind, Oriss, Baluchistan and Qandahar succumbed within a decade. Repenting its earlier submission to Akbar, Khandesh resumed its independent status, only to be reoccupied in 1601, at the same time that the provinces of Ahmadnagar and Barar were added to Akbar's rapidly burgeoning Empire.

In relation to the world as a whole, the crucial years of Akbar's reign were those during which the sultanate expanded into an empire through acquisition of the wealth and commerce of Gujarat, the establishment of contacts with Europe through the Jesuit missions, and the painstaking reform of the administration. Essentially, those were Akbar's years at Fathpur Sikri—years in which Akbar first conceived of Moslem India in pan-Indian terms.

J. BURTON-PAGE

A celebration: the costumes show the strong Western influence that Akbar encouraged.

A lion hunt.

In the years between the Battle of Lepanto and the defeat of the Spanish Armada the center of gravity of European politics shifted from the Mediterranean to the Netherlands—and the sea power exemplified in those key naval actions was of fundamental importance in the Dutch struggle for independence from Spain. William of Orange had issued letters of marque to the "Beggars of the Sea," nationalist free-booters whose small craft plundered Spanish shipping in the Channel. The Beggars initially worked out of English harbors, and when these facilities were closed to them they captured Brielle, a Dutch seaport fourteen miles west of Rotterdam, and used it as their base. In 1572 William was elected Stadtholder, or governor, by the provinces of Holland, Friesland and Zeeland. He promised to rid the Low Countries of Fernando Alva, Charles v's commander-in-chief, and led a Dutch army into the field. Although Haarlem fell to the Spanish, Alva failed to take Alkmaar. Finding his advance checked, the general asked Philip II to recall him. The Dutch rebels regained Zeeland in 1574 and saved Leyden by opening the dikes. A year later Don Louis Requesens, Alva's successor, cut communications between Holland and Zeeland, and a desperate William of

Part of the *Entry of Henri IV into Paris* in 1594 by Gerard.

William the Silent of Orange-Nassau.

Orange offered the sovereignty of the Netherlands to Elizabeth I, who sensibly refused his offer.

The Orangemen's war of independence was becoming an international affair: English adventurers were fighting in William's army, while the Duke of Anjou, heir to the French throne, and John Casimir of the Palatinate were both leading mercenary forces against the Spanish. Philip II appointed his half brother, Don Juan of Austria, victor of Lepanto, as military governor of the Netherlands. Before Don

Juan could reach his new command, the Spanish army—unpaid for many months as a result of financial crises in Spain—mutinied and sacked Antwerp. Before a month was out, representatives of all seventeen Dutch provinces had signed the Pacification of Ghent, a document which demanded that Philip recall his soldiers and grant religious toleration in the Netherlands.

Differences between the Flemish southern provinces and the Dutch northern provinces had grown steadily as a result of conflicting religious allegiances, and in 1579 matters came to a head. By the Union of Utrecht, Holland, Zeeland and the five other "Dutch" provinces banded together to defend themselves against Spain. William of Orange was so dismayed that the Union excluded the southern provinces that he delayed adding his signature. The Union, ratified, in 1581 by the Act of Abjuration (which renounced all

allegiance to Philip II), was in effect the constitutional beginning of the Dutch Republic.

The Duke of Parma, greatest soldier of his day, was gradually making headway against William of Orange during this period. The Catholic Duke of Anjou, abetted by Elizabeth I (to whom he was betrothed), fought episodic campaigns in the south, but was chiefly concerned with carving out a principality for himself. In 1583 his troops sacked Antwerp with such violence that their action became known as the "French Fury." A year later Anjou died and Parma liberated Ypres and Ghent. On July 10 of that year William, the hero of the revolt, was assassinated at Philip II's instigation. Parma captured Antwerp in August, 1585.

War of the Three Henry's

With the death of the Duke of Anjou in 1584, the Huguenots' struggle for recognition became merged with the war of succession, for the heir to that throne was the Protestant Henry of Navarre. The House of Guise united the various Catholic factions into a league to oppose Navarre's claim, and Philip of Spain agreed to support their candidate, Henry, Cardinal of Bourbon, in return for territorial concessions. Henry III capitulated to the Guises' demands for revoking all religious toleration and France was plunged into another war. That conflict, known as the War of the

Henri III of France.

Three Henrys, was more extensive than earlier campaigns.

Henry III at last stirred himself against the Guise, only to have the Duke of Guise make himself master of Paris on May 12, 1588, the Day of Barricades. The King escaped, and from exile agreed to the Catholic League's terms for summoning the States General. When the congress met at Blois in December, Henry arranged for the assassination of both the Duke of Guise and the Cardinal of Guise and had the Cardinal of Bourbon and others arrested. "At last am I King of France, no more a prisoner and slave," he remarked. In truth, Henry was far from independent.

Catherine de' Medici did not live to see her third son's assassination at Blois, nor to witness the accession of her fourth. During her forty years as Queen Mother, Catherine had tried in vain to dictate policy to four equally mindless kings of France, but she had found events too complex for her and the House of Guise more than a match for the House of Valois. Catherine had as great an interest in self-preservation and as great a taste for intrigue as Elizabeth I, but she failed to match the English Queen's successes.

Parma's death robbed the League of its greatest resource, and although Catholic troops continued to hold Paris, Navarre won ground steadily. In 1593, Navarre became a Roman Catholic, and the following year he was crowned Henry IV at Chartres and entered Paris.

Mass" and ends the civil wars

Catherine de' Medici, mother of four kings.

Gregorian Calendar

In 1582 Pope Gregory XIII promulgated a reformed calendar, which was adopted in all Catholic countries in place of the Julian Calendar. Under the Gregorian Calendar, October 4, 1582 was followed by October 15—to compensate for the days lost over the centuries through the use of the inaccurate Julian Calendar. Most Protestant countries gradually realized the folly of continuing with the Julian system, but Holland held out until 1700, Great Britain until 1752, and Russia until the 1917 Revolution.

If Gregory left his mark on chronology, Sixtus V (1585–90) left his on history. He rid the ecclesiastical estates of bandits and made his rule respected, overhauled the Church's administrative system, limited the College of Cardinals to seventy members and set higher standards for men who hoped to be elevated to the cardinalate. In his short pontificate he built roads and bridges, laid out the Lateran and attempted to drain the Pontine marshes. His lack of historical sense led him to use the ancient Roman columns of Trajan and Antoninus as pedestals for statues of St. Peter and St. Paul, but he did give Rome a new grandeur. He demanded that the dome of St. Peter's be completed, and employed six hundred men working around-the-clock to finish the work in twenty-two months.

Germany and Western Europe

Germany, like France, suffered from inadequate leadership in the sixteenth century. Emperor Rudolf II (1576–1612), a scholarly man with a predilection for astronomy and astrology, seemed to be a throwback to Frederick III. He was incapable of government and was eventually forced to resign most of his responsibilities. Rudolf patronized the Jesuits and under their direction the Counter Reformation gained ground in all the Hapsburg lands. The seeds of the Thirty Years' War germinated during Rudolf's long reign.

In 1572 Sigismund II—the last of the Jagellon dynasty that had ruled Poland since 1386—died and the Estates declared the monarchy elective. Through Catherine de' Medici's intriguing, her son Henry was elected King on the condition that he would neither marry nor declare war without the Estates' consent. After a year as a constitutional monarch, Catherine's son returned to France to succeed his brother as Henry III. In Henry's absence the Poles deposed him and elected Stephen Bathory to be their king. Bathory, an intrepid soldier, ended Russian encroachments.

Sebastian I of Portugal invaded Morocco and was killed at the Battle of Alcazar in 1578, leaving his throne to Cardinal Henry of Guise, who was already an old man. Following the Cardinal's death in 1580, five claimants to the throne emerged. Alva was hastily summoned home to command the invasion of Spain's kingless neighbor, and he defeated the supporters of Don Antonio, Prior of Crato, at Alcantana, near Lisbon. As a result of Alva's campaign, Philip II doubled his colonial empire.

Elizabeth I of England

Queen Elizabeth I realized that it was necessary to enforce religious conformity to achieve national unity—and by promoting a broad, national church she hoped to end the religious uncertainties of the previous two decades. Elizabeth regarded herself as the instrument of "God's Providence," but she did not consider it part of her mission to introduce Calvinistic theology or the Presbyterian system of church government to England. She stressed the continuity of the Church of England and the medieval Church by emphasizing the similarity of their episcopal governments.

Initially, Elizabeth had fewer problems with those who opposed her church settlement than with those Puritans and Catholics in Parliament who pressed her to settle the succession and marry. But she steadily refused to name her successor, claiming that within a month of doing so, she would find herself in the Tower. The Queen knew from her experience during Mary's reign that an heir apparent inevitably became the focus of opposition. Proposals of marriage came from various princes, and Elizabeth embarked upon a series of lengthy courtships—first with the Archduke Charles and later with Francois, Duke of Alençon (and later Anjou). The latter genuinely fascinated Elizabeth, but the difficulties of selecting a Catholic husband proved insuperable. If Robert Dudley's wife, Amy Robsart, had not died under suspicious circumstances, Elizabeth might well have married Dudley. He remained her favorite, although his position was successively challenged by Raleigh, Hatton and Essex.

For most of Elizabeth's reign England was isolated in a hostile Europe. The Queen stretched her friendship with Catholic Spain as far as she dared, permitting her seamen to harry Spanish shipping. Those incidents did not provoke an outbreak of hostilities—but the seizure of three Spanish treasure ships that had taken refuge in Plymouth did. Spain severed all commercial relations with England for six years (1568–74), and in the spring of 1572, Elizabeth signed a defensive treaty with France. That treaty proved to be a durable one: it survived the St. Bartholomew's Massacre, Elizabeth's imprisonment of Mary Queen of Scots and England's subsidies to the Huguenots—all events that exacerbated already tense Catholic-Protestant relations. In July, 1585, the Guises overturned the alliance, but its existence had postponed the day of reckoning with Spain for more than a decade.

Sir Francis Drake's maraudings along the Spanish Main opened a new chapter in the history of privateering. In 1573 he brought home $96,000 from raids upon

Robert Dudley, Earl of Leicester.

Nombre de Dios, and four years later Drake became a national hero when he circumnavigated the globe. His raids on Spanish settlements in the New World and his capture of a hoard of Peruvian silver from the *Cacafuego* netted Drake's investors a return of 1,400 per cent on their initial investments. And when the *Golden Hind* put in to Deptford, after its globe-girdling voyage, Elizabeth knighted "her pirate."

In 1585 Drake sailed to the Caribbean and sacked Santo Domingo and Cartagena. The Queen provided $24,000 in cash and two of her ships for the undertaking. Her action constituted a declaration of war against Spain. Drake's leaving Plymouth on an obvious errand of plunder provoked the confiscation of all English shipping in Spanish ports. That same year, through Sir Water Raleigh's initiative, an English expedition under Grenville and Lane planted England's first colony in the New World. They named the ill-fated colony Virginia, in deference to the Queen.

The problem of a successor was heightened by Mary Queen of Scots' arrival in England in 1568, for despite her obvious disadvantages, Mary was fundamentally a more suitable successor than any representative of the Suffolk claimants. The Northern Rebellion, a last attempt to reverse the course of England's religious and political development, coupled with the Duke of Norfolk's treason in the Ridolfi plot, insured Mary's continued captivity, while Pius V's 1570 Bull (which deposed Elizabeth and absolved her subjects from their allegiance to her) brought a spate of penal legislation against the English Catholics. Catholic opposition to Elizabeth's regime grew increasingly desperate under these circumstances: they now conspired for nothing less than Mary's release, and Elizabeth's assassination.

Walsingham's discovery of the Babington Plot, which implicated Mary in plans for Elizabeth's murder, led to the Scottish queen's trial in 1586. Mary was found guilty of treason and duly sentenced, but Elizabeth—who had often saved Mary from the militant Puritans in Parliament—could not bring herself to sign the warrant for her execution until February, 1587. She ultimately accepted the argument that she could never feel safe while Mary—the center and soul of every plot against her—was alive and she sent Mary to her death.

The Invincible Armada

There was a time when England and Spain seemed destined for a firm alliance if not an outright political union, but the differences between the Protestant island kingdom and the Catholic monarchy to the south proved irreconcilable. By early 1588, Spain was arming the mightiest naval force ever assembled. The Armada's commander, the Duke of Medina Sidonia, was totally ignorant of naval warfare, and had a distressing tendency to seasickness—yet, pressed by King Philip II, he led the Enterprise northward that summer. A nervous England waited—Queen Elizabeth unhappily contemplating the costs of a large standing army to defend her realm against invasion; the English seadogs eager to have at the Spaniard. The first clashes were inconclusive; then—according to hallowed English legend—"God breathed" and winds dispersed the invading fleet.

Lord Howard of Effingham, Earl of Nottingham, Lord High Admiral. His knowledge of naval tactics was as limited as that of the Spanish commander, the Duke of Medina Sidonia.

Opposite A symbolic picture of the triumphant Elizabeth.

A long peace between England and Spain seemed assured with the marriage, in 1554, of the Catholic Queen Mary and the Hapsburg Prince Philip, soon to be King Philip II of Spain. But within four years Mary died, childless, and was succeeded on the throne of England by her half-sister, the decidedly Protestant Elizabeth. Initially the new queen remained at peace with Philip II, but two decades later she reversed herself and entered an alliance with the people of the Low Countries, who were trying to throw off the Spanish yoke. In 1585 Elizabeth sent an army led by Robert Dudley, Earl of Leicester, to fight alongside the Dutch rebels against Philip's troops. The fiction of peace with Spain, further jeopardized by the privateering raids of John Hawkins and Francis Drake against Spain's New World possessions, could no longer be maintained.

Philip II confiscated all English ships docked in Spanish ports, and plans for a combined naval and military expedition against England were drawn up by the Marquis of Santa Cruz. When news of the execution of Mary Queen of Scots reached Spain, Philip ordered preparations to go forward speedily. A grand fleet was collected and outfitted, and supplies were gathered for the 8,000 mariners and 22,000 soldiers who were to be transported to Calais, a French seaport across the Channel from Dover, to rendezvous with the Duke of Parma's army. The meeting with Parma required perfect timing, if the expedition were to succeed. Philip anticipated that the combined Spanish forces would be welcomed as liberators by some 25,000 English Catholics. Pro-Spanish sentiment was indeed high in certain regions, and long-range culverins or heavy cannon, made in Sussex and Gloucestershire in 1587, were smuggled to Spain by unpatriotic iron-masters.

England prepared for the anticipated invasion by training county militia and by establishing along the coastal headlands a system of beacons to warn of the enemy's approach. Sir John Hawkins, prudent

treasurer and comptroller of the Royal Navy, assured Elizabeth that the fleet was ready for action, but the Queen, who could not afford to keep her "wooden walls" permanently in commission, was obliged to defer mobilization until the last moment. At the time, attack seemed the best method of defense, and in the spring of 1587, Sir Francis Drake boldly led twenty-three vessels into Cadiz harbor, where they destroyed some thirty Spanish ships. On the way home, Drake's fleet captured and burned thousands of empty barrels and other cooper's stores that were being shipped to French ports for use in victualling the Armada. Drake's raid, dubbed the "singeing of the King of Spain's beard," prevented the Spaniards from launching an invasion that year.

European seers had long been predicting that 1588 would be a year of disaster, encompassing the fall of empires and perhaps the Armageddon itself. An early setback for Philip, the death of his admiral Santa Cruz, seemed to confirm those portents. Philip chose the Duke of Medina Sidonia, a thirty-eight-year-old grandee from Castile, as Santa Cruz' successor. Although ignorant of naval warfare and prone to seasickness, Medina Sidonia was a brave and level-headed commander, and he accepted the post against his will. The new commander found the preparations for the invasion inadequate, the vessels poorly equipped and the victualling arrangements deplorable (water casks made of green wood had been substituted for those burned by Drake's raiders, and the water supply was tainted). Medina Sidonia held out for more time, but Philip, usually reluctant to move, insisted on pushing ahead. The fleet now consisted of thirty-two first-line ships: twenty galleons; four Mediterranean galleys (which later found Atlantic conditions so impossible that they turned back); four galleasses, crosses between galleon and galley that used oars when the wind dropped; and four armed merchantmen. These warships, organized in squadrons, were supported by

CORONO

EXHILER

ELIZA, TRIVMPHANS

Gunhelmus Rogerus sculp. P. 1589

Two admirals with no knowledge of seamanship

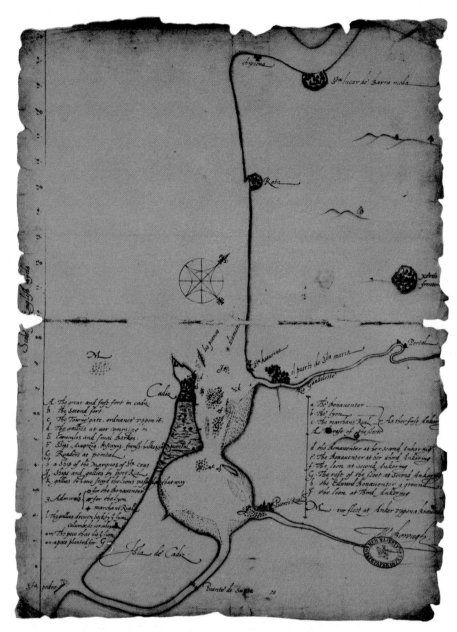

Above Cadiz Harbor with the positioning of the Spanish and English ships at the time of Drake's bold attack in 1587.

Below Part of Drake's letter to Queen Elizabeth, describing his action at Cadiz.

forty merchantmen, twenty-three freighters and two dozen pinnaces, which were used as scout ships.

Pope Sixtus v had blessed the Spanish Enterprise although he had withheld his financial support, and on April 15, 1588, the banners to be carried in the crusade against the heretic Queen were hallowed in Lisbon Cathedral; and every man in the expedition took the Sacrament. By April 30, the fleet was ready to leave, but gales delayed the actual sailing until May 20. Progress up the coast was painfully slow and the weather treacherous, and on June 9 Medina Sidonia anchored at the Spanish seaport of Corunna to wait for stragglers. Finding storm damage extensive and supplies low, he wrote to Philip asking whether he should continue. The King was adamant, and on July 12 the Armada left Corunna. The invaders were in good spirits, but even pro-Spanish Frenchmen were laying 6 to 1 odds that the Armada would never pass Ushant, an island off the Brittany coast.

The English fleet's first line was composed of eighteen large galleons and seven smaller vessels. Elizabeth's ships were more heavily armed than their Spanish counterparts, and their longer and more slender hulls gave them greater maneuverability. Privately-owned armed merchantmen and small pinnaces brought the fleet's total to 197 vessels.

In December, 1587, Elizabeth had appointed Lord Howard of Effingham to command her fleet. Like his Spanish opponent, Lord Howard was an aristocrat and—despite his administrative office of Lord High Admiral of England—he had little knowledge of naval tactics. Yet he was able, by force of his strong personality, to impose obedience on the unruly English captains Drake, Hawkins and Frobisher. Initially, Lord Howard's fleet was based at Queenborough, to defend the Thames; Lord Henry Seymour, based at Dover, patrolled the Straits, while Drake's Plymouth-based fleet stood ready to scour the western approaches to the Channel. In May, 1588, Howard moved his main fleet to join Drake's in Plymouth Sound, but the Queen refused to permit the combined force to go marauding— partly because of the cost of stores, and partly because she feared that the Armada might elude Howard and enter the Channel unopposed.

When word reached England in early July that the Spaniards were at Corunna, Howard received fresh authority for loading victuals—and a hint from Elizabeth that he might now seek out the enemy in their own port. An English fleet of ninety ships left Plymouth in haste on July 7 and raced towards Biscay on a strong northeast wind. As Howard's ships neared the northern coast of Spain, the wind suddenly shifted to the south and the fleet was forced to return to Plymouth, reaching port on July 12, the very day Medina Sidonia left Corunna. A week later the captain of an English scouting ship brought news that some Spanish ships were off the coastal Scilly Islands with their sails struck, waiting for stragglers. The English left the Sound by the night tide, and anchored in deep water. The following morning, Saturday, July 20, Howard led fifty-four

ships to leeward of the Eddystone Rocks and sailed straight south—a brilliant move that enabled him to double back on the enemy.

Medina Sidonia formed his fleet into a great crescent, with the strongest galleons at the points and flanks and the weakest in the middle, so that they appeared to Howard as an imposing enemy "with lofty towers, castle-like, in front like a crescent moon." This defensive formation limited the English to an attack on the Armada only where the Spanish were strongest.

The English needed to maneuver into a position in which their cannon could be used effectively, while the Spanish needed to close in with grappling-irons and board the enemy. Grand sea duels between fleets composed of ships-of-the-line were unheard of in warfare, and the tactics were as yet unwritten. The stalemate continued as the fleets moved up the Channel; English attacks on the points of the crescent failed to draw blood, and the only Spanish casualties in the five days of sailing were two ships lost in accidents. The Spanish had wasted 100,000 cannon balls with nothing to show for their fusillades, and the English were also running short of shot.

Though the Cornish beacons had been lit on July 19, not until the Armada was off Portland Bill, four miles south of Weymouth on the southern coast, four days later, did the order go out for the main army to assemble at Tilbury and for the second army, which was to defend the Queen's person, to go to St. James's. On that day, July 23, 1588, Leicester was named lieutenant-general for the defense of the realm, and from all over England the mustered levies began converging on the southeast. Booms were improvised across the Thames to prevent a Spanish raid on London.

Medina Sidonia anchored off Calais on July 27, only to discover that Parma had no flat-bottomed boats available to transport 18,000 men camped between Dunkirk and Nieuport out to the Armada. Howard, too, was in a quandary, for he could not get within gunshot range of the Spanish. He called a council of war, and it was decided to attempt to break up the Spaniard's formation by sending a fleet of large fire ships into the Armada's midst.

Drake volunteered his own ship, the 200-ton *Thomas*, and seven other owners proffered theirs as well. The vessels were filled with anything that would

The Ark Royal, flagship of Elizabeth's fleet.

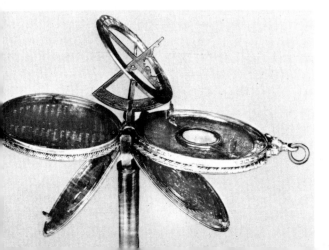

"Drake's dial," a sixteenth-century navigational instrument used by Drake.

Fire ships—England's secret weapon

The English attack the Spanish off Calais. The use of fireships threw the Armada into confusion from which it never recovered.

burn and their guns were double-shotted so that they would explode from the intense heat. The Spanish had feared a secret weapon—and here it was. Soon after midnight the fireships, lashed together, approached the anchorage, cutting through the cordon of pinnaces. In great confusion the Spanish galleons slipped their cables and stood out to sea. None of the Armada's vessels caught fire, but the impregnable crescent had been broken.

At dawn on July 28, Lord Howard divided his squadrons to deal with the scattered enemy. Drake, in the *Revenge*, was to lead the fight and, aided by Frobisher and Hawkins, he pounded the Spanish flagship, whose defenders were reduced to using muskets. Howard had driven the rudderless *San Lorenzo* ashore, and in the four hours of close fighting that ensued the Spanish suffered major casualties. The duel at Gravelines, a French port fifteen miles southwest of Dunkirk, clearly demonstrated the superiority of the English in handling their vessels— but Medina Sidonia still would not give in. Squalls and blinding rain saved the Spanish from certain defeat; when the weather cleared, the English discovered that the Spanish had drifted out of range and reformed the old crescent formation. Two Spanish ships had sunk, however, and most were leaking. His ammunition nearly spent, Howard could not repeat the attack—but he pursued the enemy north along the Netherlands coast.

Early on July 30, when it seemed certain that the Spanish fleet would be driven on the perilous lee shore of the Zeeland sands, the wind suddenly backed to west-southwest, enabling the Spanish to maneuver into the deep waters of the North Sea. At a war council on board the *San Martin*, casualties and damage were reported and it was agreed that if the wind changed again, the Armada would fight its way through the Straits of Dover and attempt to take an English harbor. If the wind held, the fleet would have to sail westward around the British Isles.

The wind did not change, and Medina Sidonia, who had already lost seven of his first-line ships, knew he must at all costs bring the rest of his limping vessels home. The long, hazardous voyage around the Orkney and Shetland islands and west of Ireland would have to be made on meager rations. Seventeen ships broke away from the fleet in a desperate attempt to secure food and water in Ireland, and all but two were wrecked. The remainder battled on. Their fight was now only with the elements, for Howard had given up the chase north of Berwick, on the Scottish border, on August 2, when it became clear that the enemy would not attempt a landing.

The Queen, hedged in by her guards at St. James's,

NETHERLANDS

NEW ALBION

VIRGINIA

NEW SPAIN

ATLANTIC OCEAN

AFRICA

NEW ANDALUSIA

NEW GRANADA

SOUTH AMERICA

PERU

BRAZIL

- Spanish
- Portuguese
- English
- Holy Roman Empire

Spanish Possessions 1588

The Armada Portrait of Queen Elizabeth.

felt left out, and decided to visit the coast. Leicester politely forbade the journey, so Elizabeth then decided to visit Tilbury. The Earl did not have the heart to disuade her, and she went by barge on August 8 to inspect the men. A steel corselet was found for her, and the Queen rode through the ranks "like some Amazonian empress." She stayed nearby and returned to the camp the next day to review the troops and make the speech that, Leicester said, "so inflamed the hearts of her poor subjects as I think the weakest person among them is able to match the proudest Spaniard that dares now land":

... Let tyrants fear. I have always so behaved myself that under God, I have placed my chiefest strength and goodwill in the loyal hearts and goodwill of my subjects; and therefore I come amongst you, as you see, at this time, not for my recreation and disport, but being resolved, in the midst and heat of the battle, to live or die amongst you all; to lay down for God, my kingdom and for my people, my honour and my blood, even in the dust. I know I have but the body of a weak and feeble woman;

Sir Francis Drake, pirate, explorer and naval captain. Legend obscured history and made Drake the hero of the campaign against the Armada.

England saved—by a Protestant wind

One of a pack of playing cards produced to celebrate the victory of 1588: the king of hearts represents the army of the Earl of Leicester, Lieutenant-General for the Defense of the Realm.

The Army of 1000 horse, and 22000 Foot, which yᵉ Earle of Leicester comanded when hee Pitched his Tents att Tilbury

The Armada, a contemporary engraving showing the crescent formation of the Spanish fleet.

but I have the heart and stomach of a king, and a King of England too, and think it foul scorn that Parma or Spain, or any Prince of Europe, should dare to invade the borders of my realm; to which, rather than any dishonour should grow by me, I myself will take up arms . . .

Elizabeth assured her troops that they would be paid for their services and asserted that she did not doubt that they would shortly have a great victory. The cheers were thunderous. During dinner in Leicester's tent that night, news came that Parma was embarking from Dunkirk and would cross on the spring tide. Those eager for action were disappointed, however: Parma's chances had been dashed eleven days before, when the British fireships scattered the Armada.

Lord Howard was later criticized for not having destroyed more ships—although the English had not lost a single ship and no more than one hundred men in the whole engagement. Little was heard about the crews still on shipboard—many of whom died like flies from typhus while their officers quarreled about their pay. The significance of the Armada's defeat soon pierced the haze, and court and capital celebrated. The captured flags were placed in St. Paul's, and the Queen journeyed to London on November 24 to attend a Thanksgiving. John Piers, Bishop of Salisbury, preached on the "Protestant wind"—the same wind that had wrecked Pharaoh's chariots in the Red Sea—and his impassioned oratory earned him promotion to the Archbishopric of York.

To mark the English fleet's victory, Elizabeth took the novel step of issuing various medals, with

her bust on the obverse and a suitable engraving of the storm on the reverse; "God breathed and they were scattered," ran one of the inscriptions. She sat for a special portrait that included views of the English galleons proudly returning from Calais and of the Spanish ships foundering, and Sir Thomas Heneage gave her "the Armada jewel," a brooch that incorporated a miniature of herself by Hilliard. The following year, Elizabeth asked Burghley to draw up an honors list including six earldoms, but they both thought better of the idea before the peerages were announced. In 1597 she belatedly advanced Howard to the Earldom of Nottingham; his patent described his brilliant service in 1588.

By the time the Spanish flagship *San Martin* reached Santander on September 13, many on board had died from scurvy or typhus and Medina Sidonia himself was delirious from dysentery. Among the thousands who later died were the Spanish commander's stalwarts, Recalde and Oquendo. The sick Admiral was unable to organize relief for his men; he never returned to sea and never lived down the obloquy of the campaign that was unfairly heaped on him. Philip II took the defeat with dignity, never realizing that the Armada had been set an impossible task, with inadequate provisions and ammunition. No one praised Medina Sidonia for succeeding in bringing home sixty-seven battered ships.

Legends soon obscured history: Drake became the hero of the campaign, and the Queen was credited with the idea of the fireships (which purportedly actually burned some galleons). Above all,

The medal struck to celebrate the victory of 1588: the Spanish fleet is scattered and destroyed.

the wind was made "God's instrument" in England's victory—when, in truth, the weather had favored the Spanish all along.

The campaign did not cause Philip II to sue for peace with England or lead him to recognize Dutch independence, nor did it end England's fear of invasion. The action was decisive primarily in that it checked the colossus of Spain—which had grown considerably since the Battle of Lepanto and the conquest of Portugal. The fact that the Enterprise had been a holy crusade—and an unsuccessful one—shows that the Counter-Reformation, no less than Spanish prestige, had passed its apogee. French Huguenots no longer felt that the world had ended with St. Bartholomew, or Dutch Calvinists that hope had been buried with William the Silent. The events of 1588 put new hearts into the Protestant cause.

NEVILLE WILLIAMS

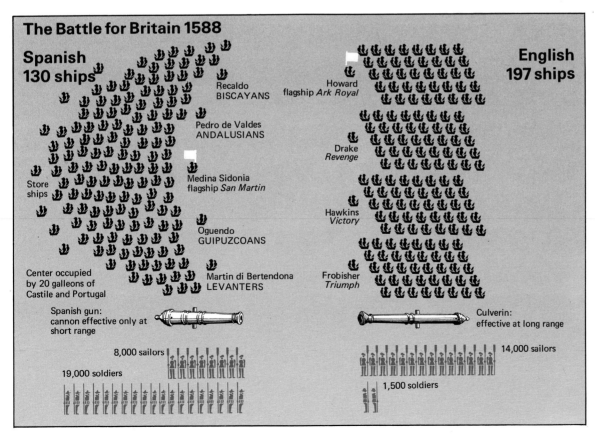

The Battle for Britain 1588

Spanish 130 ships

Recaldo BISCAYANS

Pedro de Valdes ANDALUSIANS

Store ships

Medina Sidonia flagship *San Martin*

Oguendo GUIPUZCOANS

Center occupied by 20 galleons of Castile and Portugal

Martin di Bertendona LEVANTERS

Howard flagship *Ark Royal*

English 197 ships

Drake *Revenge*

Hawkins *Victory*

Frobisher *Triumph*

Spanish gun: cannon effective only at short range

Culverin: effective at long range

8,000 sailors

14,000 sailors

19,000 soldiers

1,500 soldiers

Route of the Armada

1215

Agreement at Runnymede — England's King John signs Magna Carta, and unwittingly speeds the decline of "divine right" monarchs

1275

When East Met West — The travels of Marco Polo, recorded in a famous book, arouse Europe's curiosity about the mysterious Orient

1240

The Russian Giant Stirs — The victories of Alexander Nevski help a great nation take shape on Europe's eastern borders

Gregory IX 1145-1241
Pope

Simon de Montfort c.1208-65
Leader in English Barons' War

Philip III the Bold 1245-85
King of France

Simon de Montfort the Elder c. 1160-1218 *French Crusader*

Louis IX (St.) 1214-70
King of France

John Balliol 1249-1315
King of Scotland

John c. 1167-1216
King of England

Roger Bacon c. 1214-94
English scholar

Marco Polo c. 1254-1324
Venetian traveler

William Marshall, Earl of Pembroke d. 1219
Regent for Henry III of England

Kublai Khan c. 1215-94
Mongol Emperor

Osman I c. 1259-1326
Turkish Sultan

Robert Grosseteste c. 1170-1253
Oxford Franciscan scholar

Hulagu 1217-65
Il-Khan of Persia

Meister Eckhart c. 1260-1328
German theologian

Edmund Rich (St.) c. 1170-1240
Archbishop of Canterbury

Rudolf I of Hapsburg 1218-92
German Emperor

Sciarra Colonna d. 1329
Ghibelline leader in Rome

Snorri Sturleson 1178-1241
Icelandic politician and writer

Alexander Nevski (St.) 1219-63
Prince of Novgorod and Vladimir

Guillaume de Nogaret c. 1265-1313
Chancellor of France

Saadi 1184-1283
Persian poet

Niccolo Pisano c. 1220-80
Italian sculptor and architect

Clement V 1265-1314
Pope

Hermann von Salza d. 1239
Grand Master of Teutonic Knights

Alfonso X the Learned c. 1221-84
King of Castile

John Duns Scotus c. 1265-1308
British scholastic philosopher

Hubert de Burgh d. 1243
Justiciar of England

Michael VIII Palaeologus 1124-82
Byzantine Emperor

Dante Alighieri 1265-1321
Italian poet

Blanche of Castile c. 1185-1252
Queen of France

Thomas Aquinas (St.) 1224-74
Italian philosopher

Giotto 1266-1337
Florentine painter

Innocent IV d. 1254
Pope

Charles of Anjou 1226-85
King of Naples

Philip IV the Fair
King of France

Batu d. 1255
Leader of Mongol Golden Horde

Manfred c. 1230-66
Hohenstaufen King of Sicily

Louis VIII 1187-1226
King of France

Otakar II 1230-78
King of Bohemia

Albert the Great (St.) 1193-1280
German scholar at Paris

Boniface VIII 1235-1303
Pope

Raymond VI
Count of Toulouse

Peter III c. 1239-85
King of Aragon

Ferdinand III 1199-1252
King of Castile

Edward I 1239-1307
King of England

Birger Magnusson d. 1266
Swedish jarl (earl), regent

Cimabue c. 1240-1302
Florentine painter

Haakon IV c. 1204-62
King of Norway and Iceland

Alexander III 1241-86
King of Scotland

Henry III 1207-72
King of England

Llewelyn the Great d. 1282
Prince of Wales

● **1214** Battle of Bouvines: French conquer Normandy and Poitou

c. **1200** University of Paris founded

Seventh Crusade, led by St. Louis ● **1248**

● **1265** De Montfort's "Great Parliament"

● **1226** Order of Teutonic Knights reorganized by Frederick II

1253-99 ● Venetian-Genoese struggle over trade in the Levant and Black Sea

● **1266** Battle of Benevento: Charles of Anjou takes Sicily from Germans

Indus valley and Afghanistan ● **1221** conquered by Mongols

Florin first coined **1252** ●

● **1258** Sack of Baghdad by Mongol Hulagu

● **1267-73** St. Thomas Aquinas' *Summa Theologiae*

Cordova, Moorish capital, ● taken by Castile **1236**

● **1268** Battle of Tagliacozzo

Albigensian crusade begun ● **1208**

Golden Horde established ● in southern Russia by Batu **1242**

Fourth Lateran Council ● **1215**

1244 ● Jerusalem taken by Egyptian Moslems

1264-5 ● Barons' War in England against Henry III

● **1273**

Genghis Khan takes Peking ● **1215**

1275	1300	1325	1350	1375	AD 1400

1320
"The Divine Comedy" — In composing his epic poem, Dante gives expression to new ideologies and helps create the modern Italian language

1351
The Black Death — Trading vessels returning to fourteenth-century Europe from Asian ports carry a new and deadly cargo: bubonic plague

1381
Wat Tyler "Captures" London — England's boy King averts civil war, but cannot ignore his subjects' demands for a larger voice in Parliament

Petrarch 1304-74
Italian poet

Timur the Great c. 1336-1405
Mongol conqueror

John Huss 1369-1415
Czech religious reformer

Etienne Marcel d. 1358
Provost of Paris merchants

Charles V 1337-80
King of France

John Ziska d. 1424
Czech military leader

Stephen Dushan c. 1308-55
King of Serbia

Jean Froissart c. 1337-1410
French chronicler

John the Fearless 1371-1419
Duke of Burgundy

Casimir III the Great 1310-70
King of Poland

Philip van Arteveld 1340-82
Leader of Flemish weavers' rebellion

Isabella of Bavaria 1371-1435
Queen of France

Edward III 1312-77
King of England

Gerard Groote 1340-84
Dutch Monastic reformer

Lorenzo Ghiberti 1378-1455
Florentine sculptor

Giovanni Boccaccio 1313-75
Italian writer

John of Gaunt 1340-99
Duke of Lancaster

Thomas à Kempis (St.) c. 1380-1471
German monk

Cola di Riezi 1313-54
Roman tribune

Geoffrey Chaucer c. 1340-1400
English poet

Procup d. 1434
Taborite leader

Charles IV of Luxemburg 1316-78
Holy Roman Emperor

John 1340-1416
Duke of Berry

Eugenius IV 1383-1447
Pope 1431-47

Urban VI c. 1318-89
Pope 1378-89

Philip the Bold 1342-1404
Duke of Burgundy

John Hunyadi c. 1385-1456
Hungarian national hero

John II 1319-64
King of France

Catherine of Siena (St.) 1347-80
Italian Dominican nun

John of Capistrano (St.) c. 1385-1456
Italian preacher

Peter I the Cruel 1320-67
King of Portugal

John Ball d. 1381
English preacher

Donatello c. 1386-1466
Florentine sculptor

1268-1314

Bertrand Du Guesclin c. 1320-80
Constable of France

Wat Tyler d. 1381
Leader of English Peasants' Revolt

Henry V 1387-1422
King of England

William Wallace c. 1272-1305
Scottish rebel leader

William of Wykeham 1324-1404
English churchman and educationist

John I c. 1357-1433
King of Portugal

John of Lancaster 1389-1435
Duke of Bedford, Protector of England

Robert Bruce 1274-1329
King of Scotland 1306-29

Louis I the Great 1326-82
King of Hungary

Wenceslas 1361-1419
German Emperor

Cosimo de' Medici 1389-1464
Ruler of Florence

Diniz 1279-1325
King of Portugal

John Wyclif c. 1328-84
English religious reformer

Richard II 1367-1400
King of England

John VIII Palaeologus 1390-1448
Byzantine Emperor

Edward II 1284-1327
King of England

Chu Yuan-chang 1328-98
Founder of Ming Dynasty China

Henry IV (Bolingbroke) 1367-1413
King of England

Humphrey Duke of Gloucester 1391-1447 *Son of Henry IV of England*

Ludwig IV of Bavaria 1287-1847
German Emperor

Edward the Black Prince 1330-76
Prince of Wales

Charles VI 1368-1422
King of France

Henry the Navigator 1394-1460
Portuguese prince

Marsiglio of Padua c. 1290-1343
Italian political philosopher

Gregory XI 1330-78
Pope

Martin V 1368-1431
Pope

Alfonso V the Magnanimous 1396-1450 *King of Aragon, Sicily and Naples*

William of Occam 1290-1349
English philosopher

Charles II the Bad 1332-87
King of Navarre

Sigismund 1368-1437
German Emperor

Philip the Good 1396-1467
Duke of Burgundy

Philip VI 1293-1328
King of France

Henry II of Trastamara c. 1333-79
King of Castile and Leon

Yoshimitsu d. 1395
Japanese Shogun

Nicholas V 1397-1455
Pope 1447-55

1276
Paper manufactured in Italy

1280 Yuan (Mongol) Dynasty established in China (Peking)

1282
Sicilian Vespers: French lose Sicily to Aragon

1291
Turks capture Acre

Accession of Rudolf I as Emperor ends German Interregnum (since 1254)

English Parliament acquires right to approve taxation **1297**

1307
Papal court moved to Avignon

1314
Scots rout English at Bannockburn

1315
Battle of Morgarten: Ludwig IV recognizes Swiss confederation

First Venetian trading expedition to Flanders **1317**

Hundred Years' War begun **1337**

1340
Asia Minor controlled by Turks

Formation of Hanseatic League **1344**

Battle of Crecy **1346**

Naples overrun by Louis I of Hungary **1347**

1325
Aztec Empire established in Mexico at Tenochtitlan

Adrianople Turkish capital **1360**

Jacquerie peasant revolt in France **1358**

Ming Dynasty established in China **1368**

Resumption of Hundred Years' War **1369**

1356
Poitiers: John II of France captured by English

Turks conquer Serbia and Balkans at Kossovo **1389**

Venetians definitively defeat Genoese **1380**

Russians defeat Mongols at Kulikovo **1380**

1381

Venice cedes Dalmatia to Louis I of Hungary **1385**

Battle of Aljubarrota: Portuguese independence

1378 The Great Schism

1391

1391
Golden Horde defeated by Timur

1396
Union of Kalmar: Sandinavia under Danish rule

1397
Delhi sacked by Mongol Timur

Bolingbroke deposes **1399** Richard II of England

1431
The Maid of Orleans — Saint or witch, a peasant girl from Orleans sways a nation — and is burned at the stake for fulfilling her mission

1453
The Fall of Constantinople — The inexorable advance of the Ottoman Turks spells the end for the once-brilliant Roman Empire of the East

1492
Landfall at San Salvador — Seeking the elusive Orient, Christopher Columbus happens upon America and opens a new world to Europe

John Gutenberg c. 1400-68
German printer

Ivan III the Great 1440-1505
Prince of Muscovy

Alfonso de Albuquerque 1453-1515
Portuguese admiral

Leo X 1475-1521
Pope

Thomas Cranmer 1489-1556
English prelate

Francesco I Sforza 1401-66
Condottiere of Milan

Edward IV 1442-83
King of England

Amerigo Vespucci 1454-1512
Italian discoverer

Michelangelo 1475-1564
Italian sculptor and painter

Ignatius Loyola (St.) 1491-1556
Spanish founder of Jesuits

Murad II 1403-51
Ottoman Sultan

Matthias I Corvinus c. 1443-90
King of Hungary

Henry VII 1457-1509
King of England

Cesare Borgia c. 1476-1507
Italian ruler

Henry VIII 1491-1547
King of England

Charles VII 1403-61
King of France

Julius II 1443-1513
Pope

Maximilian I 1459-1519
Holy Roman Emperor

William Tyndale 1492-1536
English humanist and reformer

Constantine XI Palaeologus 1404-53
Byzantine Emperor

Sandro Botticelli c. 1444-1510
Florentine painter

Jacob Fugger 1459-1525
German merchant prince

Titian 1477-1576
Venetian painter

Paracelsus c. 1493-1541
Swiss physician

Pius II 1405-64
Pope

Lorenzo de' Medici (the Magnificent) 1449-92 *Florentine ruler*

Vasco da Gama c. 1460-1524
Portuguese navigator

Clement VII 1478-1534
Pope

Francis I 1494-1547
King of France

Richard Duke of York 1411-60
Pretender to English throne

John Cabot c. 1450-98
Italian explorer for England

Louis XII 1462-1515
King of France

Thomas More, Sir 1478-1535
English humanist and statesman

Suleiman I the Magnificent 1494-1566 *Ottoman Sultan*

Joan of Arc (St.) c. 1412-31
French national heroine

Bartholemew Diaz 1450-1500
Portuguese navigator

Pico della Mirandola 1463-94
Italian humanist

Montezuma c. 1480-1520
Mexican Emperor

Gustavus I Vasa
King of Sweden

Sixtus IV 1414-84
Pope

Francisco de Almeida c. 1450-1510
Portuguese admiral

Desiderius Erasmus c. 1466-1536
Dutch humanist

Ferdinand Magellan 1480-1521
Portuguese navigator

Frederick III 1415-93
German Emperor

Aldus Manucci 1450-1515
Venetian printer, humanist

Selim I 1467-1520
Ottoman Sultan

Charles, Duke of Bourbon 1480-1527
Constable of France

Henry VI 1421-71
King of England

Isabella I 1451-1504
Queen of Castile and Leon

Paul III 1468-1549
Pope

Christian II 1481-1559 (deposed 1523)
King of Denmark, Sweden, Norway

William Caxton c. 1421-91
English printer

Christopher Columbus c. 1451-1506
Italian discoverer

Niccolo Machiavelli 1469-1527
Florentine statesman

Raphael 1483-1520
Italian painter

Louis XI 1423-83
King of France

Ludovico Sforza "Il Moro" 1451-1508 *Duke of Milan*

Charles VIII 1470-98
King of France

Babar 1483-1530
Founder of Mogul Empire

Richard Neville 1428-71
Earl of Warwick, "Kingmaker"

Richard III 1452-85
King of England

Francisco Pizarro 1470-1541
Spanish conquistador

Martin Luther 1483-1546
German religious reformer

Mehmet II 1429-81
Ottoman Sultan

Girolamo Savonarola 1452-98
Italian religious reformer

Albrecht Durer 1471-1528
German artist

Ulrich Zwingli 1484-1531
Swiss religious reformer

Alexander VI 1431-1503
Pope

Ferdinand V the Catholic 1452-1516
King of Aragon

Thomas Wolsey c. 1472-1530
English cardinal and statesman

Thomas Cromwell c. 1485-1540
English statesman

Edward c. 1506-52

Charles the Bold 1433-77
Duke of Burgundy

Leonardo da Vinci 1452-1519
Italian artist and inventor

Lukas Cranach 1472-1553
German painter

Hernán Cortés 1485-1547
Spanish conquistador

Marsilio Ficino 1433-99
Florentine humanist

Ferdinand I d. 1494
King of Naples

Nicholas Copernicus 1473-1543
Polish astronomer

Atahualpa d. 1533
Last Inca of Peru

● **1414-17**
Council of Constance: end of Great Schism

● **1436**
Gutenberg's invention of moveable type for printing

1455-85 ●
Wars of the Roses

Inquisition established in ● Spain
1478

Leonardo's Last Supper ● **1495-98**

1489 ● Venice annexes Cyprus

● **1415**
Battle of Agincourt

● **1439**
Council of Florence attempt to end East-West schism

Diaz rounds Cape of ● Good Hope
1487-88

● **1402**
Turks defeated by Timur at Ankara

● **1419-35**
Hussite Wars

● **1456**
Turks checked by Hungarians at Belgrade

Venetian-Turkish peace ● treaty
1479

● **1492**
Granada taken: Moors and Jews expelled from Spain

● **1420**
Treaty of Troyes

● **1435**
Treaty of Arras: alliance of Charles VII and Philip of Burgundy

End of Tartar rule in ● Russia **1480**

Cabot discovers Newfoundland **1497**

● **1415**
Huss burned for heresy

● **1453**
Castillon: end of Hundred Years' War

Battle of Nancy: **1477** ● Burgundy annexed to France

Treaty of Tordesillas ● divides world between 1494 Spain and Portugal

● **1410**
Baghdad captured by Turks (from Timurid Mongols)

● **1431-35**
Council of Basel

Diet of Worms abolishes ● private warfare in Germany **1495**

1512
Frescoes for Pope Julius — Michelangelo's triumphant achievement in painting the ceiling of the Sistine Chapel marks a high point of the Italian Renaissance

1521
The Conquest of Mexico — Luck, ingenuity and courage— and the skillful use of horses and firearms—enables Cortes to topple the mighty Aztec empire

1533
A Bible for the Masses — Martin Luther's secretly-published vernacular translation of the New Testament proves the power of the popular press in Europe

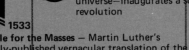

1543 The Earth Dethroned — Copernicus' theory of planetary motion—making the sun and not the earth the center of the universe—inaugurates a scientific revolution

1571
Cutting the Sultan's Beard — Two vast navies— one Christian, one Moslem—engage in a sea duel that determines the course of trade in the eastern Mediterranean

1573
A New Empire for India — By conquering the province of Gujarat, the Mogul Emperor Akbar lays the foundation for a pan-Indian nation.

1588
The Invincible Armada — As Spain's mighty naval force approaches, England seems doomed—but "God breathes" and the island kingdom is spared

---

John Calvin 1509-64 *French Protestant leader*

Philip II 1527-98 *King of Spain*

Mary Stuart 1542-87 *Queen of Scots*

Robert Devereux, Earl of Essex 1567-1601 *English nobleman*

Humayun d. 1556 *Mogul Emperor*

Emmanuel Philibert 1528-80 *Duke of Savoy*

Maurice of Nassau 1567-1625 *Dutch national leader*

Gerard Mercator 1512-94 *Flemish cartographer*

Louis I de Condé 1530-69 *French Protestant leader*

Akbar the Great 1542-1605 *Mogul Emperor*

Felix Lope de Vega 1562-1635 *Spanish dramatic poet*

Mary of Guise 1515-60 *Wife of James V of Scotland*

Ivan IV the Terrible 1530-84 *Tsar of Russia*

Tokugawa Ieyasu 1543-1616 *Japanese Shogun*

Jahangir 1569-1627 *Mogul Emperor*

Mary I 1516-58 *Queen of England*

Robert Dudley c. 1532-88 *Earl of Leicester*

Francis II 1544-60 *King of France*

Johannes Kepler 1571-1630 *German astonomer*

Henry II 1519-59 *King of France*

John Hawkins 1532-95 *English privateer and slavetrader*

Alexander Farnese 1545-92 *Duke of Parma and Piacenza*

Francis of Lorraine 1519-63 *Duke of Guise*

William of Orange (the Silent) 1533-84 *Leader of Netherlands revolt*

Tycho Brahe 1546-1601 *Danish astronomer*

1496-1560 Gaspard de Coligny 1519-72 *French Protestant admiral*

Stephen Báthory 1533-92 *King of Poland*

Don Juan of Austria c. 1547-78 *Spanish admiral, Governor General of Netherlands*

Philip Melancthon 1497-1560 *German humanist*

Catherine de' Medici 1519-89 *Queen of France*

Miguel de Cervantes 1547-1616 *Spanish novelist*

Charles V 1500-58 *Holy Roman Emperor and King of Spain*

Sigismund II 1520-72 *King of Poland*

Michel de Montaigne 1533-92 *French writer*

Charles IX 1550-74 *King of France*

John III 1502-57 *King of Portugal*

Sixtus V 1521-90 *Pope*

Henry of Lorraine 1550-88 *Duke of Guise*

Ferdinand I 1503-64 *Archduke, then German Emperor*

Count Egmont 1522-68 *Flemish leader*

Elizabeth I 1533-1603 *Queen of England*

Medina Sidonia 1550-1615 *Commander of Armada*

John Knox c. 1505-72 *Scottish religious reformer*

Margaret of Parma 1522-86 *Regent of the Netherlands*

Ota Nobunaga 1534-82 *Japanese warlord*

Henry III 1551-89 *King of France and Poland*

Pius V 1505-72 *Pope*

Selim II c. 1524-74 *Ottoman Sultan*

Rudolf II 1552-1612 *Holy Roman Emperor*

Louis II 1506-26 *King of Hungary*

Ali Pasha d. 1571 *Ottoman general*

Toyotomi Hideyoshi c. 1536-98 *Japanese dictator*

Walter Raleigh, Sir c.1552-1618 *English statesman*

Seymour, Duke of Somerset *Lord Protector of England*

Charles of Guise 1525-74 *Cardinal of Lorraine*

Francis Drake c. 1540-96 *English admiral*

Henry IV (of Navarre) 1553-1610 *King of France*

Francis Xavier (St.) 1506-52 *Jesuit missionary*

Giovanni Palestrina c. 1525-94 *Italian composer*

Francis, Duke of Alençon and Anjou c. 1554-84 *French prince*

Fernando, Duke of Alva 1508-82 *Spanish general, Regent of Netherlands*

Maximilian II 1527-76 *Holy Roman Emperor*

El Greco c. 1541-1614 *Cypriot painter in Spain*

Abbas I the Great 1557-1629 *Shah of Persia*

● **1509** Egyptians and Indians routed by Portuguese in Indian Ocean off Diu

1521 ● Diet of Worms: Luther under Imperial ban

● **Suleiman invades Hungary 1541**

● **Adoption of 39 Articles 1562** and establishment of Anglican Church

1525 ● French defeated at Pavia

● **1530** Antwerp: new Bourse financial hub of Europe

● **1541** Calvin organizes Geneva as theocratic state

● **1555** Peace of Augsburg: Lutheranism tolerated in Germany

● **1572** St. Bartholemew's Day Massacre in France

Marignano: Francis I ● takes Milan **1515**

● **1542** Inquisition established in Rome

● **1557-82** Russian-Livonian war

1516-17 ● Turks conquer Syria and Egypt

1521-9 ● War between France and Spain

● **1585-98** French War of Succession

1545 ● Silver deposits discovered at Potosi, Peru

● **1568** Revolt of the Netherlands

Luther's 95 Theses ● **1517**

● **1534** Foundation of Jesuit Order

● Mogul Empire established **1526** in North India by Babar

● Treaty of Cateau-Cambresis: **1559** end of Hapsburg-Valois strife

● **1590** Unification of Japan under Hideyoshi

1519 ● Magellan's circumnavigation

● Mohacs: Turks defeat **1526** Hungarians

1545-63 Council of Trent reforms Roman Catholic Church

● **1562-80** French Wars of Religion

Acknowledgments

The authors and publishers wish to thank the following individuals and the authorities of the following museums and art galleries by whose kind permission the illustrations are reproduced:

BERLIN: Provincial Museum, 114/1
BRUSSELS: Bibliothèque Royale, 50/2
  Musée Royale de Beaux Arts, 131/2
CAMBRIDGE: Corpus Christi College, 55/1
COMO: Museo Civico, 83
DUBLIN: Chester Beatty Library, 142/1
ESCORIAL: 128
EDINBURGH: University Library, 30/2, 31/2
FLORENCE: Bargello, 37
  Biblioteca Laurenziana, 49/2, 104/1, 106/1
  Cathedral, 40/1
  Horne Collection, 115/2
  Museo dell'Opera del Duomo, 36
  Museo St. Marco, 90/2
  Orfanotrionfo Bigallo, 43/2
  Pitti, 98/1, 134/1
  Raccolta, 80/1
  St. Apollonia, 47, 54/2
  St. Maria Novella, 38, 41/3
  Uffizi, 92, 98/2, 103
GENEVA: Bibliothèque Nationale et
  Universitaire, 109/2
KONINGSEGG, COUNT OF: 62/2
LILLE: Bibliothèque Municipale, 68/2
LISBON: Archivio de Indias, 118/1
LONDON: British Museum, 14/1, 16/2, 17/1,
  18, 27/2, 34/2, 44/1, 58, 59/1, 59/2, 60/1,
  60/2, 61, 68/1, 75, 91/3, 91/4, 104/2, 113/2,
  127/3, 135/2, 152/1
  India Office Library, 137, 143
  Lambeth Palace Library, 42/2, 81/3
  National Gallery, 55/2, 79
  National Maritime Museum, 132/2, 148/2,
  149/1, 150/1, 150/2, 151/2, 153/1
  National Portrait Gallery, 80/2, 80/3, 81/1,
  108/3, 109/1, 118/3, 126/3, 145/3, 146
  Public Record Office, 148/1
  Royal Academy, 73/1
  Royal Society, 120, 123/1, 142/2, 145
  Science Museum, 124/2
  Society of Antiquaries, 99/2
  Victoria and Albert Museum, 115/1, 136,
  139/1, 140/2, 141/2
  Westminster Abbey, 19
MADRID: Biblioteca Nacionale, 106/2
  Prado, 130/1
MEXICO CITY: National Anthropological
  Museum, 102
MUNICH: Staatsbibliothek, 116/2
NANTES: Biblicthèque, 64
OXFORD: Bodleian Library, 28, 32/2, 33,
  106/3, 106/4
  Campion Hall, 126/2
  Hertford College, 119/3
  Museum of History of Science, 124/1
  New College, 62/1
NEW YORK: American Museum of Natural
  History, 105/2
  Frick Collection, 119/1, 119/2
PALERMO: Galleria Nazionale, 46/1

PARIS: Archives Nationale, 19, 65
  Bibliothèque Nationale, 54/1, 68/3, 69, 71/1,
  127/1, 127/2, 144/3
  Hotel Cluny, 26/1
  Louvre, 18, 66/2, 144/2
PEGLI: Naval Museum, 85/1, 85/2
PISA: Camposanto, 41/2, 52/2
PRINSENHOF, HET: Stadelik Museum, 144/1
ROME: Ambroziana, 91/1
  Istituto di Studi Romani, 45/2, 145/2
  Palazzo Medici-Riccardi, 78
  Palazzo Roma, 93/3
ROUEN: Bibliothèque Nationale, 67
SIENNA: Palazzo Publico, 42/1
  Pinakoteka, 48
SUBIACO: Sacro Spaco, 13
TOLEDO: Cathedral, 88
VATICAN: Library, 34/1
VERSAILLES: 145/1
VIENNA: Kunsthistorisches Museum, 63/1
  Österreiches Nationale Bibliothèque, 27/1
VITTO, BARON: 81/2
WINDSOR: Royal Library, 91/2

Photographs were kindly supplied by the following:

Aerofilms, 72/1
Alinari, 13, 38, 39/1, 41/2, 41/3, 47/1, 48, 51/2,
  52/2, 54/2, 94/1, 99
Anderson, 39/2, 39/3, 94/2, 95, 98/1
Arland, Jean, 118/2
British Travel Association, 12, 26
Photo Bulloz, 26/1, 65, 68/2, 69, 81/2, 134/3,
  145/1
Burn, Richard, 59/3
Buchall, Elea, 76
Cash, J. Allan, 77/1
Connaissance de Arts, (R. Bonnefoy), 124/1
Courtauld Institute, 115/2
Dingjam, A. 144/1
Dundas, Kerry, 130/2
Foliot, Francoise, 54/1
Fleming, R. B., 152/1
Freeman, John, 112, 126/1, 135/1, 135/2, 52/1,
  52/3, 53, 148/2
Gabinetto Fotografico Nazionale, 90/1, 96/2,
  97/1, 98/2, 134/1
Giraudon, 18/1, 19/2, 30/1, 39/1, 64/1, 66/1,
  66/3, 67, 68/3, 71/1, 85/3, 144/2, 144/3
Goldschmidt, E. P., 123/2
Graham, Ian, 77/2
Held, André, 117/2
Holford, Michael, 70/1
Mansell Collection, 31/1, 37, 63/2, 73/2, 81,
  84, 90/2, 90/3, 91/1, 108/2, 149/2, 153/2
Foto Marburg, 62/3, 116/2, 118/1
Foto Mas, 54/3, 74, 88, 106
Mella, Frederico Arborio, 62/2
Ministry of Public Buildings and Works, 36/3
Novosti, 20–22, 24–25
Picturepoint, 98, 99/1
Radio Times Hulton Picture Library, 23/2, 29,
  50/1, 122, 124/3, 134/2
Rizzoli-Editore, 93

Roberts, Rex, 142/1
Ronan Picture Library, 123/2
Scala, 37, 40/1, 42/1, 43, 46/1, 49/2, 78, 89,
  92, 102, 103
Society for Cultural Relations with the
  U.S.S.R., 23/1
Thomas Photos, 119/3
Ullstein, Bilderdienst, 111, 114/1, 115/3
Witty, Derrick, 120/1

Index